THE THEATRE OF TENNESSEE WILLIAMS

Volume VI

By TENNESSEE WILLIAMS

PLAYS

Baby Doll (a screenplay)
Camino Real
Cat on a Hot Tin Roof
Dragon Country
The Glass Menagerie
A Lovely Sunday for Creve Coeur
Small Craft Warnings
A Streetcar Named Desire
Sweet Bird of Youth
THE THEATRE OF TENNESSEE WILLIAMS, VOLUME I
Battle of Angels, A Streetcar Named Desire, The Glass Menagerie
THE THEATRE OF TENNESSEE WILLIAMS, VOLUME II
The Eccentricities of a Nightingale, Summer and Smoke, The Rose Tattoo, Camino Real
THE THEATRE OF TENNESSEE WILLIAMS, VOLUME III
Cat on a Hot Tin Roof, Orpheus Descending, Suddenly Last Summer
THE THEATRE OF TENNESSEE WILLIAMS, VOLUME IV
Sweet Bird of Youth, Period of Adjustment, The Night of the Iguana
THE THEATRE OF TENNESSEE WILLIAMS, VOLUME V
The Milk Train Doesn't Stop Here Anymore, Kingdom of Earth (The Seven Descents of Myrtle), Small Craft Warnings, The Two-Character Play
THE THEATRE OF TENNESSEE WILLIAMS, VOLUME VI
27 Wagons Full of Cotton and Other Short Plays
THE THEATRE OF TENNESSEE WILLIAMS, VOLUME VII
In the Bar of a Tokyo Hotel and Other Plays
27 Wagons Full of Cotton and Other Plays
The Two-Character Play
Vieux Carré

POETRY

Androgyne, Mon Amour
In the Winter of Cities

PROSE

Eight Mortal Ladies Possessed
Hard Candy and Other Stories
The Knightly Quest and Other Stories
One Arm and Other Stories
The Roman Spring of Mrs. Stone
Where I Live: Selected Essays

THE THEATRE OF
TENNESSEE WILLIAMS

Volume VI

27 Wagons Full of Cotton
and Other Short Plays

A NEW DIRECTIONS BOOK

ACKNOWLEDGMENTS

Most of the plays included in *The Theatre of Tennessee Williams, Vol. VI* were first published in 1953 as *27 Wagons Full of Cotton and Other One-Act Plays*, subsequently issued as New Directions Paperbook 217 in 1966. To that original collection three plays have been added: *The Unsatisfactory Supper* (first published with the screenplay for *Baby Doll* in 1956); *Steps Must Be Gentle* (first published in a limited edition by William Targ in 1980); and *The Demolition Downtown* (first published in *Esquire* in 1971).

Excerpts from Hart Crane's "Chaplinesque" (used as an epigraph to *The Strangest Kind of Romance*) and "The Broken Tower" (quoted in *Steps Must Be Gentle*) are reprinted from *The Collected Poems of Hart Crane* (Copyright 1933 by Liveright Publishing Corporation) by permission of W. W. Norton & Company, Inc.

Contents

27 Wagons Full of Cotton   3

The Purification   41

The Lady of Larkspur Lotion   81

The Last of My Solid Gold Watches   93

Portrait of a Madonna   109

Auto-Da-Fé   131

Lord Byron's Love Letter   155

The Strangest Kind of Romance   171

The Long Good-bye   203

Hello from Bertha   231

This Property Is Condemned   247

Talk to Me Like the Rain . . .   265

Something Unspoken   275

The Unsatisfactory Supper   299

Steps Must be Gentle   317

The Demolition Downtown   331

27 WAGONS FULL OF COTTON

A Mississippi Delta Comedy

———

*Now Eros shakes my soul, a wind on the
mountain, falling on the oaks.*

SAPPHO

CHARACTERS

JAKE MEIGHAN, a cotton-gin owner

FLORA MEIGHAN, his wife

SILVA VICARRO, superintendent of the Syndicate Plantation

The scene is the front porch of the Meighans' cottage near Blue Mountain, Mississippi. The porch is narrow and rises into a single narrow gable. There are spindling white pillars on either side supporting the porch roof and a door of Gothic design and two Gothic windows on either side of it. The peaked door has an oval of richly stained glass, azure, crimson, emerald, and gold. At the windows are fluffy white curtains gathered coquettishly in the middle of baby-blue satin bows. The effect is not unlike a doll's house.

It is early evening and there is a faint rosy dusk in the sky. Shortly after the curtain rises, Jake Meighan, a fat man of sixty, scrambles out the front door and races around the corner of the house carrying a gallon can of coal oil. A dog barks at him. A car is heard starting and receding rapidly in the distance. A moment later Flora calls from inside the house.

FLORA: Jake! I've lost m' white kid purse! [*Closer to the door*] Jake? Look'n see 'f uh laid it on th' swing. [*There is a pause.*] Guess I could've left it in th' Chevy? [*She comes up to screen door.*] Jake. Look'n see if uh left it in th' Chevy. Jake? [*She steps outside in the fading rosy dusk. She switches on the porch light and stares about, slapping at gnats attracted by the light. Locusts provide the only answering voice. Flora gives a long nasal call.*] Ja-ay—a-a-ake! [*A cow moos in the distance with the same inflection. There is a muffled explosion somewhere about half a mile away. A strange flickering glow appears, the reflection of a burst of flame. Distant voices are heard exclaiming.*]

VOICES [*shrill, cackling like hens*]:
You heah that noise?
Yeah! Sound like a bomb went off!
Oh, look!
Why, it's a fire!
Where's it at? You tell?

Th' Syndicate Plantation!

Oh, my God! Let's go! [*A fire whistle sounds in the distance.*]

Henry! Start th' car! You all wanta go with us?

Yeah, we'll be right out!

Hurry, honey! [*A car can be heard starting up.*]

Be right there!

Well, hurry.

VOICE [*just across the dirt road*]: Missus Meighan?

FLORA: Ye-ah?

VOICE: Ahn't you goin' th' fire?

FLORA: I wish I could but Jake's gone off in th' Chevy.

VOICE: Come awn an' go with us, honey!

FLORA: Oh, I cain't an' leave th' house wide open! Jake's gone off with th' keys. What do you all think it is on fire?

VOICE: Th' Syndicate Plantation!

FLORA: Th' Syndicate Plan-*ta*-tion? [*The car starts off and recedes.*] Oh, my Go-od! [*She climbs laboriously back up on the porch and sits on the swing which faces the front. She speaks tragically to herself.*] Nobody! Nobody! Never! Never! Nobody! [*Locusts can be heard. A car is heard approaching and stopping at a distance back of house. After a moment Jake ambles casually up around the side of the house.*]

FLORA [*in a petulant babyish tone*]: Well!

JAKE: Whatsamatter, Baby?

FLORA: I never known a human being could be that mean an' thoughtless!

4

JAKE: Aw, now, that's a mighty broad statement fo' you to make, Mrs. Meighan. What's the complaint this time?

FLORA: Just flew out of the house without even sayin' a word!

JAKE: What's so bad about that?

FLORA: I told you I had a headache comin' on an' had to have a dope, there wassen a single bottle lef' in th' house, an' you said, Yeah, get into yuh things 'n' we'll drive in town right away! So I get into m' things an' I cain't find m' white kid purse. Then I remember I left it on th' front seat of th' Chevy. I come out here t' git it. Where are you? Gone off! Without a word! Then there's a big explosion! Feel my heart!

JAKE: Feel my baby's heart? [*He puts a hand on her huge bosom.*]

FLORA: Yeah, just you feel it, poundin' like a hammer! How'd I know what happened? You not here, just disappeared some-where!

JAKE [*sharply*]: Shut up! [*He pushes her head roughly.*]

FLORA: Jake! What did you do that fo'?

JAKE: I don't like how you holler! Holler ev'rything you say!

FLORA: What's the matter with you?

JAKE: Nothing's the matter with me.

FLORA: Well, why did you go off?

JAKE: I didn' go off!

5

FLORA: You certainly *did* go off! Try an' tell me that you never went off when I just now seen an' heard you drivin' back in th' car? What uh you take me faw? No sense a-tall?

JAKE: If you got sense you keep your big mouth shut!

FLORA: Don't talk to me like that!

JAKE: Come on inside.

FLORA: I won't. Selfish an' inconsiderate, that's what you are! I told you at supper, There's not a bottle of Coca-Cola left on th' place. You said, Okay, right after supper we'll drive on over to th' White Star drugstore an' lay in a good supply. When I come out of th' house—

JAKE [*standing in front of her and gripping her neck with both hands*]: Look here! Listen to what I tell you!

FLORA: *Jake!*

JAKE: Shhh! Just listen, Baby.

FLORA: Lemme go! G'damn you, le' go my throat!

JAKE: Jus' try an' concentrate on what I tell yuh!

FLORA: Tell me what?

JAKE: I ain't been off th' po'ch.

FLORA: Huh!

JAKE: I ain't been off th' front po'ch! Not since supper! Understand that, now?

6

FLORA: Jake, honey, you've gone out of you' mind!

JAKE: Maybe so. Never you mind. Just get that straight an' keep it in your haid. I ain't been off the porch of this house since supper.

FLORA: But you sure as God *was* off it! [*He twists her wrist.*] Ouuuu! Stop it, stop it, stop it!

JAKE: Where have I been since supper?

FLORA: Here, here! On th' porch! Fo' God's sake, quit that twistin'!

JAKE: Where have I been?

FLORA: Porch! Porch! Here!

JAKE: Doin' what?

FLORA: *Jake!*

JAKE: Doin' what?

FLORA: Lemme go! Christ, Jake! Let loose! Quit twisting, you'll break my wrist!

JAKE [*laughing between his teeth*]: Doin' what? What doin'? Since supper?

FLORA [*crying out*]: How in hell do I know!

JAKE: 'Cause you was right here with me, all the time, for every second! You an' me, sweetheart, was sittin' here together on th' swing, just swingin' back an' forth every minute since supper! You got that in your haid good now?

FLORA [*whimpering*]: Le' go!

JAKE: Got it? In your haid good now?

FLORA: Yeh, yeh, yeh—leggo!

JAKE: What was I doin', then?

FLORA: Swinging! For Christ's sake—swingin'! [*He releases her. She whimpers and rubs her wrist but the impression is that the experience was not without pleasure for both parties. She groans and whimpers. He grips her loose curls in his hand and bends her head back. He plants a long wet kiss on her mouth.*]

FLORA [*whimpering*]: Mmmm-hmmmm! Mmmm! Mmmm!

JAKE [*huskily*]: Tha's my swee' baby girl.

FLORA: Mmmmm! Hurt! Hurt!

JAKE: Hurt?

FLORA: Mmmm! Hurt!

JAKE: Kiss?

FLORA: Mmmm!

JAKE: Good?

FLORA: Mmmm . . .

JAKE: Good! Make little room.

FLORA: Too hot!

8

JAKE: Go on, make little room.

FLORA: Mmmmm . . .

JAKE: Crosspatch?

FLORA: Mmmmmm.

JAKE: Whose baby? Big? Sweet?

FLORA: Mmmmm! Hurt!

JAKE: Kiss! [*He lifts her wrist to his lips and makes gobbling sounds.*]

FLORA [*giggling*]: Stop! Silly! Mmmm!

JAKE: What would I do if you was a big piece of cake?

FLORA: Silly.

JAKE: Gobble! Gobble!

FLORA: Oh, you—

JAKE: What would I do if you was angel food cake? Big white piece with lots of nice thick icin'?

FLORA [*giggling*]: Quit!

JAKE: Gobble, gobble, gobble!

FLORA [*squealing*]: Jake!

JAKE: Huh?

FLORA: You *tick*-le!

JAKE: Answer little question!

FLORA: Wh-at?

JAKE: Where I been since supper?

FLORA: Off in the Chevy! [*He instantly seizes the wrist again. She shrieks.*]

JAKE: Where've I been since supper?

FLORA: Po'ch! Swing!

JAKE: Doin' what?

FLORA: *Swingin'!* Oh, Christ, Jake, let loose!

JAKE: Hurt?

FLORA: Mmmmm . . .

JAKE: Good?

FLORA [*whimpering*]: Mmmmm . . .

JAKE: Now you know where I been an' what I been doin' since supper?

FLORA: Yeah . . .

JAKE: Case anybody should ask?

FLORA: Who's going to ast?

10

JAKE: Never mind who's goin' t' ast, just you know the answers! Uh-huh?

FLORA: Uh-huh [*lisping babyishly*]. This is where you been. Settin' on th' swing since we had supper. Swingin'—back an' fo'th—back an' fo'th. . . . You didn' go off in th' Chevy [*slowly*] an' you was awf'ly surprised w'en th' Syndicate fire broke out! [*Jake slaps her.*] Jake!

JAKE: Everything you said is awright. But don't you get ideas.

FLORA: Ideas?

JAKE: A woman like you's not made to have ideas. Made to be hugged an' squeezed!

FLORA [*babyishly*]: Mmmm. . . .

JAKE: But not for ideas. So don't you have ideas. [*He rises.*] Go out an' get in th' Chevy.

FLORA: We goin to th' fire?

JAKE: No. We ain' goin' no fire. We goin' in town an' get us a case a dopes because we're hot an' thirsty.

FLORA [*vaguely, as she rises*]: I lost m' white—kid—purse . . .

JAKE: It's on the seat of th' Chevy whe' you left it.

FLORA: Whe' *you* goin'?

JAKE: I'm goin in t' th' toilet. I'll be right out. [*He goes inside, letting the screen door slam. Flora shuffles to the edge of the steps and stands there with a slight idiotic smile. She begins to descend, letting herself down each time with the same foot,*

11

like a child just learning to walk. She stops at the bottom of the steps and stares at the sky, vacantly and raptly, her fingers closing gently around the bruised wrist. Jake can be heard singing inside.]

My baby don' care fo' rings
or other expensive things—
My baby just cares—fo'—me!

CURTAIN

*It is just after noon. The sky is the color of the satin bows on
the window curtains—a translucent, innocent blue. Heat devils
are shimmering over the flat Delta country and the peaked white
front of the house is like a shrill exclamation. Jake's gin is busy,
heard like a steady pulse across the road. A delicate lint of cotton is drifting about in the atmosphere.*

*Jake appears, a large and purposeful man with arms like hams
covered with a fuzz of fine blond hair. He is followed by Silva
Vicarro who is the Superintendent of the Syndicate Plantation
where the fire occurred last night. Vicarro is a rather small and
wiry man of dark Latin looks and nature. He wears whipcord
breeches, laced boots, and a white undershirt. He has a Roman
Catholic medallion on a chain about his neck.*

JAKE [*with the good-natured condescension of a very large
man for a small one*]: Well, suh, all I got to say is you're a
mighty lucky little fellow.

VICARRO: Lucky? In what way?

JAKE: That I can take on a job like this right now! Twenty-
seven wagons full of cotton 's a pretty big piece of bus'ness, Mr.
Vicarro. [*Stopping at the steps*] Baby! [*He bites off a piece of
tobacco plug.*] What's yuh firs' name?

VICARRO: Silva.

JAKE: How do you spell it?

VICARRO: S-I-L-V-A.

JAKE: Silva! Like a silver lining! Ev'ry cloud has got a silver
lining. What does that come from? The Bible?

13

VICARRO [*sitting on the steps*]: No. The Mother Goose Book.

JAKE: Well, suh, you sure are lucky that I can do it. If I'd been busy like I was two weeks ago, I would 've turned it down. *BABY! COME OUT HERE A MINUTE!* [*There is a vague response from inside.*]

VICARRO: Lucky, Very lucky. [*He lights a cigarette. Flora pushes open the screen door and comes out. She has on her watermelon pink silk dress and is clutching against her body the big white kid purse with her initials on it in big nickel plate.*]

JAKE [*proudly*]: Mr. Vicarro—I want you to meet Mrs. Meighan. Baby, this is a very down-at-the-mouth young fellow I want you to cheer up fo' me. He thinks he's out of luck because his cotton gin burnt down. He's got twenty-seven wagons full of cotton to be ginned out on a hurry-up order from his most impo'tant customers in Mobile. Well, suh, I said to him, Mr. Vicarro, you're to be congratulated—not because it burnt down, but because I happen to be in a situation to take the business over. Now you tell him just how lucky he is!

FLORA [*nervously*]: Well, I guess he don't see how it was lucky to have his gin burned down.

VICARRO [*acidly*]: No, ma'am.

JAKE [*quickly*]: Mr. Vicarro. Some fellows marry a girl when she's little an' tiny. They like a small figure. See? Then, when the girl gets comfo'tably settled down—what does she do? Puts on flesh—of cou'se!

FLORA [*bashfully*]: Jake!

JAKE: Now then! How do they react? Accept it as a matter of cou'se, as something which 'as been ordained by nature?

14

Nope! No, suh, not a bit! They sta't to feeling abused. They think that fate must have a grudge against them because the little woman is not so little as she used to be. Because she's gone an' put on a matronly figure. Well, suh, that's at the root of a lot of domestic trouble. However, Mr. Vicarro, I never made that mistake. When I fell in love with this baby-doll I've got here, she was just the same size then that you see her today.

FLORA [*crossing shyly to porch rail*]: Jake . . .

JAKE [*grinning*]: A woman not large but tremendous! That's how I liked her—tremendous! I told her right off, when I slipped th' ring on her finger, one Satiddy night in a boathouse on Moon Lake—I said to her, Honey, if you take off one single pound of that body—I'm going to quit yuh! I'm going to quit yuh, I said, the minute I notice you've started to take off weight!

FLORA: Aw, Jake—please!

JAKE: I don't want nothing little, not in a woman. I'm not after nothing *petite*, as the Frenchmen call it. This is what I wanted—and what I *got!* Look at her, Mr. Vicarro. Look at her blush! [*He grips the back of Flora's neck and tries to turn her around.*]

FLORA: Aw, quit, Jake! Quit, will yuh?

JAKE: See what a doll she is? [*Flora turns suddenly and spanks him with the kid purse. He cackles and runs down the steps. At the corner of the house, he stops and turns.*] Baby, you keep Mr. Vicarro comfo'table while I'm ginnin' out that twenty-seven wagons full of cotton. Th' good-neighbor policy, Mr. Vicarro. You do me a good turn an' I'll do you a good one! Be see'n' yuh! So long, Baby! [*He walks away with an energetic stride.*]

VICARRO: The good-neighbor policy! [*He sits on the porch steps.*]

FLORA [*sitting on the swing*]: Izzen he out-*ray*-juss! [*She laughs foolishly and puts the purse in her lap. Vicarro stares gloomily across the dancing brilliance of the fields. His lip sticks out like a pouting child's. A rooster crows in the distance.*]

FLORA: I would'n' dare to expose myself like that.

VICARRO: Expose? To what?

FLORA: The sun. I take a terrible burn. I'll never forget the burn I took one time. It was on Moon Lake one Sunday before I was married. I never did like t' go fishin' but this young fellow, one of the Peterson boys, insisted that we go fishin'. Well, he didn't catch nothin' but jus' kep' fishin' an' fishin' an' I set there in th' boat with all that hot sun on me. I said, Stay under the willows. But he would'n' lissen to me, an' sure enough I took such an awful burn I had t' sleep on m' stummick th' nex' three nights.

VICARRO [*absently*]: What did you say? You got sunburned?

FLORA: Yes. One time on Moon Lake.

VICARRO: That's too bad. You got over it all right?

FLORA: Oh, yes. Finally. Yes.

VICARRO: That must 've been pretty bad.

FLORA: I fell in the lake once, too. Also with one of the Peterson boys. On another fishing trip. That was a wild bunch of boys, those Peterson boys. I never went out with 'em but something happened which made me wish I hadn't. One time, sun-

16

burned. One time, nearly drowned. One time—poison ivy! Well, lookin' back on it, now, we had a good deal of fun in spite of it, though.

VICARRO: The good-neighbor policy, huh? [*He slaps his boot with the riding crop. Then he rises from steps.*]

FLORA: You might as well come up on th' po'ch an' make you'-self as comfo'table as you can.

VICARRO: Uh-huh.

FLORA: I'm not much good at—makin' conversation.

VICARRO [*finally noticing her*]: Now don't you bother to make conversation for my benefit, Mrs. Meighan. I'm the type that prefers a quiet understanding. [*Flora laughs uncertainly.*] One thing I always notice about you ladies . . .

FLORA: What's that, Mr. Vicarro?

VICARRO: You always have something in your hands—to hold onto. Now that kid purse . . .

FLORA: My purse?

VICARRO: You have no reason to keep that purse in your hands. You're certainly not afraid that I'm going to snatch it!

FLORA: Oh, God, no! I wassen afraid of that!

VICARRO: That wouldn't be the good-neighbor policy, would it? But you hold onto that purse because it gives you something to get a grip on. Isn't that right?

FLORA: Yes. I always like to have something in my hands.

17

VICARRO: Sure you do. You feel what a lot of uncertain things there are. Gins burn down. The volunteer fire department don't have decent equipment. Nothing is any protection. The afternoon sun is hot. It's no protection. The trees are back of the house. They're no protection. The goods that dress is made of— is no protection. So what do you do, Mrs. Meighan? You pick up the white kid purse. It's solid. It's sure. It's certain. It's something to hold *on* to. You get what I mean?

FLORA: Yeah. I think I do.

VICARRO: It gives you a feeling of being attached to something. The mother protects the baby? No, no, no—the baby protects the mother! From being lost and empty and having nothing but lifeless things in her hands! Maybe you think there isn't much connection!

FLORA: You'll have to excuse me from thinking. I'm too lazy.

VICARRO: What's your name, Mrs. Meighan?

FLORA: Flora.

VICARRO: Mine is Silva. Something not gold but—Silva!

FLORA: Like a silver dollar?

VICARRO: No, like a silver dime! It's an Italian name. I'm a native of New Orleans.

FLORA: Then it's not sunburn. You're natcherally dark.

VICARRO [*raising his undershirt from his belly*]: Look at this!

FLORA: Mr. Vicarro!

18

VICARRO: Just as dark as my arm is!

FLORA: You don't have to show me! I'm not from Missouri!

VICARRO [*grinning*]: Excuse me.

FLORA [*laughing nervously*]: Whew! I'm sorry to say we don't have a Coke in the house. We meant to get a case of Cokes las' night, but what with all the excitement going on—

VICARRO: What excitement was that?

FLORA: Oh, the fire and all.

VICARRO [*lighting a cigarette*]: I shouldn't think you all would of been excited about the fire.

FLORA: A fire is always exciting. After a fire, dogs an' chickens don't sleep. I don't think our chickens got to sleep all night.

VICARRO: No?

FLORA: They cackled an' fussed an' flopped around on the roost—took on something awful! Myself, I couldn't sleep neither. I jus' lay there an' sweated all night long.

VICARRO: On account of th' fire?

FLORA: An' the heat an' mosquitoes. And I was mad at Jake.

VICARRO: Mad at Mr. Meighan? What about?

FLORA: Oh, he went off an' left me settin' here on this ole po'ch last night without a Coca-Cola on the place.

VICARRO: Went off an' left you, did he?

19

FLORA: Yep. Right after supper. An' when he got back the fire 'd already broke out an' instead of drivin' into town like he said, he decided to go an' take a look at your burnt-down cotton gin. I got smoke in my eyes an' my nose an' throat. It hurt my sinus an' I was in such a wo'n-out, nervous condition, it made me cry. I cried like a baby. Finally took two teaspoons of paregoric. Enough to put an elephant to sleep. But still I stayed awake an' heard them chickens carryin' on out there!

VICARRO: It sounds like you passed a very uncomfortable night.

FLORA: Sounds like? Well, it *was.*

VICARRO: So Mr. Meighan—you say—disappeared after supper? [*There is a pause while Flora looks at him blankly.*]

FLORA: Huh?

VICARRO: You say Mr. Meighan was out of the house for a while after supper? [*Something in his tone makes her aware of her indiscretion.*]

FLORA: Oh—uh—just for a moment.

VICARRO: Just for a moment, huh? How long a moment? [*He stares at her very hard.*]

FLORA: What are you driving at, Mr. Vicarro?

VICARRO: Driving at? Nothing.

FLORA: You're looking at me so funny.

VICARRO: He disappeared for a moment! Is that what he did? How long a moment did he disappear for? Can you remember, Mrs. Meighan?

20

FLORA: What difference does that make? What's it to you, anyhow?

VICARRO: Why should you mind me asking!

FLORA: You make this sound like I was on trial for something!

VICARRO: Don't you like to pretend like you're a witness?

FLORA: Witness of what, Mr. Vicarro?

VICARRO: Why—for instance—say—a case of arson!

FLORA [*wetting her lips*]: Case of—? What is—arson?

VICARRO: The willful destruction of property by fire. [*He slaps his boots sharply with the riding crop.*]

FLORA [*startled*]: Oh! [*She nervously fingers the purse.*] Well, now, don't you go and be getting any—funny ideas.

VICARRO: Ideas about what, Mrs. Meighan?

FLORA: My husband's disappearin'—after supper. I can explain that.

VICARRO: Can you?

FLORA: Sure I can.

VICARRO: Good! How do you explain it? [*He stares at her. She looks down.*] What's the matter? Can't you collect your thoughts, Mrs. Meighan?

FLORA: No, but—

VICARRO: Your mind's a blank on the subject?

FLORA: Look here, now— [*She squirms on the swing.*]

VICARRO: You find it impossible to remember just what your husband disappeared for after supper? You can't imagine what kind of errand it was that he went out on, can you?

FLORA: No! No, I can't!

VICARRO: But when he returned—let's see . . . The fire had just broken out at the Syndicate Plantation?

FLORA: Mr. Vicarro, I don't have the slightest idear what you could be driving at.

VICARRO: You're a very unsatisfactory witness, Mrs. Meighan.

FLORA: I never can think when people—stare straight at me.

VICARRO: Okay. I'll look away, then. [*He turns his back to her.*] Now does that improve your memory any? Now are you able to concentrate on the question?

FLORA: Huh . . .

VICARRO: No? You're not? [*He turns around again, grinning evilly.*] Well . . . shall we drop the subject?

FLORA: I sure do wish you would.

VICARRO: It's no use crying over a burnt-down gin. This world is built on the principle of tit for tat.

FLORA: What do you mean?

22

VICARRO: Nothing at all specific. Mind if I . . . ?

FLORA: What?

VICARRO: You want to move over a little an' make some room? [*Flora edges aside on the swing. He sits down with her.*] I like a swing. I've always liked to sit an' rock on a swing. Relaxes you. . . . You relaxed?

FLORA: Sure.

VICARRO: No, you're not. Your nerves are all tied up.

FLORA: Well, you made me feel kind of nervous. All of them questions you ast me about the fire.

VICARRO: I didn' ask you questions about the fire. I only asked you about your husband's leaving the house after supper.

FLORA: I explained that to you.

VICARRO: Sure. That's right. You did. The good-neighbor policy. That was a lovely remark your husband made about the good-neighbor policy. I see what he means by that now.

FLORA: He was thinking about President Roosevelt's speech. We sat up an' lissened to it one night last week.

VICARRO: No, I think that he was talking about something closer to home, Mrs. Meighan. You do me a good turn and I'll do you one, that was the way that he put it. You have a piece of cotton on your face. Hold still—I'll pick it off. [*He delicately removes the lint.*] There now.

FLORA [*nervously*]: Thanks.

23

VICARRO: There's a lot of fine cotton lint floating round in the air.

FLORA: I know there is. It irritates my nose. I think it gets up in my sinus.

VICARRO: Well, you're a delicate woman.

FLORA: Delicate? Me? Oh, no. I'm too big for that.

VICARRO: Your size is part of your delicacy, Mrs. Meighan.

FLORA: How do you mean?

VICARRO: There's a lot of you, but every bit of you is delicate. Choice. Delectable, I might say.

FLORA: Huh?

VICARRO: I mean you're altogether lacking in any—coarseness. You're soft. Fine-fibered. And smooth.

FLORA: Our talk is certainly taking a personal turn.

VICARRO: Yes. You make me think of cotton.

FLORA: Huh?

VICARRO: Cotton!

FLORA: Well! Should I say thanks or something?

VICARRO: No, just smile, Mrs. Meighan. You have an attractive smile. Dimples!

FLORA: No . . .

VICARRO: Yes, you have! Smile, Mrs. Meighan! Come on—smile! [*Flora averts her face, smiling helplessly.*] There now. See? You've got them! [*He delicately touches one of the dimples.*]

FLORA: Please don't touch me. I don't like to be touched.

VICARRO: Then why do you giggle?

FLORA: Can't help it. You make me feel kind of hysterical, Mr. Vicarro. Mr. Vicarro—

VICARRO: Yes?

FLORA: I hope you don't think that Jake was mixed up in that fire. I swear to goodness he never left the front porch. I remember it perfeckly now. We just set here on the swing till the fire broke out and then we drove in town.

VICARRO: To celebrate?

FLORA: No, no, no.

VICARRO: Twenty-seven wagons full of cotton's a pretty big piece of business to fall in your lap like a gift from the gods, Mrs. Meighan.

FLORA: I thought you said that we would drop the subjeck.

VICARRO: You brought it up that time.

FLORA: Well, please don't try to mix me up any more. I swear to goodness the fire had already broke out when he got back.

VICARRO: That's not what you told me a moment ago.

FLORA: You got me all twisted up. We went in town. The fire broke out an' we didn't know about it.

VICARRO: I thought you said it irritated your sinus.

FLORA: Oh, my God, you sure put words in my mouth. Maybe I'd better make us some lemonade.

VICARRO: Don't go to the trouble.

FLORA: I'll go in an' fix it direckly, but right at this moment I'm too weak to get up. I don't know why, but I can't hardly hold my eyes open. They keep falling shut. . . . I think it's a little too crowded, two on a swing. Will you do me a favor an' set back down over there?

VICARRO: Why do you want me to move?

FLORA: It makes too much body heat when we're crowded together.

VICARRO: One body can borrow coolness from another.

FLORA: I always heard that bodies borrowed heat.

VICARRO: Not in this case. I'm cool.

FLORA: You don't seem like it to me.

VICARRO: I'm just as cool as a cucumber. If you don't believe it, touch me.

FLORA: Where?

VICARRO: Anywhere.

FLORA [*rising with great effort*]: Excuse me. I got to go in. [*He pulls her back down.*] What did you do that for?

VICARRO: I don't want to be deprived of your company yet.

26

FLORA: Mr. Vicarro, you're getting awf'ly familiar.

VICARRO: Haven't you got any fun-loving spirit about you?

FLORA: This isn't fun.

VICARRO: Then why do you giggle?

FLORA: I'm ticklish! Quit switching me, will yuh?

VICARRO: I'm just shooing the flies off.

FLORA: Leave 'em be, then, please. They don't hurt nothin'.

VICARRO: I think you like to be switched.

FLORA: I don't. I wish you'd quit.

VICARRO: You'd like to be switched harder.

FLORA: No, I wouldn't.

VICARRO: That blue mark on your wrist—

FLORA: What about it?

VICARRO: I've got a suspicion.

FLORA: Of what?

VICARRO: It was twisted. By your husband.

FLORA: You're crazy.

VICARRO: Yes, it was. And you liked it.

FLORA: I certainly didn't. Would you mind moving your arm?

27

VICARRO: Don't be so skittish.

FLORA: Awright. I'll get up then.

VICARRO: Go on.

FLORA: I feel so weak.

VICARRO: Dizzy?

FLORA: A little bit. Yeah. My head's spinning round. I wish you would stop the swing.

VICARRO: It's not swinging much.

FLORA: But even a little's too much.

VICARRO: You're a delicate woman. A pretty big woman, too.

FLORA: So is America. Big.

VICARRO: That's a funny remark.

FLORA: Yeah. I don't know why I made it. My head's so buzzy.

VICARRO: Fuzzy?

FLORA: Fuzzy an'—buzzy. . . . Is something on my arm?

VICARRO: No.

FLORA: Then what 're you brushing?

VICARRO: Sweat off.

FLORA: Leave it alone.

VICARRO: Let me wipe it. [*He brushes her arm with a handker-chief.*]

FLORA [*laughing weakly*]: No, please, don't. It feels funny.

VICARRO: How does it feel?

FLORA: It tickles me. All up an' down. You cut it out now. If you don't cut it out I'm going to call.

VICARRO: Call who?

FLORA: I'm going to call that nigger. The nigger that's cutting the grass across the road.

VICARRO: Go on. Call, then.

FLORA [*weakly*]: Hey! Hey, boy!

VICARRO: Can't you call any louder?

FLORA: I feel so funny. What is the matter with me?

VICARRO: You're just relaxing. You're big. A big type of woman. I like you. Don't get so excited.

FLORA: I'm not, but you—

VICARRO: What am I doing?

FLORA: Suspicions. About my husband and ideas you have about me.

VICARRO: Such as what?

FLORA: He burnt your gin down. He didn't. And I'm not a big piece of cotton. [*She pulls herself up.*] I'm going inside.

29

VICARRO [*rising*]: I think that's a good idea.

FLORA: I said I was. Not you.

VICARRO: Why not me?

FLORA: Inside it might be crowded, with you an' me.

VICARRO: Three's a crowd. We're two.

FLORA: You stay out. Wait here.

VICARRO: What'll you do?

FLORA: I'll make us a pitcher of nice cold lemonade.

VICARRO: Okay. You go on in.

FLORA: What'll you do?

VICARRO: I'll follow.

FLORA: That's what I figured you might be aiming to do. We'll both stay out.

VICARRO: In the sun?

FLORA: We'll sit back down in th' shade. [*He blocks her.*] Don't stand in my way.

VICARRO: You're standing in mine.

FLORA: I'm dizzy.

VICARRO: You ought to lie down.

FLORA: How can I?

30

VICARRO: Go in.

FLORA: You'd follow me.

VICARRO: What if I did?

FLORA: I'm afraid.

VICARRO: You're starting to cry.

FLORA: I'm afraid!

VICARRO: What of?

FLORA: Of you.

VICARRO: I'm little.

FLORA: I'm dizzy. My knees are so weak they're like water. I've got to sit down.

VICARRO: Go in.

FLORA: I can't.

VICARRO: Why not?

FLORA: You'd follow.

VICARRO: Would that be so awful?

FLORA: You've got a mean look in your eyes and I don't like the whip. Honest to God he never. He didn't, I swear!

VICARRO: Do what?

FLORA: The fire . . .

31

VICARRO: Go on.

FLORA: Please don't!

VICARRO: Don't what?

FLORA: Put it down. The whip, please put it down. Leave it out here on the porch.

VICARRO: What are you scared of?

FLORA: You.

VICARRO: Go on. [*She turns helplessly and moves to the screen. He pulls it open.*]

FLORA: Don't follow. Please don't follow! [*She sways uncertainly. He presses his hand against her. She moves inside. He follows. The door is shut quietly. The gin pumps slowly and steadily across the road. From inside the house there is a wild and despairing cry. A door is slammed. The cry is repeated more faintly.*]

CURTAIN

It is about nine o'clock the same evening. Although the sky behind the house is a dusky rose color, a full September moon of almost garish intensity gives the front of the house a ghostly brilliance. Dogs are howling like demons across the prostrate fields of the Delta.

The front porch of the Meighans is empty.

After a moment the screen door is pushed slowly open and Flora Meighan emerges gradually. Her appearance is ravaged. Her eyes have a vacant limpidity in the moonlight, her lips are slightly apart. She moves with her hands stretched gropingly before her till she has reached a pillar of the porch. There she stops and stands moaning a little. Her hair hangs loose and disordered. The upper part of her body is unclothed except for a torn pink band about her breasts. Dark streaks are visible on the bare shoulders and arms and there is a large discoloration along one cheek. A dark trickle, now congealed, descends from one corner of her mouth. These more apparent tokens she covers with one hand when Jake comes up on the porch. He is now heard approaching, singing to himself.

JAKE: By the light—by the light—by the light—Of the sil-very mo-o-on! [*Instinctively Flora draws back into the sharply etched shadow from the porch roof. Jake is too tired and triumphant to notice her appearance.*] How's a baby? [*Flora utters a moaning grunt.*] Tired? Too tired t' talk? Well, that's how I feel. Too tired t' talk. Too goddam tired t' speak a friggin' word! [*He lets himself down on the steps, groaning and without giving Flora more than a glance.*] Twenty-seven wagons full of cotton. That's how much I've ginned since ten this mawnin'. A man-size job.

FLORA [*huskily*]: Uh-huh. . . . A man-size—job. . . .

JAKE: *Twen*-ty *sev*-en *wa*-gons *full* of *cot*-ton!

FLORA [*senselessly repeating*]: *Twen*-ty *sev*-en *wa*-gons *full* of *cot*-ton! [*A dog howls. Flora utters a breathless laugh.*]

JAKE: What're you laughin' at, honey? Not at me, I hope.

FLORA: No. . . .

JAKE: That's good. The job that I've turned out is nothing to laugh at. I drove that pack of niggers like a mule skinner. They don't have a brain in their bodies. All they got is bodies. You got to drive, drive, drive. I don't even see how niggers eat without somebody to tell them to put the food in their moufs! [*She laughs again, like water spilling out of her mouth.*] Huh! You got a laugh like a— Christ. A terrific day's work I finished.

FLORA [*slowly*]: I would'n' brag—about it. . . .

JAKE: I'm not braggin' about it, I'm just sayin' I done a big day's work, I'm all wo'n out an' I want a little appreciation, not cross speeches. Honey. . . .

FLORA: I'm not—[*She laughs again.*]—makin' cross speeches.

JAKE: To take on a big piece of work an' finish it up an' mention the fack that it's finished I wouldn't call braggin'.

FLORA: You're not the only one's—done a big day's—work.

JAKE: Who else that you know of? [*There is a pause.*]

FLORA: Maybe you think that I had an easy time. [*Her laughter spills out again.*]

JAKE: You're laughin' like you been on a goddam jag. [*Flora laughs.*] What did you get pissed on? Roach poison or citronella? I think I make it pretty easy for you, workin' like a mule

34

skinner so you can hire you a nigger to do the wash an' take the housework on. An elephant woman who acks as frail as a kitten, that's the kind of a woman I got on m' hands.

FLORA: Sure. ·. . . [*She laughs.*] You make it easy!

JAKE: I've yet t' see you lift a little finger. Even gotten too lazy t' put you' things on. Round the house ha'f naked all th' time. Y' live in a cloud. All you can think of is "Give me a Coca-Cola!" Well, you better look out. They got a new bureau in the guvamint files. It's called U.W. Stands for Useless Wimmen. Tha's secret plans on foot t' have 'em shot! [*He laughs at his joke.*]

FLORA: Secret—plans—on foot?

JAKE: T' have 'em *shot.*

FLORA: That's good. I'm glad t' hear it. [*She laughs again.*]

JAKE: I come home tired an' you cain't wait t' peck at me. What 're you cross about now?

FLORA: I think it was a mistake.

JAKE: What was a mistake?

FLORA: Fo' you t' fool with th' Syndicate—Plantation. . . .

JAKE: I don't know about that. We wuh kind of up against it, honey. Th' Syndicate buyin' up all th' lan' aroun' here an' turnin' the ole croppers off it without their wages—mighty near busted ev'ry mercantile store in Two Rivers County! An' then they build their own gin to gin their own cotton. It looked for a while like I was stuck up high an' dry. But when the gin burnt down an' Mr. Vicarro decided he'd better throw a little bus'ness my way—I'd say the situation was much improved!

FLORA [*laughing weakly*]: Then maybe you don't understand th' good-neighbor—policy.

JAKE: Don't understand it? Why, I'm the boy that invented it.

FLORA: Huh-huh! What an—*invention!* All I can say is—I hope you're satisfied now that you've ginned out—twenty-seven wagons full of—cotton.

JAKE: Vicarro was pretty well pleased w'en he dropped over.

FLORA: Yeah. He was—pretty well—pleased.

JAKE: How did you all get along?

FLORA: We got along jus' fine. Jus' fine an'—dandy.

JAKE: He didn't seem like a such a bad little guy. He takes a sensible attitude.

FLORA [*laughing helplessly*]: He—sure—does!

JAKE: I hope you made him comfo'table in the house?

FLORA [*giggling*]: I made him a pitcher—of nice cold—lemonade!

JAKE: With a little gin in it, huh? That's how you got pissed. A nice cool drink don't sound bad to me right now. Got any left?

FLORA: Not a bit, Mr. Meighan. We drank it *a-a-ll* up! [*She flops onto the swing.*]

JAKE: So you didn't have such a tiresome time after all?

FLORA: No. Not tiresome a bit. I had a nice conversation with Mistuh—Vicarro. . . .

JAKE: What did you all talk about?

FLORA: Th' good-neighbor policy.

JAKE [*chuckling*]: How does he feel about th' good-neighbor policy?

FLORA: Oh—[*She giggles.*]—He thinks it's a—good idea! He says—

JAKE: Huh? [*Flora laughs weakly.*] Says what?

FLORA: Says—[*She goes off into another spasm of laughter.*]

JAKE: What ever he said must've been a panic!

FLORA: He says—[*controlling her spasm*]—he don't think he'll build him a new cotton gin any more. He's gonna let you do a-a-lll his ginnin'—fo' him!

JAKE: I told you he'd take a sensible attitude.

FLORA: Yeah. Tomorrow he plans t' come back—with lots more cotton. Maybe another twenty-seven wagons.

JAKE: Yeah?

FLORA: An' while you're ginnin' it out—he'll have me entertain him with—nice lemonade! [*She has another fit of giggles.*]

JAKE: The more I hear about that lemonade the better I like it. Lemonade highballs, huh? Mr. Thomas Collins?

FLORA: I guess it's—gonna go on fo'—th' rest of th'—summer. . . .

JAKE [*rising and stretching happily*]: Well, it'll . . . it'll soon be fall. Cooler nights comin' on.

FLORA: I don't know that that will put a—stop to it—though. . . .

JAKE [*obliviously*]: The air feels cooler already. You shouldn't be settin' out here without you' shirt on, honey. A change in the air can give you a mighty bad cold.

FLORA: I couldn't stan' nothin' on me—nex' to my—skin.

JAKE: It ain't the heat that gives you all them hives, it's too much liquor. Grog-blossoms, that's what you got! I'm goin' inside to the toilet. When I come out—[*He opens the screen door and goes in.*]—we'll drive in town an' see what's at th' movies. You go hop in the Chevy! [*Flora laughs to herself. She slowly opens the huge kid purse and removes a wad of Kleenex. She touches herself tenderly here and there, giggling breathlessly.*]

FLORA [*aloud*]: I really oughtn' t' have a white kid purse. It's wadded full of—Kleenex—to make it big—like a baby! Big—in my arms—like a baby!

JAKE [*from inside*]: What did you say, Baby?

FLORA [*dragging herself up by the chain of the swing*]: I'm not—Baby. Mama! Ma! That's—me. . . . [*Cradling the big white purse in her arms, she advances slowly and tenderly to the edge of the porch. The moon shines full on her smiling and ravaged face. She begins to rock and sway gently, rocking the purse in her arms and crooning.*] Rock-a-bye Baby—in uh tree-tops! If a wind blows—a cradle will rock! [*She descends a step.*] If a bough bends—a baby will fall! [*She descends another step.*] Down will come Baby—cradle—an'—all! [*She laughs and stares raptly and vacantly up at the moon.*]

CURTAIN

THE PURIFICATION

FOR MARGO JONES

A play in verse to be performed with a musical accompaniment on the guitar. The action takes place in the Western ranchlands over a century ago. The characters are Spanish ranchers and Indians.

The placenames used in this play are associated mainly with the country around Taos, New Mexico, but that is merely because those names and that country come most familiarly to my mind: it is the clear, breathtaking sort of country that I like to imagine as the background for the play. Actually I do not know whether or not people of this type ever lived there and I don't believe it matters. The characters are as follows:

THE JUDGE, an aristocratic rancher of middle age

THE SON, a youth of twenty, handsome, irrationally tense of feeling

THE MOTHER, pure blooded Castillian with iron-gray hair, dressed in rich mourning

THE FATHER, tall and gaunt, a steady wine-drinker: brooding and slow of movement

THE RANCHER FROM CASA ROJO, the burnt-out shell of a longing that drove to violence. His blood is coarser than the people from Casa Blanca. But he is a man of dignity and force.

LUISA, an Indian servant-woman—some Spanish blood. A savage nature. She wears a good deal of jewelry and a brilliant shawl

AN INDIAN YOUTH

A CHORUS OF THREE MEN AND THREE WOMEN, ranchers

THE GUITAR PLAYER, he wears a domino and a scarlet-lined cape—he sits on a stool beside the wide arched doorway

ELENA OF THE SPRINGS AND THE DESERT ELENA, two visions of the same character—the lost girl

ıııllllllllllllllllllllllllllllllllllllllllllllllllllllllllllllllllllllllllllllllllllllllllllllllllllllllllllllllllllllllll

A bare room, white or pearl gray. A number of plain wooden benches, a small square table for the Judge. Skull of a steer on wall. The wide arched door admits a vista of plain and sky: the sky is a delicate aquamarine: the plain pale gold. A range of purplish mountains between. Two high-set windows with sunlight slanting through them.

A crime has been committed: an informal trial is being conducted. The Chorus file silently onto the stage and seat themselves on the benches as the curtain rises. Next comes The Guitar Player. He plays softly as the main characters come in. The Judge remains standing back of the table till the others are seated.

ıııllllllllllllllllllllllllllllllllllllllllllllllllllllllllllllllllllllllllllllllllllllllllllllllllllllllllllllllllllllllll

THE JUDGE:

Well, my neighbors, I know about as much of court procedure
as any reasonably well-informed jackrabbit.
Nevertheless I seem to be the Judge.
And I was put in office more, I hope,
for what you know about me than what I know.
I do not believe in one man judging another:
I'd rather that those who stand in need of judgment
would judge themselves.
Honor being
more than a word amongst us
I have no doubt
that this is the kind of judgment which will prevail.
We're all of us ranchers—neighbors—
Our enmities, sometimes bloody, are usually brief.
Our friendships—longer lasting.
And that is good. . . . What I mean to say is simply this—
We know each other sufficiently well, I think,
to get along without much ceremony.
An evil thing has occurred.
The reasons are still beclouded.
This much we know: the rains are long delayed.

41

The season is parched.
Our hearts, like forests stricken by the drought,
are quick to flame.
Well, flames have broken out, not only in the Lobos,
but here, between two ranches.
Rain is needed.
Rain's the treatment for a forest fire.
For violent deeds likewise the rain is needed.
The rain I speak of is the rain of truth,
for truth between men is the only purification.
How is it over the Lobos, Señor Moreno?

RANCHER [*the one nearest the door*]: Clouded a little.

JUDGE: Bueno!
[*catching sight of a flask*]
Drinking inside is forbidden—outside is not my business
So let's get on with what we have come to do.
You neighbors from Casa Blanca—
I ask you first
to speak concerning your daughter—
[*facing The Mother*]
You, the mother,
what do you have to say?

[*The Mother bows her head.*]

FATHER: She cannot speak.

JUDGE: Can you?

FATHER: Not like a man with any of his senses.

JUDGE:
Then like a man without them, if you will—
But speak up freely—

42

Speak out the broken language of your hearts
and we'll supply the sense where it seems to be needed.

[*Chord on guitar*]

FATHER:
It is not easy to tell you
about our daughter.
Her name was Elena.

SON:
She had no name
for no one here could name her.

MOTHER: Her name—was Elena.

SON:
Her skeleton,
much too elastic,
stitched together
the two lost frozen blue poles!

[*A murmur among The Chorus*]

LUISA: The tainted spring—is bubbling.

FATHER:
He means to say
she went beyond our fences.

SON:
I mean to say
she went beyond all fences.
The meadow grasses
continued entirely too far

43

beyond where the gate
was broken—in several—places . . .

LUISA [*mockingly*]: Listen—bubbling, bubbling!

FATHER: Our son is demented.

MOTHER: Since the death of our daughter.

LUISA: The tainted spring—is bubbling!

[*The Chorus murmur. The Judge raises his hand to warn them.*]

JUDGE: The boy would speak?

MOTHER [*quickly*]: He is not able to speak!

JUDGE:
I think he can speak,
but in the language of vision.
Rosalio, would you
speak concerning your sister?

SON [*slowly rising*]:
Her eyes were always
excessively clear in the morning.
Transparency is a bad omen
in very young girls!
It makes flight
                   necessary
                              sometimes!
[*facing his parents*]
You should have bought her
        the long crystal beads that she wanted . . .

44

MOTHER [*gently, not looking up*]:
But how could we know
she would have been satisfied with them?

SON:
Oh, I know, Mother,
you fear that she might have desired
to discover reflections in them
of something much farther away
than those spring freshets she bathed in,
naked, clasping her groin
rigidly, with both palms,
against the cold
immaculate kiss of snow-water!

[*The Chorus murmur*]

LUISA: The tainted spring—is bubbling!

[*The Rancher places a restraining hand on Luisa's shoulder.*]

FATHER:
He means to say
she went beyond our fences.

SON:
Beyond all fences, Father.
She knew also
glaciers, intensely blue,
valleys, brilliant with sunlight,
lemon-yellow, terrific!
        And desolation
that stretched too widely apart
the white breastbones of her body!

LUISA: Bubbling—bubbling!

45

[*The Father touches his arm but he continues, facing the door.*]

SON [*violently*]:
Not even noon's
        thundering
                statement
                        crescendo
                                of distance!
Knocking down walls
        with two
                blue
                        brutal
                              bare fists
                                    clenched over quicksilver
could ever—[*tenderly*]
        could certainly never—enclose
such longing as was my sister's!
How much less night,
fearlessly stating with stars
        that breathless inflection—
                              Forever?

[*The wordless singing rises. The wide arched portal that gives on the aquamarine of the desert sky now lightens with a ghostly radiance. Bells toll softly. The guitar weaves a pattern of rapture.*
Rosalio's sister, Elena of the Springs, steps into the doorway. She wears a sheer white robe and bears white flowers. With slender candlelike fingers she parts the shawl that covers her head and reveals her face. Her lips are smiling. But only The Son, Rosalio, is aware of the apparition—he and The Guitar Player. The others stare at the Indian woman, Luisa, who rises stiffly from the bench beside The Rancher from Casa Rojo.]

LUISA [*clutching her wooden beads*]:

You have heard the dead lady compared to mountain water.
A very good comparison, I think.
I once led goats through the mountains:
we stopped to drink.
It seemed the purest of fountains.
Five of the goat herd died.
I only survived because I had promised the master
that I would return
in time for the Feast of the Virgin . . .
The water was crystal—but it was fouled at the source.
The water was—tainted water!

[*The girl of the vision lowers her head and covers her face and her garland with the shawl. The guitar plays—sad and sinister. She turns and withdraws from the doorway.*]

SON [*springing furiously at the servant*]: *Madre de Dios!*

JUDGE: Restrain him!

[*The Father holds him back, dramatic chords on the guitar.*]

SON: This whore should be made to taste of the bastinado!

MOTHER:
Patience, my son.
The *zopilote* will croak—we cannot prevent it!

JUDGE: You people from Casa Blanca will serve us best in advancing your own satisfaction by holding the peace until this witness has finished.
[*to Luisa*]
Go on, Señora. But please to avoid uncalled-for offense to these people.

LUISA:
The youth's demented. That's true.

47

He used to ride on his pony past our place.
He cried out loud to some invisible creatures as even a moment ago you saw his rapturous gaze at an empty doorway.
The moon, I suspect,
has touched his head too fondly.

CHORUS:
The moon, we suspect,
has touched his head too fondly.

[*They nod and mumble.*]

LUISA:
You know how it is in August?
In August the heavens
take on more brilliance, more fire.
They become—unstable.
And then I believe it is well to stay indoors,
to keep yourself at a sensible occupation.
This one lacked prudence, however.
He rode at night, bareback,
through the Sangre de Cristo,
shouting aloud and making ridiculous gestures.
[*The guitar plays—lyrical chords.*]
You know how it is in August?

CHORUS: Yes, in August!

LUISA:
The stars make—sudden excursions.
The moon's—lopsided.
The dogs go howling like demons about the ranches.

CHORUS: Howling like demons!

LUISA:
I'm wise—I stay indoors.

But this one here, this youth from Casa Blanca,
continually raced and raced
through the mountain larches—
until exhaustion stopped him.
When he stopped—
it was not always in his own enclosures.

[*The Chorus gossip and nod. The Judge warns them.*]

No—
He pastured his pony some nights at Casa Rojo.
His visits were unannounced except by the pony's
neighing in the distance, borne down windward.
On one such occasion as this
I climbed upstairs to notify the mistress.
This was unnecessary: her bed was empty:
the covers—thrown aside.

[*Guitar. The Chorus whisper. The Judge silences them.*]

I did not trouble the master, he was sleeping,
but went alone through the meadow:
the grasses were chill: I shivered:
I bore no lantern—the starlight proved sufficient.
I had not come to the barn
when suddenly through the window of the loft,
that was lit with the wavering radiance of a candle—
two naked figures appeared in a kind of—dance . . .

[*Loud dramatic chords on the guitar. Castanets and drums.
Shocked murmur among the women. The Chorus rise and
talk among themselves.*]

RANCHER: *Basta! Basta*, Luisa!

[*He clenches his hands in torment.*]

49

LUISA: Someone has got to speak!

MOTHER [*rising*]:
So at last it is out—
this infamous slander whispered against our house!

[*Silence.*]

FATHER [*choked*]: What man of this woman's people will answer for it?

LUISA:
I am alone.
I'll answer for it myself.

THE JUDGE:
Resume your seats, *mis vecinos.*
It is foolish to feign surprise at the charge now spoken.
A thing so persistently whispered in our kitchens
is better spoken out in the presence of all.
So now it is necessary to face it squarely.

[*The guitar plays—tragic, tormented. The Son looks down without moving.*]

LUISA [*smiling*]: Why doesn't he stand?

FATHER: Rosalio, stand!—And speak!

MOTHER [*rising*]: No!—Wait!
[*She speaks softly, tenderly, and makes delicate gestures with her hands which are ringed with rubies and sapphires.*]
My son is the victim of an innocent rapture.
His ways are derived of me.
I also rode on horseback through the mountains
in August as well as in March—

50

I also shouted and made ridiculous gestures
before I grew older and learned the uselessness of it . . .
If this imputes some dark guilt on the doer,
Then I, his mother, must share in this public censure.
Sangre mala—call it.

CHORUS [*whispering*]: *Sangre mala! Sangre mala!*

MOTHER:
Our people—were Indian-fighters . . .
The Indians now are subdued—
So what can we do but contend with our own queer shadows?

THE JUDGE: Señora—

MOTHER:
Bear with me a while,
for I must explain things to you.

FATHER:
Callate, Maria!
Rosalio, stand and speak!

[*The Son looks at The Judge.*]

THE JUDGE: Yes, Rosalio, speak.

[*The Son rises slowly, twisting the length of white rope between his hands.*]

SON: What do you want me to tell you?

THE JUDGE [*smiling*]: Simply the truth.

SON:
The truth?

Why ask me for that?
Ask it of him, the player—
for truth is sometimes alluded to in music.
But words are too loosely woven to catch it in . . .
A bird can be snared as it rises
or torn to earth by the falcon.
His song, which is truth,
is not to be captured ever.
It is an image, a dream,
it is the link to the mother,
the belly's rope that dropped our bodies from God
a longer time ago than we remember!
I—forget.

[*The Chorus murmur.*]

LUISA: The tainted spring—is bubbling.

SON: Player! Prompt me with music.

[*The Guitar Player sweeps the strings.*]

SON [*with a sudden smile*]:
How shall I describe
the effect that a song had on us?
On nights of fiesta
the ranch-boys, eager with May,
surrounded our fences
with little drum-gourds, with guitars.
   [*facing The Mother*]
You, Mother, would wash
the delicate white lace curtains,
sweep down the long stairs
and scent the alcoves with lemon.
   [*Chord on the guitar.*]
How shall I describe

the effect that a song had on us?
Our genitals were too eager!

MOTHER [*involuntarily*]: No!

LUISA: Listen!

SON:
Player, prompt me with music
For I have lost the thread.
Weave back my sister's image.
[*Music*]
No. She's lost,
Snared as she rose,
      or torn to earth by the falcon!
      No, she's lost,
      Irretrievably lost,
Gone out among Spanish-named ranges.
     [*He smiles vaguely.*]
Too far to pursue
      except on the back of that lizard . . .

LUISA: Bubbling! Bubbling!

MOTHER: Rosalio!

[*The Father touches her shoulder.*]

SON:
. . . Whose green phosphorescence,
      scimitar-like,
            disturbs midnight
wtih hissing, metallic sky-prowling . . .

JUDGE:
Is this the chimera you,

you moon-crazed youth,
pursued through the mountains?

SON: No . . .

[*Luisa laughs harshly.*]

LUISA:
How shall he describe
the effect that a song had on him!

SON: I washed my body in snow.

LUISA: Because it was shameful!

SON:
Yes!
And now you may know
How well indeed I succeeded
in putting out fires.
My sister is free.
    [*To The Rancher*]
His hand gave liberty to her.
But mine—a less generous agent—
Only gave her—longings . . .

[*The Mother cries out. The Father rises. The Chorus murmur.*]

LUISA: *Sangre mala!*

[*A peal of thunder outside.*]

JUDGE:
A house that breeds in itself
will breed destruction.

LUISA: *Sangre mala!*

FATHER [*passionately*]:
In our blood
was the force that carved this country!
Sangre mala, you call it?

THE JUDGE:
Your pride turned inward too far,
excluded the world and lost itself in a mirror.

MOTHER:
No, we admitted too much of the world, I think.
We should have put up more fences.
The Conquistadors must not neglect their fences.

FATHER: Ours were neglected.

MOTHER: We poured our blood in the desert to make it flower.

FATHER: The flowers were not good flowers.

[*The sky through the doorway darkens. Wind moans.*]

MOTHER: They were neglected.

SON [*tormented*]: Mother!

MOTHER: I never should have poured—dark wine—at supper.

SON: Mother!

MOTHER:
Yes—yes, lately the place
        has grown a great deal wilder
because of neglect

              or maybe because
winds take more liberty with it.
Storms seem to come more often.

FATHER:
Year after year it's the same.
I step out the door, a little bit drunk after supper,
to watch down the valley—
          Five miles off, even ten,
the rainstorms advancing
          like armies of tall, silent men.
          Nothing changes . . .

MOTHER:
But isn't it strange
how things grow up in a life?
Like trees—
One spring planted—accepted—forgotten almost,
Then all of a sudden—crowding the backyard with shadows!

FATHER:
Invaders!
We are invaders ourselves.
These ranches, these golden valleys—
A land so fiercely contested as this land was.
Father's blood and mother's anguish bought it!
Is it to be merely used for cattle to graze on?
Are we to build on it nothing but barns and fences?
No, no, we are invaders. We used the land—gave nothing!
But even so—
This man has killed our daughter.
We ask in return his life.

MOTHER: Demand his life in return.

LUISA: Hear how the blood-lust in them cries out loud!

THE JUDGE:
Rosalio, in your presence your sister was slain.
It is for you to accuse the man who . . .

SON [*springing up*]: Yes, I accuse him!

LUISA:
Your tongue should be torn from your mouth and flung to
buzzards!
Shameless—Shameless!

SON:
Yes, I am shameless—shameless.
The kitchen-woman has spoken her kitchen truth.
The loft of the barn was occupied by lovers
not once, not twice, but time and time again,
whenever our blood's rebellion broke down bars.
Resistless it was,
this coming of birds together
in heaven's center . . .
Plumage—song—the dizzy spirals of flight
all suddenly forced together
in one brief, burning conjunction!
Oh—oh—
a passionate little spasm of wings and throats
that clutched—and uttered—darkness . . .
Down
        down
                down
Afterwards, shattered,
we found our bodies in grass.
   [*Soft music*]
The coolness healed us,
        the evening drained our fever,
bandaged the wounded part in silk of stars . . .

57

And so did the wind take back the startling pony—
and hurl him down arroyos toward the dawn!

[*He sinks down on the bench between his parents.*]

THE JUDGE [*rising*]:
Enough for a while—enough. The court is thirsty.
   [*He crosses to door and shouts.*]
Muchachos! Run to the well and bring us water!
Or if you prefer—*habanero!*
Musician—play!

[*Smiling cavalierly, The Guitar Player moves sinuously forward. He stands in the light through the window and plays a
danson. Gourds and buckets of water are brought inside and
passed among the benches.*

The Judge returns from the doorway.]

THE JUDGE:
The clouds are darkening still.
If heaven is good enough to send us rain,
the court will be suspended until tomorrow.
Now let us get on.

[*He pauses before the people from Casa Blanca.*]

Rosalio, could you not guess
that this violation of blood which you have acknowledged
would certainly—sooner or later—
bring shame—disaster?

SON:
We knew—and we did not know.
We were oblivious of this sun-bleached man
who sullenly dreamed to possess her.
But he of us derived his green suspicion,
    the only green thing in him,
watered and tended by this sly Indian woman.
He, our former repair man,
mender of our broken fences,
which almost without our knowledge had grown to be his,
till he seized on the girl—instead of Casa Blanca.
Finding that all of his clutching was finally gainless,
clutched an axe!
For he would be owner of something—or else destroy it!

[*The guitar sounds. He faces The Rancher.*]

You, repair man, come early,
before daybreak can betray you.
Now clasp in your hand
the smooth white heft of the axe!
But wait! Wait—first—

59

Fill up the tin buckets
with chalky white fluid, the milk
of that phosphorescent green lizard—
Memory, passion.

LUISA: The tainted spring . . .

SON:
Unsatisfied old appetites—
And stir these together—
carefully, not to slop over—

LUISA: . . . is bubbling!

SON [*to Luisa*]:
You, too,
assist in this business.
Bring a scapular blade
to remove the stained parts of the lumber—
collection of rags
to scrub the splatterings off.

MOTHER [*moaning*]: Ahhh—ahhh . . .

SON [*deliriously*]:
For often toward daybreak that rime
of the reptile's diamond-like progress . . .

LUISA [*mockingly*]: He wanders again. The tainted spring is
bubbling!

SON:
. . . makes following easy
for those who desire to pursue him.
He depends on his tail's rapid motion,
scimitar-like—green lightning—

60

to stave off hunters!
You have to skip rope lightly, handyman,
our former repair man,
you have to skip rope lightly—lightly!—lightly!
Carry your axe and your bucket
slow-clanking past frozen hen-houses
where sinister stalactite fowls make rigid comment
claw—beak—
barely, perceptibly stirring their russet feathers—
on purpose of your quiet passage.
Go on—go on to where
the barn,
that moon-paled building,
large
and church-like in arch of timber,
tumescent between the sensual fingers of vines,
intractably waits
this side of your death-coition!
There halt, repair man,
for surely the light will halt you if nothing else does.

[*Guitar*]

RANCHER [*trance-like*]:
It stood
in a deep well of light.
It stood like a huge wrecked vessel—in deep seas of light!

SON: You halted . . .

CHORUS [*like an echo*]: Halt!

RANCHER: Yes.

SON: At this immemorial vault,

61

CHORUS: Vault!

SON:
this place of plateaux
and ranges of Spanish-named mountains . . .

CHORUS: Mountains!

RANCHER:
Yes.
I set up the ladder.

SON:
Set up the steep, steep ladder—
Narrow . . .

RANCHER:
Narrow!—Enquiring
If Christ be still on the Cross!

CHORUS: Cross!

SON: Against the north wall set it . . .

RANCHER:
Set it and climbed . . .
[*He clutches his forehead.*] Climbed!

CHORUS: Climbed!

SON:
Climbed!
To the side of the loft
that gave all things to the sky.
The axe—

for a single moment—
saluted the moon—then struck!

CHORUS: Struck!

SON: And she didn't cry . . .

RANCHER:
Struck?
Aye, struck—struck—*struck!*

CHORUS: Struck!

[*Dissonant chords on the guitar, with cymbals. The two men surge together and struggle like animals till they are torn apart. There is a rumble of thunder.*]

THE JUDGE:
Thunder?—Over the Lobos.
Señores,
Your passion is out of season.
This is the time for reflection to calm the brain,
as later, I hope, the rain will cool our ranches.
I know that truth
evades the certain statement
but gradually and obliquely filters through
the mind's unfettering in sleep and dream.
The stammered cry gives more of truth than the hand
could put on passionless paper . . .
My neighbor from Casa Rojo,
Stand and speak your part in this dark recital.
You say that the woman Elena
never allowed you freely the right of marriage?

RANCHER:
Never freely, and never otherwise.

63

It was no marriage.
They have compared her to water—and water, indeed, she was.
Water that ran through my fingers when I was athirst.
Oh, from the time that I worked at Casa Blanca,
a laborer for her people, as they have mentioned,
I knew there was something obscure—subterranean—
cool—from which she drew her persistence,
when by all rights
of what I felt to be nature,
she should have dried—as fields in a rainless summer,
a summer like this one that presently starves our grainfields,
she should have dried, this seemingly loveless woman,
and *yet* she *didn't*.
Yes, she was cool, she was water,
even as they have described her—
but water sealed under the rock—where I was concerned.
I burned.
I burned.
I burned . . .

[*Three dissonant notes are sounded on the guitar. There is a feverish, incessant rustling sound like wind in a heap of dead leaves.*]

RANCHER [*hoarsely*]:
I finally said to her once,
in the late afternoon it was, and she stood in the doorway . . .

[*The dissonant notes are repeated. The rustling is louder. A sound of mocking laughter outside the door, sudden and brief.*
The Desert Elena appears. It is the same lost girl, but not as the brother had seen her. This is the vision of the loveless bride, the water sealed under rock from the lover's thirst— not the green of the mountains and the clear swift streams, but the sun-parched desert. Her figure is closely sheathed in a coarse-fibered bleached material, her hair bound tight to her

64

*skull. She bears a vessel in either hand, like balanced scales,
one containing a cactus, the other a wooden grave-cross with
a wreath of dry, artificial flowers on it. Only The Rancher
observes her.*]

RANCHER:
'Woman,' I said to her, 'Woman, what keeps you alive?'
'What keeps you sparkling so, you make-believe fountain?'
[*to the vision*]
'You and the desert,' I told her,
'You are sisters—sisters beneath the skin!'
But even the desert is sometimes pregnant with something,
distorted progeny,
twisted, dry, imbecilic,
gives birth to the cacti,
the waterless Judas tree.
The blood of the root makes liquor to scorch the brain and
put foul oaths on the tongue.
But you—you, woman, bear nothing,
nothing ever but death—which is all you will get
with your pitiful—stone kind of body.

ELENA: Oh, no—I will get something more.

THE JUDGE:
More? You will get something more?
Where will it come from—lovely, smiling lady?

[*The dead leaves rustle.*]

Will it come singing and shouting and plunging bareback down
canyons
and run like wild birds home to Sangre de Cristo
when August crazes the sky?

ELENA [*smiling*]: Yes!

65

RANCHER [*to the Judge*]:
Yes, she admitted, yes!
For in their house, these people from Casa Blanca—no one
can say they fear to speak the truth!

ELENA:
Perhaps it will come as you say—but until then
The fences are broken—mend them.
The moon is needing a new coat of whitewash on it!
Attend to that, repair man! Those are your duties.
But keep your hands off me!

RANCHER: My hands are empty—starved!

ELENA: Fill them with chicken feathers! Or buzzard feathers.

RANCHER: My lips are dry.

ELENA:
Then drink from the cistern. Or if the cistern is empty, moisten
your lips with the hungry blood of the fox that kills our fowls.

RANCHER: The fox-blood burns!

ELENA:
Mine, too.
I have no coolness for you:
my hands are made of the stuff in the dried sulphur pools.
These are my gifts:
the cactus, the bleached grave-cross with the wreath of dead
vines on it.
Listen! The wind, when it blows,
is rattling dry castanets in the restless grave-yard.
The old monks whittle—they make prayer-beads in the cellar.
Their fingers are getting too stiff to continue the work.
They dread the bells. For the bells are heavy and iron
and have no wetness in them.

The bones of the dead have cracked from lack of moisture.
The sisters come out in a quick and steady file and their black
skirts whisper dryer and dryer and dryer,
until they halt
before their desperate march has reached the river.
The river has turned underground.
The sisters crumble: beneath their black skirts crumble,
the skirts are blown and the granular salty bodies
go whispering off among the lifeless grasses . . .
I must go too,
For I, like these, have glanced at a burning city.
Now let me go!

[*She turns austerely and moves away from the door. Three
dissonant notes on the guitar and the sound of dead rustling
leaves is repeated. A yellow flash of lightning in the portal,
now vacant, and the sound of wind.*]

RANCHER:
My hand shot out, whip-like, to catch at her wrist,
But she had gone . . .
My wife—that make-believe fountain—had fled from the door.

[*He covers his face with his hands.*]

THE JUDGE [*rising*]:
Player, give us the music
of wind that promises rain.
The time is dry.
But clouds have come,
and the sound of thunder is welcome.
Now let the Indian women tread the earth
in the dance that destroys the locust!

[*The three white-robed women rise from their bench and
move in front. They perform a slow, angular dance to drums*]

67

and guitar. Their movements slow. The music softens. The
dance and the music become a reticent background for the
speech.]

RANCHER:

Elena had fled through the door as the storm broke on us.
She had fled through the open door, out over the fields
darkening down the valley
where rain was advancing
its tall silent squadrons of silver.
Her figure was lost
in a sudden convulsion of shadows
heaved by the eucalyptus.

[*The dancers raise their arms.*]

The rain came down
as sound of rapturous trumpets rolled over the earth,
and still
the delicate warmthless yellow
of late afternoon persisted
behind
that transparent curtain of silver.
At once the clouds
had changed their weight into motion,
their inkiness thinned,
their cumulous forms rose higher,
their edges were stirred
as radiant feathers, upwards, above the mountains.

[*Distant choral singing. Wordless. "La Golondrina" is woven*
into the music.]

RANCHER:

A treble choir
now sang in the eucalyptus,

an Angelus rang!
  [*Bells*]
The whole wide vault of the valley,
the sweep of the plain
assumed a curious lightness under the rain.
The birds already, the swallows,
before the rainstorm ceased,
had begun to climb
the atmosphere's clean spirals.
Ethereal wine
intoxicated these tipplers,
their notes were wild
and prodigal as fool's silver.
The moon,
unshining, blank, bone-like,
stood over the Lobos mountains
and grinned and grinned
like a speechless idiot where
the cloud-mass thinned . . .
I saw her once more—briefly,
running along by the fence at the end of the meadow.
The long and tremendous
song of the eucalyptus described this flight:
the shoulders inclined stiffly forward,
the arms flung out, throat arched,
more as though drunk
with a kind of heroic abandon—than blinded—by fright.
  [*He covers his face.*]
Forgive me . . .

  [*The cloud that darkened the sun passes over. The stream of
  fierce sunlight returns through the door and the windows.
  The women return to the bench.*]

The Judge pours water from a gourd to wet his handkerchief and wipes his forehead.

THE JUDGE:
The clouds have cheated again—and crossed away.
Our friend the sun comes back like an enemy now.
We want the rain—the coolness—the shade . . .
It is not given us yet.

THE WOMEN [*softly chanting*]:
Rojo—rojo
Rojo de sangre es el sol.

THE JUDGE:
It is the lack of what he desires most keenly
that twists a man out of nature.
When you were a boy, my friend from Casa Rojo,
you were gentle—withdrew too much from the world.
This reticence, almost noble, persisted through youth,
but later, as you grew older,
an emptiness, still unfilled, became a cellar,
a cellar into which blackness dripped and trickled,
a slow, corrosive seepage.
Then the reticence
was no longer noble—but locked—resentful,
and breeding a need for destruction.
What was clear?

RANCHER: Nothing was clear.

THE JUDGE: What was straight?

RANCHER: Nothing was straight.

THE JUDGE: How did the light come through?

RANCHER: Through the crookedest entrance, the narrowest areaway!

THE JUDGE: And where you walked—what was it you walked among?

RANCHER: A pile of my own dead bones—like discarded lumber.

THE JUDGE: The day was still.

RANCHER: Oppressively still.

THE JUDGE:
Noon—breathless. The sky was vacant.
White—plague-like—exhausted.

RANCHER:
Once it disgorged
a turbulent swarm of locusts.
Heat made wave-like motions
over the terrible
desert statement of distance.
Giants came down,
invisibly,
pounding huge—huge—drums!

THE WOMEN [*softly*]:
*Rojo—rojo
rojo de sangre es el sol!*

[*A low drumming*]

RANCHER:
Drummers!
            Drummers!

71

Go back under my skull.
There is a time for nightmare's reality later!
Ahhh—ahhh—with disgust.
With fur on the tongue,
with mucous-inflamed eyeballs,
fever enlarging the horrible chamber at night!

THE WOMEN:
Rojo—rojo
rojo de sangre es el sol!

RANCHER:
Now do you wonder
that with no divining rod excepting my thirst
I looked for coolness of springs
in the woman's body?
That finding none,
or finding it being cut off—drained away
at the source—by the least suspected,
I struck?
And *struck?*
And tore the false rock open?

THE WOMEN: *Rojo—rojo.*

RANCHER:
I own my guilt.
I own it before you ranchers, before you women.
I say that I struck with an axe
at the wife's false body
and would have struck him, too,
but my strength went from me.
I found the two together
and clove them apart
with that—the axe.

72

No more,
there is no more.

THE WOMEN:
Rojo de sangre es el sol!
Rojo—rojo.
Rojo de sangre es el sol!

[*The Rancher sinks to the bench. The Son rises. A cloud again passes over the sky. There is a glimmer of lightning and the fretful murmur of wind. A dimness replaces the glare that was in the room. The women murmur and draw their shawls about them.*]

SON [*facing The Rancher*]:
You shall not defame her,
nor shall you defile her,
this quicksilver girl,
this skyward diver,
this searcher after pearls,
terrestrial striver!
Blue—
    Blue—
        Immortally blue
is space at last . . .
I think she always knew
that she would be lost in it.
Lost in it? Where!
In which if any direction!
Player, with music lead us!
Lead us—Where?

[*The Guitar Player, with an assenting smile, rises by the door.*]

SON [*with gestures of infinite longing*]:
O stallion lover

73

the night is your raped white mare!
The meadow grasses continued entirely too far
beyond where the gate—is broken in several places.
Cling to it, dark child,
till it carries you further than ever.
O make it swing out
to the wildest and openest places!
The most—indestructible places!
For nothing contains you now,
no, nothing contains you,
lost little girl, my sister,
not even those—little—blue veins
that carried the light to your temples,
O springtime jets
so torrential they burst their vessels
and spattered the sky!

[*Bells toll softly once more and the girl reappears in the doorway. It is the first vision again—Elena of the Springs. The Son stumbles toward her.*]

SON: Elena.

[*She shakes her head with a sorrowful smile.*]

Elena!

[*He whips a knife from his belt and holds it above him.*]

Witness—in this thrust—our purification!

[*He plunges the knife into his breast. Everyone rises with a soft intake of breath. The Guitar Player stands and sweeps back his crimson cape. He accompanies the speech and action wtih delicate chords.*]

MOTHER [*unbearably*]: My son!

SON: Elena . . .

[*The vision retreats smiling, transcendent. The Son drops the knife and leans in the open doorway. The sky darkens and there is a rumble of thunder. A voice in the distance cries "Rain!"*]

SON [*looking out with a smile*]:
Peeto, our pony,
catches the scent in his nostrils
of thunderstorms coming . . .

[*A delicate chord on the guitar.*]

When Peeto was born
he stood on his four legs at once, and accepted the world.
He was wiser than I.
When Peeto was one year old,
he was wiser than God!

A VOICE [*nearer*]: The rain! The rain! The rain!

SON [*with a faint smile, glancing up*]:
Peeto! Peeto!
The Indian boys call after . . .

VOICE [*still nearer*]: the rain!

SON:
. . . trying to stop him,
trying to stop—the wind . . .

[*He lurches forward and falls to the floor. An Indian Youth in a wet blue shirt and sombrero bursts in the doorway, shouting.*]

YOUTH: The rain! The rain! The . . .

[*He tears off his sombrero and flings the rain from the brim across the courtroom. Then he suddenly observes the body on the floor. He falls respectfully silent and bows his head. Outside is heard the faint and haunting music of guitars, accompanied by the wordless singing of women. Rain can be heard falling steadily and gently on the roof.*]

MOTHER [*quietly, rising from her knees, facing The Rancher*]:
Pass him the knife.

RANCHER:
I thank you, Señora.
This generous offer, however, is unrequired.

[*He removes from his belt a silver knife.*]

I also came prepared for—purification.

[*He turns to the Indian.*]

What did you say?—The rain?
As one who has suffered overlong from drought
I'd like the cooling taste of rain on my lips.

[*He bows.*]

Señoras—Señores . . .
Follow me if you will—I go outside.

[*He moves to the door.*]

LUISA: Stop him!

[*She faces the chorus pleadingly but all are motionless. With a sob, she tries to rush outside with The Rancher. Indians at*

*either side of the door clutch her arms and hold her pinioned
in the archway. She writhes between them. The Guitar Player
strikes a somber chord.*]

THE JUDGE:
It needs no witness.

[*He crosses in front of the table.*]

Here on this plain,
between these mountain ranges,
we seem to have bred
some feeling of honor amongst us,
deeper than law.
That is good.
It is good that we keep it bright against the time
when lesser breeds than we,
invaders!—honorless thieves and killers without any conscience,
come—as they someday will
to try that honor.
If men keep honor, the rest can be arranged.
The rest will arrange itself—in the course of time.

[*Outside an alarum of trumpets. Luisa screams. The Guitar
Player tosses his hat in the middle of the floor.*]

THE JUDGE [*turning and bowing to the audience*]: *Mañana es
otro dio.*
The play is done!

[*The Guitar Player sweeps his strings as the curtain falls
slowly.*]

CURTAIN

THE LADY OF LARKSPUR LOTION*

* *Larkspur Lotion is a common treatment for body vermin.*

CHARACTERS

MRS. HARDWICKE-MOORE

MRS. WIRE

THE WRITER

THE LADY OF LARKSPUR LOTION

A wretchedly furnished room in the French Quarter of New Orleans. There are no windows, the room being a cubicle partitioned off from several others by imitation walls. A small slanting skylight admits the late and unencouraging day. There is a tall, black armoire, whose doors contain cracked mirrors, a swinging electric bulb, a black and graceless dresser, an awful picture of a Roman Saint and over the bed a coat-of-arms in a frame.

Mrs. Hardwicke-Moore, a dyed-blonde woman of forty, is seated passively on the edge of the bed as though she could think of nothing better to do.

There is a rap at the door.

MRS. HARDWICKE-MOORE [*in a sharp, affected tone*]: Who is at the door, please?

MRS. WIRE [*from outside, bluntly*]: Me! [*Her face expressing a momentary panic, Mrs. Hardwicke-Moore rises stiffly.*]

MRS. HARDWICKE-MOORE: Oh. . . . Mrs. Wire. Come in. [*The landlady enters, a heavy, slovenly woman of fifty.*] I was just going to drop in your room to speak to you about something.

MRS. WIRE: Yeah? What about?

MRS. HARDWICKE-MOORE [*humorously, but rather painfully smiling*]: Mrs. Wire, I'm sorry to say that I just don't consider these cockroaches to be the most desirable kind of room-mates—do you?

MRS. WIRE: Cockroaches, huh?

MRS. HARDWICKE-MOORE: Yes. Precisely. Now I have had very little experience with cockroaches in my life but the few that

I've seen before have been the pedestrian kind, the kind that *walk*. These, Mrs. Wire, appear to be *flying* cockroaches! I was shocked, in fact I was literally stunned, when one of them took off the floor and started to whiz through the air, around and around in a circle, just missing my face by barely a couple of inches. Mrs. Wire, I sat down on the edge of this bed and *wept*, I was just so shocked and disgusted! Imagine! Flying cockroaches, something I never dreamed to be in existence, whizzing around and around and around in front of my face! Why, Mrs. Wire, I want you to know—

MRS. WIRE [*interrupting*]: Flying cockroaches are nothing to be surprised at. They have them all over, even uptown they have them. But that ain't what I wanted to—

MRS. HARDWICKE-MOORE [*interrupting*]: That may be true, Mrs. Wire, but I may as well tell you that I have a horror of roaches, even the plain old-fashioned, pedestrian kind, and as for this type that flies—! If I'm going to stay on here these flying cockroaches have got to be gotten rid of and gotten rid of at *once!*

MRS. WIRE: Now how'm I going to stop them flying cockroaches from coming in through the windows? But that, however, is not what I—

MRS. HARDWICKE-MOORE [*interrupting*]: I don't know *how*, Mrs. Wire, but there certainly must be a method. All I know is they must be gotten rid of before I will sleep here one more night, Mrs. Wire. Why, if I woke up in the night and found one on my bed, I'd have a convulsion, I swear to goodness I'd simply *die* of convulsions!

MRS. WIRE: If you'll excuse me for sayin' so, Mrs. Hardshell-Moore, you're much more likely to die from over-drinkin' than cockroach convulsions! [*She seizes a bottle from the dresser.*] What's this here? Larkspur Lotion! *Well!*

MRS. HARDWICKE-MOORE [*flushing*]: I use it to take the old polish off my nails.

MRS. WIRE: Very fastidious, yes!

MRS. HARDWICKE-MOORE: What do you mean?

MRS. WIRE: There ain't an old house in the Quarter that don't have roaches.

MRS. HARDWICKE-MOORE: But not in such enormous quantities, do they? I tell you this place is actually crawling with them!

MRS. WIRE: It ain't as bad as all that. And by the way, you ain't yet paid me the rest of this week's rent. I don't want to get you off the subjeck of roaches, but, nevertheless, I want to colleck that money.

MRS. HARDWICKE-MOORE: I'll pay you the rest of the rent as soon as you've exterminated these roaches!

MRS. WIRE: You'll have to pay me the rent right away or get out.

MRS. HARDWICKE-MOORE: I intend to get out unless these *roaches* get out!

MRS. WIRE: Then get out then and quit just talking about it!

MRS. HARDWICKE-MOORE: You must be out of your mind, I can't get out right now!

MRS. WIRE: Then what did you mean about roaches?

83

MRS. HARDWICKE-MOORE: I meant what I said about roaches, they are not, in my opinion, the most desirable roommates!

MRS. WIRE: Okay! Don't room with them! Pack your stuff and move where they don't have roaches!

MRS. HARDWICKE-MOORE: You mean that you *insist* upon having the roaches?

MRS. WIRE: No, I mean I insist upon having the rent you owe me.

MRS. HARDWICKE-MOORE: Right at the moment that is out of the question.

MRS. WIRE: Out of the question, is it?

MRS. HARDWICKE-MOORE: Yes, and I'll tell you why! The quarterly payments I receive from the man who is taking care of the rubber plantation have not been forwarded yet. I've been expecting them to come in for several weeks now but in the letter that I received this morning it seems there has been some little misunderstanding about the last year's taxes and—

MRS. WIRE: Oh, now stop it, I've heard enough of that goddam rubber plantation! The Brazilian rubber plantation! You think I've been in this business seventeen years without learning nothing about your kind of women?

MRS. HARDWICKE-MOORE [*stiffly*]: What is the implication in that remark?

MRS. WIRE: I suppose the men that you have in here nights come in to discuss the Brazilian rubber plantation?

MRS. HARDWICKE-MOORE: You must be crazy to say such a thing as that!

84

MRS. WIRE: I hear what I hear an' I know what's going on!

MRS. HARDWICKE-MOORE: I know you spy, I know you listen at doors!

MRS. WIRE: I never spy and I never listen at doors! The first thing a landlady in the French Quarter learns is not to *see* and not to *hear* but only collect your *money!* As long as that comes in—okay, I'm blind, I'm deaf, I'm dumb! But soon as it stops, I recover my hearing and also my sight and also the use of my voice. If necessary I go to the phone and call up the chief of police who happens to be an in-law of my sister's! I heard last night that argument over money.

MRS. HARDWICKE-MOORE: What argument? What money?

MRS. WIRE: He shouted so loud I had to shut the front window to keep the noise from carrying out on the streets! I heard no mention of any Brazilian plantation! But plenty of other things were plainly referred to in that little midnight conversation you had! Larkspur Lotion—to take the polish off nails! Am I in my infancy, am I? That's on a par with the wonderful *rubber* plantation! [*The door is thrown open. The Writer, wearing an ancient purple bathrobe, enters.*]

WRITER: Stop!

MRS. WIRE: *Oh!* It's *you!*

WRITER: Stop persecuting this woman!

MRS. WIRE: The second Mr. Shakespeare enters the scene!

WRITER: I heard your demon howling in my sleep!

MRS. WIRE: *Sleep?* Ho-*ho!* I think that what you *mean* is your *drunken stupor!*

WRITER: I rest because of my illness! Have I no right—

MRS. WIRE [*interrupting*]: Illness—*alcoholic!* Don't try to pull that beautiful wool over my eyes. I'm glad you come in now. Now I repeat for your benefit what I just said to this woman. I'm *done* with *deadbeats!* Now is that plain to yuh? Completely fed-up with all you Quarter rats, half-breeds, drunkards, degenerates, who try to get by on promises, lies, delusions!

MRS. HARDWICKE-MOORE [*covering her ears*]: *Oh, please, please, please stop shrieking!* It's not necessary!

MRS. WIRE [*turning on Mrs. Hardwicke-Moore*]: You with your Brazilian rubber plantation. That coat-of-arms on the wall that you got from the junk-shop—the woman who sold it *told* me! One of the Hapsburgs! Yes! A titled lady! *The Lady of Larkspur Lotion! There's* your *title!* [*Mrs. Hardwicke-Moore cries out wildly and flings herself face down on the sagging bed.*]

WRITER [*with a pitying gesture*]: Stop badgering this unfortunate little woman! Is there no mercy left in the world anymore? What has become of compassion and understanding? Where have they all gone to? Where's God? Where's Christ? [*He leans trembling against the armoire.*] What if there *is* no Brazilian rubber plantation?

MRS. HARDWICKE-MOORE [*sitting passionately erect*]: I tell you there is, there *is!* [*Her throat is taut with conviction, her head thrown back.*]

WRITER: What if there *is* no rubber king in her life! There *ought* to be rubber kings in her life! Is she to be blamed because it is necessary for her to compensate for the cruel deficiencies of reality by the exercise of a little—what shall I say?—God-given—imagination?

MRS. HARDWICKE-MOORE [*throwing herself face down on the bed once more*]: No, no, no, no, it *isn't*—imagination!

MRS. WIRE: I'll ask you to please stop spitting me in the face those high-flown speeches! You with your 780-page masterpiece—right on a par with the Lady of Larkspur Lotion as far as the use of imagination's concerned!

WRITER [*in a tired voice*]: Ah, well, now, what if I am? Suppose there *is* no 780-page masterpiece in existence. [*He closes his eyes and touches his forehead.*] Supposing there is in existence no masterpiece whatsoever! What of that, Mrs. Wire? But only a few, a very few—vain scribblings—in my old trunk-bottom. . . . Suppose I wanted to be a great artist but lacked the force and the power! Suppose my books fell short of the final chapter, even my verses languished uncompleted! Suppose the curtains of my exalted fancy rose on magnificent dramas—but the houselights darkened before the curtain fell! Suppose all of these unfortunate things are true! And suppose that I—stumbling from bar to bar, from drink to drink, till I sprawl at last on the lice-infested mattress of this brothel—suppose that I, to make this nightmare bearable for as long as I must continue to be the helpless protagonist of it—suppose that I ornament, illuminate—glorify it! With dreams and fictions and fancies! Such as the existence of a 780-page masterpiece—impending Broadway productions—marvelous volumes of verse in the hands of publishers only waiting for signatures to release them! Suppose that I live in this world of pitiful fiction! What satisfaction can it give you, good woman, to tear it to pieces, to crush it—call it a *lie*? I tell you this—now listen! There are no lies but the lies that are stuffed in the mouth by the hard-knuckled hand of need, the cold iron fist of necessity, Mrs. Wire! So I am a liar, yes! But your world is built on a lie, your world is a hideous fabrication of lies! Lies! Lies! . . . Now I'm tired and I've said my say and I have no money to give you so get away and leave this woman in peace! Leave her alone. Go on, get out, get away! [*He shoves her firmly out the door.*]

MRS. WIRE [*shouting from the other side*]: Tomorrow morning! Money or out you go! Both of you. Both together! 780-page masterpiece and Brazilian rubber plantation! *BALONEY!* [*Slowly the derelict Writer and the derelict woman turn to face each other. The daylight is waning grayly through the skylight. The Writer slowly and stiffly extends his arms in a gesture of helplessness.*]

MRS. HARDWICKE-MOORE [*turning to avoid his look*]: Roaches! Everywhere! Walls, ceiling, floor! The place is infested with them.

WRITER [*gently*]: I know. I suppose there weren't any roaches on the Brazilian rubber plantation.

MRS. HARDWICKE-MOORE [*warming*]: No, of course there weren't. Everything was immaculate always—always. *Immaculate!* The floors were so bright and clean they used to shine like—mirrors!

WRITER: I know. And the windows—I suppose they commanded a very lovely view!

MRS. HARDWICKE-MOORE: Indescribably lovely!

WRITER: How far was it from the Mediterranean?

MRS. HARDWICKE-MOORE [*dimly*]: The Mediterranean? Only a mile or two!

WRITER: On a very clear morning I daresay it was possible to distinguish the white chalk cliffs of Dover? . . . Across the channel?

MRS. HARDWICKE-MOORE: Yes—in very clear weather it *was.*

[*The Writer silently passes her a pint bottle of whisky.*] Thank you, Mr.—?

WRITER: Chekhov! Anton Pavlovitch Chekhov!

MRS. HARDWICKE-MOORE [*smiling with the remnants of co-quetry*]: Thank you, Mr.—Chekhov.

CURTAIN

THE LAST OF MY SOLID GOLD WATCHES

Ce ne peut être que la fin du monde, en avançant.

RIMBAUD

THIS PLAY IS INSCRIBED TO MR. SIDNEY GREENSTREET,
FOR WHOM THE PRINCIPAL CHARACTER WAS HOPEFULLY CONCEIVED.

CHARACTERS

MR. CHARLIE COLTON

A NEGRO, a porter in the hotel

HARPER, a traveling salesman

THE LAST OF MY
SOLID GOLD WATCHES

||||||||||||||||||||||||||||||||||||||||||||||||||||||||||||||||||||||||||||||||||||||||||||||||||||||||||||||||||||||||||||||||||||

A hotel room in a Mississippi Delta town. The room has looked the same, with some deterioration, for thirty or forty years. The walls are mustard-colored. There are two windows with dull green blinds, torn slightly, a ceiling fan, a white iron bed with a pink counterpane, a washstand with rosebuds painted on the pitcher and bowl, and on the wall a colored lithograph of blind-folded Hope with her broken lyre.

The door opens and Mr. Charlie Colton comes in. He is a legendary character, seventy-eight years old but still "going strong." He is lavish of flesh, superbly massive and with a kingly dignity of bearing. Once he moved with a tidal ease and power. Now he puffs and rumbles; when no one is looking he clasps his hand to his chest and cocks his head to the warning heart inside him. His huge expanse of chest and belly is criss-crossed by multiple gold chains with various little fobs and trinkets suspended from them. On the back of his head is a derby and in his mouth a cigar. This is "Mistuh Charlie"—who sadly but proudly refers to himself as "the last of the Delta drummers." He is followed into the room by a Negro porter, as old as he is—thin and toothless and grizzled. He totes the long orange leather sample cases containing the shoes which Mr. Charlie is selling. He sets them down at the foot of the bed as Mr. Charlie fishes in his pocket for a quarter.

||||||||||||||||||||||||||||||||||||||||||||||||||||||||||||||||||||||||||||||||||||||||||||||||||||||||||||||||||||||||||||||||||||

MR. CHARLIE [*handing the coin to the Negro*]: Hyunh!

NEGRO [*breathlessly*]: Thankyseh!

MR. CHARLIE: Huh! You're too old a darkey to tote them big heavy cases.

NEGRO [*grinning sadly*]: Don't say that, Mistuh Charlie.

MR. CHARLIE: I reckon you'll keep right at it until yuh drop some day.

NEGRO: That's right, Mistuh Charlie. [*Mr. Charlie fishes in his pocket for another quarter and tosses it to the Negro, who crouches and cackles as he receives it.*]

MR. CHARLIE: Hyunh!

NEGRO: Thankyseh, thankyseh!

MR. CHARLIE: Now set that fan in motion an' bring me in some ice water by an' by!

NEGRO: De fan don' work, Mistuh Charlie.

MR. CHARLIE: Huh! Deterioration! Everything's going downhill around here lately!

NEGRO: Yes, suh, dat's de troof, Mistuh Charlie, ev'ything's goin' downhill.

MR. CHARLIE: Who all's registered here of my acquaintance? Any ole-timers in town?

NEGRO: Naw, suh, Mistuh Charlie.

MR. CHARLIE: "Naw-suh-Mistuh-Charlie" 's all I get any more! You mean to say I won't be able to scare up a poker game?

NEGRO [*chuckling sadly*]: Mistuh Charlie, you's de bes' judge about dat!

MR. CHARLIE: Well, it's mighty slim pickin's these days. Ev'ry time I come in a town there's less of the old and more of the new and by God, nigguh, this new stand of cotton I see around

94

the Delta's not worth pickin' off th' ground! Go down there an' tell that young fellow, Mr. Bob Harper, to drop up here for a drink!

NEGRO [*withdrawing*]: Yes, suh.

MR. CHARLIE: It looks like otherwise I'd be playin' solitaire!

[*The Negro closes the door. Mr. Charlie crosses to the window and raises the blind. The evening is turning faintly blue. He sighs and opens his valise to remove a quart of whisky and some decks of cards which he slaps down on the table. He pauses and clasps his hand over his chest.*]

MR. CHARLIE [*ominously to himself*]: Boom-boom-boom-boom-boom! Here comes th' parade! [*After some moments there comes a rap at the door.*] Come awn in! [*Harper, a salesman of thirty-five, enters. He has never known the "great days of the road" and there is no vestige of grandeur in his manner. He is lean and sallow and has a book of colored comics stuffed in his coat pocket.*]

HARPER: How is the ole war-horse?

MR. CHARLIE [*heartily*]: Mighty fine an' dandy! How's the young squirrel?

HARPER: Okay.

MR. CHARLIE: That's the right answer! Step on in an' pour you'self a drink! Cigar?

HARPER [*accepting both*]: Thanks, Charlie.

MR. CHARLIE [*staring at his back with distaste*]: Why do you carry them comic sheets around with yuh?

HARPER: Gives me a couple of laughs ev'ry once and a while.

MR. CHARLIE: Poverty of imagination! [*Harper laughs a little resentfully.*] You can't tell me there's any real amusement in them things. [*He pulls it out of Harper's coat pocket.*] "Superman," "The Adventures of Tom Tyler!" Huh! None of it's half as fantastic as life itself! When you arrive at my age—which is seventy-eight—you have a perspective of time on earth that astounds you! Literally astounds you! Naw, you say it's not true, all of that couldn't have happened! And for what *reason?* Naw! You begin to wonder. . . . Well . . . You're with Schultz and Werner?

HARPER: That's right, Charlie.

MR. CHARLIE: That concern's comparatively a new one.

HARPER: I don't know about that. They been in th' bus'ness fo' goin' on twenty-five years now, Charlie.

MR. CHARLIE: Infancy! Infancy! You heard this one, Bob? A child in its infancy don't have half as much fun as adults—in their adultery! [*He roars with laughter. Harper grins. Mr. Charlie falls silent abruptly. He would have appreciated a more profound response. He remembers the time when a joke of his would precipitate a tornado. He fills up Harper's glass with whisky.*]

HARPER: Ain't you drinkin'?

MR. CHARLIE: Naw, suh. Quit!

HARPER: How come?

MR. CHARLIE: Stomach! Perforated!

96

HARPER: Ulcers? [*Mr. Charlie grunts. He bends with difficulty and heaves a sample case onto the bed.*] I had ulcers once.

MR. CHARLIE: *Ev'ry* drinkin' man has ulcers once. Some *twice.*

HARPER: You've fallen off some, ain't you?

MR. CHARLIE [*opening the sample case*]: Twenty-seven pounds I lost since August. [*Harper whistles. Mr. Charlie is fishing among his samples.*] Yay-ep! Twenty-seven pounds I lost since August. [*He pulls out an oxford which he regards disdainfully.*] Hmmm . . . A waste of cowhide! [*He throws it back in and continues fishing.*] A man of my age an' constitution, Bob—he oughtn't to carry so much of that—adipose tissue! It's— [*He straightens up, red in the face and puffing.*] —a terrible strain—on the *heart!* Hand me that other sample—over yonder. I wan' t' show you a little eyeful of queenly footwear in our new spring line! Some people say that the Cosmopolitan's not abreast of the times! That is an allegation which I deny and which I intend to disprove by the simple display of one little calfskin slipper! [*opening up the second case*] Here we are, Son! [*fishing among the samples*] You knew ole "Marblehead" Langner in Friar's Point, Mississippi.

HARPER: Ole "Marblehead" Langner? Sure.

MR. CHARLIE: They found him dead in his bathtub a week ago Satiddy night. *Here's* what I'm lookin' faw!

HARPER: "Marblehead"? Dead?

MR. CHARLIE: *Buried!* Had a Masonic funeral. I helped carry th' casket. Bob, I want you t' look at this Cuban-heel, shawl-tongue, perforated toe, calfskin Misses' sport-oxford! [*He elevates it worshipfully.*] I want you to look at this shoe—and tell me what you think of it in plain language! [*Harper whistles and bugs his eyes.*] Ain't that a piece of *real* merchandise, you squirrel? Well, suh, I want you t' know—!

HARPER: Charlie, that certainly is a piece of merchandise there!

MR. CHARLIE: Bob, that piece of merchandise is only a small indication—of what our spring line consists of! You don't have to pick up a piece of merchandise like that—with I.S.C. branded on it!—and examine it with the microscope t' find out if it's quality stuff as well as quality *looks!* This ain't a shoe that Mrs. Jones of Hattiesburg, Mississippi, is going to throw back in your face a couple or three weeks later because it come to pieces like *card*board in th' first *rain!* No, suh—I want you to know! We got some pretty fast-movers in our spring line—I'm layin' my samples out down there in th' lobby first thing in th' mornin'— I'll pack 'em up an' be gone out of town by *noon*— But by the Almighty Jehovah I bet you I'll have to *wire* the office to mail me a bunch of *brand*-new order-books at my next stopping-*off* place, Bob! *Hot* cakes! *That's* what I'm sellin'! [*He returns exhaustedly to the sample case and tosses the shoe back in, somewhat disheartened by Harper's vaguely benevolent contemplation of the brass light fixture. He remembers a time when people's attention could be more securely riveted by talk. He slams the case shut and glances irritably at Harper who is staring very sadly at the brown carpet.*] Well, suh— [*He pours a shot of whisky.*] It was a mighty shocking piece of news I received this afternoon.

HARPER [*blowing a smoke ring*]: What piece of news was that?

MR. CHARLIE: The news about ole Gus Hamma—one of the old war-horses from *way* back, Bob. He and me an' this boy's daddy, C. C., used t' play poker ev'ry time we hit town together in this here selfsame room! Well, suh, I want you t' know—

HARPER [*screwing up his forehead*]: I think I heard about that. Didn't he have a stroke or something a few months ago?

98

MR. CHARLIE: He *did*. An' partly *recovered*.

HARPER: Yeah? Last I heard he had t' be fed with a spoon.

MR. CHARLIE [*quickly*]: He did an' he partly recovered! He's been goin' round, y'know, in one of them chairs with a 'lectric motor on it. Goes chug-chug-chuggin' along th' road with th' butt of a cigar in his mouth. Well, suh, yestuddy in Blue Mountain, as I go out the Elks' Club door I pass him comin' in, bein' helped by th' nigguh— "Hello! Hiyuh, Gus!" That was at six-fifteen. Just half an hour later Carter Bowman stepped inside the hotel lobby where I was packin' up my sample cases an' give me the information that ole Gus Hamma had just now burnt himself to death in the Elks' Club lounge!

HARPER [*involuntarily grinning*]: What uh yuh talkin' about?

MR. CHARLIE: Yes, suh, the ole war-horse had fallen asleep with that nickel cigar in his mouth—set his clothes on fire—and burnt himself right up like a piece of paper!

HARPER: I don't believe yuh!

MR. CHARLIE: Now, why on earth would I be lyin' to yuh about a thing like that? He burnt himself right up like a piece of paper!

HARPER: Well, ain't that a bitch of a way for a man to go?

MR. CHARLIE: *One* way—*another* way—! [*gravely*] Maybe you don't *know* it—but all of us ole-timers, Bob, are disappearin' *fast!* We all gotta quit th' road one time or another. Me, I reckon I'm pretty nearly the last of th' Delta drummers!

HARPER [*restively squirming and glancing at his watch*]: The last—of th' Delta drummers! How long you been on th' road?

99

MR. CHARLIE: Fawty-six yeahs in Mahch!

HARPER: I don't believe yuh.

MR. CHARLIE: Why would I tell you a lie about something like that? No, suh, I want you t' know— I want you t' know— Hmmm. . . . I lost a mighty good customer this week.

HARPER [*with total disinterest, adjusting the crotch of his trousers*]: How's that, Charlie?

MR. CHARLIE [*grimly*]: Ole Ben Summers—Friar's Point, Mississippi . . . Fell over dead like a bolt of lightning had struck him just as he went to pour himself a drink at the Cotton Planters' Cotillion!

HARPER: Ain't that terrible, though! What was the trouble?

MR. CHARLIE: Mortality, that was the trouble! Some people think that millions now living are never going to *die*. I don't think that—I think it's a misapprehension not borne out by the facts! We go like flies when we come to the end of the summer . . . And who is going to prevent it? [*He becomes depressed.*] Who—is going—to prevent it! [*He nods gravely.*] The road is changed. The shoe industry is changed. These times are—revolution! [*He rises and moves to the window.*] I don't like the way that it looks. You can take it from me—the world that I used to know—the world that this boy's father used t' know—the world we belonged to, us old time war-horses!—is slipping and sliding away from under our shoes. Who is going to prevent it? The ALL LEATHER slogan don't sell shoes any more. The stuff that a shoe's made of is not what's going to sell it any more! No! STYLE! SMARTNESS! APPEARANCE! That's what counts with the modern shoe-purchaser, Bob! But try an' tell your style department that. Why, I remember the time when all I had to do was lay out my samples down there in the lobby. Open up my order-book an' write out orders until my fingers *ached!* A *sales*-talk was not *necessary.* A store was a place where people sold merchandise and to sell merchandise the retail-dealer had to obtain it from the wholesale manufacturer, Bob! Where they get merchandise now I do not pretend to know. But it don't look like they buy it from wholesale dealers! Out of the air—I guess it materializes! Or maybe stores don't *sell* stuff any more! Maybe I'm living in a world of illusion! I recognize that possibility, too!

HARPER [*casually, removing the comic paper from his pocket*]: Yep—yep. You must have witnessed some changes.

MR. CHARLIE: Changes? A mild expression. Young man—I have witnessed—a REVOLUTION! [*Harper has opened his comic paper but Mr. Charlie doesn't notice, for now his peroration is really addressed to himself.*] Yes, a *revolution!* The atmosphere that I *breathe* is not the same! Ah, well—I'm an old war-horse. [*He opens his coat and lifts the multiple golden chains from his vest. An amazing number of watches rise into view. Softly, proudly he speaks.*] Looky here, young fellow! You ever seen a man with this many watches? How did I *acquire* this many timepieces? [*Harper has seen them before. He glances above the comic sheet with affected amazement.*] At every one of the annual sales conventions of the Cosmopolitan Shoe Company in St. Louis a seventeen-jewel, solid gold, Swiss movement Hamilton watch is presented to the ranking salesman of the year! Fifteen of those watches have been awarded to me! I think that represents something! I think that's *something* in the way of achievement! . . . Don't *you?*

HARPER: Yes, *siree!* You bet I *do,* Mistuh Charlie! [*He chuckles at a remark in the comic sheet. Mr. Charlie sticks out his lips with a grunt of disgust and snatches the comic sheet from the young man's hands.*]

101

MR. CHARLIE: Young man—I'm talkin' to *you,* I'm talkin' for your *benefit.* And I expect the courtesy of your attention until I am through! I may be an old war-horse. I may have received— the last of my solid gold watches . . . But just the same—good manners are still a part of the road's tradition. And part of the *South's* tradition. Only a young peckerwood would look at the comics when old Charlie Colton is talking.

HARPER [*taking another drink*]: Excuse me, Charlie. I got a lot on my mind. I got some business to attend to directly.

MR. CHARLIE: And directly you shall attend to it! I just want you to know what I think of this new world of yours! I'm not one of those that go howling about a Communist being stuck in the White House now! I don't say that Washington's been took over by Reds! I don't say all of the wealth of the country is in the hands of the Jews! I like the Jews and I'm a friend to the niggers! I *do* say *this*—however. . . . The world I knew is gone—gone—gone with the wind! My pockets are full of watches which tell me that my time's just about over! [*A look of great trouble and bewilderment appears on his massive face. The rather noble tone of his speech slackens into a senile complaint.*] All of them—pigs that was slaughtered—carcasses dumped in the river! Farmers receivin' payment *not* t' grow wheat an' corn an' *not* t' plant cotton! All of these alphȧbet letters that's sprung up all about me! Meaning—unknown—to men of my generation! The rudeness—the lack of respect—the newspapers full of strange items! The terrible—fast—dark—rush of events in the world! Toward what and where and why! . . . I don't pre- tend to have any knowledge of now! I only say—and I say this very humbly—I don't understand—what's happened. . . . I'm one of them monsters you see reproduced in museums—out of the dark old ages—the giant *rep*-tiles, and the dino-whatever-you- call-ems. BUT—I *do* know *this!* And I state it without any shame! Initiative—self-reliance—independence of character! The old sterling qualities that distinguished one man from another—

the clay from the potters—the potters from the clay—are—
[*kneading the air with his hands*] How is it the old song
goes? . . . Gone with the roses of *yesterday!* Yes—with the
wind!

HARPER [*whose boredom has increased by leaps and bounds*]:
You old-timers make one mistake. You only read one side of the
vital statistics.

MR. CHARLIE [*stung*]: What do you mean by that?

HARPER: In the papers they print people *dead* in one corner
and people *born* in the next and usually *one* just about levels *off*
with the *other.*

MR. CHARLIE: Thank you for that information. I happen to be
the godfather of several new infants in various points on the
road. However, I think you have missed the whole point of
what I was saying.

HARPER: I don't think so, Mr. Charlie.

MR. CHARLIE: Oh, yes, you have, young fellow. My point is
this: the ALL-LEATHER slogan is not what sells any more—
not in shoes and not in humanity, neither! The emphasis isn't on
quality. Production, production, yes! But out of inferior goods!
Ersatz—that's what they're making 'em out of!

HARPER [*getting up*]: That's your opinion because you belong
to the past.

MR. CHARLIE [*furiously*]: A piece of impertinence, young man!
I expect to be accorded a certain amount of respect by whipper-
snappers like you!

HARPER: Hold on, Charlie.

103

MR. CHARLIE: I belong to—tradition. I am a *legend*. Known from one end of the Delta to the other. From the Peabody Hotel in Memphis to Cat-Fish Row in Vicksburg. Mistuh Charlie—*Mistuh Charlie!* Who knows *you?* What do *you* represent? A line of goods of doubtful value, some kike concern in the East! Get out of my room! I'd rather play solitaire, than poker with men who're no more solid characters than the jacks in the deck! [*He opens the door for the young salesman who shrugs and steps out with alacrity. Then he slams the door shut and breathes heavily. The Negro enters with a pitcher of ice water.*]

NEGRO [*grinning*]: What you shoutin' about, Mistuh Charlie?

MR. CHARLIE: I lose my patience sometimes. Nigger—

NEGRO: Yes, suh?

MR. CHARLIE: You remember the way it used to be.

NEGRO [*gently*]: Yes, suh.

MR. CHARLIE: I used to come in town like a conquering hero! Why, my God, nigger—they all but laid red carpets at my feet! Isn't that so?

NEGRO: That's so, Mistuh Charlie.

MR. CHARLIE: This room was like a *throne* room. My samples laid out over there on green velvet cloth! The ceiling fan *going*—now *broken!* And over here—the washbowl an' pitcher removed and the tabletop *loaded* with *liquor!* In and out from the time I arrived till the time I left, the men of the road who knew me, to whom I stood for things commanding respect! Poker—continuous! Shouting, laughing—hilarity! Where have they all gone to?

NEGRO [*solemnly nodding*]: The graveyard is crowded with folks we knew, Mistuh Charlie. It's mighty late in the day!

MR. CHARLIE: Huh! [*He crosses to the window.*] Nigguh, it ain't even late in the day any more— [*He throws up the blind.*] It's NIGHT! [*The space of the window is black.*]

NEGRO [*softly, with a wise old smile*]: Yes, suh . . . *Night,* Mistuh Charlie!

CURTAIN

PORTRAIT OF A MADONNA

|||||||||||||||||||||||||||||||||||||||||||||||||||||||||||||||||||||||||||||||||||||||||||||||||||||||||||||||

CHARACTERS

MISS LUCRETIA COLLINS

THE PORTER

THE ELEVATOR BOY

THE DOCTOR

THE NURSE

MR. ABRAMS

PORTRAIT OF A MADONNA

The living room of a moderate-priced city apartment. The furnishings are old-fashioned and everything is in a state of neglect and disorder. There is a door in the back wall to a bedroom, and on the right to the outside hall.

MISS COLLINS: Richard! [*The door bursts open and Miss Collins rushes out, distractedly. She is a middle-aged spinster, very slight and hunched of figure with a desiccated face that is flushed with excitement. Her hair is arranged in curls that would become a young girl and she wears a frilly negligee which might have come from an old hope chest of a period considerably earlier.*] No, no, no, no! I don't care if the whole church hears about it! [*She frenziedly snatches up the phone.*] Manager, I've got to speak to the manager! Hurry, oh, please hurry, there's a *man—*! [*wildly aside as if to an invisible figure*] Lost all respect, absolutely no respect! . . . Mr. Abrams? [*in a tense hushed voice*] I don't want any reporters to hear about this but something awful has been going on upstairs. Yes, this is Miss Collins' apartment on the top floor. I've refrained from making any complaint because of my connections with the church. I used to be assistant to the Sunday School superintendent and I once had the primary class. I helped them put on the Christmas pageant. I made the dress for the Virgin and Mother, made robes for the Wise Men. Yes, and now this has happened, I'm not responsible for it, but night after night after night this man has been coming into my apartment and—indulging his senses! Do you understand? Not once but repeatedly, Mr. Abrams! I don't know whether he comes in the door or the window or up the fire escape or whether there's some secret entrance they know about at the church, but he's here now, in my bedroom, and I can't force him to leave, I'll have to have some assistance! No, he isn't a thief, Mr. Abrams, he comes of a very fine family in Webb, Mississippi, but this woman has ruined his character, she's destroyed his respect for ladies! Mr. Abrams? Mr.

109

Abrams! Oh, goodness! [*She slams up the receiver and looks distractedly about for a moment; then rushes back into the bedroom.*] Richard! [*The door slams shut. After a few moments an old porter enters in drab gray coveralls. He looks about with a sorrowfully humorous curiosity, then timidly calls.*]

PORTER: Miss Collins? [*The elevator door slams open in hall and the Elevator Boy, wearing a uniform, comes in.*]

ELEVATOR BOY: Where is she?

PORTER: Gone in 'er bedroom.

ELEVATOR BOY [*grinning*]: She got him in there with her?

PORTER: Sounds like it. [*Miss Collins' voice can be heard faintly protesting with the mysterious intruder.*]

ELEVATOR BOY: What'd Abrams tell yuh to do?

PORTER: Stay here an' keep a watch on 'er till they git here.

ELEVATOR BOY: Jesus.

PORTER: Close 'at door.

ELEVATOR BOY: I gotta leave it open a little so I can hear the buzzer. Ain't this place a holy sight though?

PORTER: Don't look like it's had a good cleaning in fifteen or twenty years. I bet it ain't either. Abrams'll bust a blood vessel when he takes a lookit them walls.

ELEVATOR BOY: How comes it's in this condition?

PORTER: She wouldn't let no one in.

110

ELEVATOR BOY: Not even the paperhangers?

PORTER: Naw. Not even the plumbers. The plaster washed down in the bathroom underneath hers an' she admitted her plumbin' had been stopped up. Mr. Abrams had to let the plumber in with this here passkey when she went out for a while.

ELEVATOR BOY: Holy Jeez. I wunner if she's got money stashed around here. A lotta freaks do stick away big sums of money in ole mattresses an' things.

PORTER: She ain't. She got a monthly pension check or something she always turned over to Mr. Abrams to dole it out to 'er. She tole him that Southern ladies was never brought up to manage finanshul affairs. Lately the checks quit comin'.

ELEVATOR BOY: Yeah?

PORTER: The pension give out or somethin'. Abrams says he got a contribution from the church to keep 'er on here without 'er knowin' about it. She's proud as a peacock's tail in spite of 'er awful appearance.

ELEVATOR BOY: Lissen to 'er in there!

PORTER: What's she sayin'?

ELEVATOR BOY: Apologizin' to him! For callin' the *police!*

PORTER: She thinks police 're comin'?

MISS COLLINS [*from bedroom*]: Stop it, it's got to stop!

ELEVATOR BOY: Fightin' to protect her honor again! What a commotion, no wunner folks are complainin'!

111

PORTER [*lighting his pipe*]: This here'll be the last time.

ELEVATOR BOY: She's goin' out, huh?

PORTER [*blowing out the match*]: Tonight.

ELEVATOR BOY: Where'll she go?

PORTER [*slowly moving to the old gramophone*]: She'll go to the state asylum.

ELEVATOR BOY: Holy G!

PORTER: Remember this ole number? [*He puts on a record of "I'm Forever Blowing Bubbles."*]

ELEVATOR BOY: Naw. When did that come out?

PORTER: Before your time, sonny boy. Machine needs oilin'.

[*He takes out small oil-can and applies oil about the crank and other parts of gramophone.*]

ELEVATOR BOY: How long is the old girl been here?

PORTER: Abrams says she's been livin' here twenty-five, thirty years, since before he got to be manager even.

ELEVATOR BOY: Livin' alone all that time?

PORTER: She had an old mother died of an operation about fifteen years ago. Since then she ain't gone out of the place excep' on Sundays to church or Friday nights to some kind of religious meeting.

ELEVATOR BOY: Got an awful lot of ol' magazines piled aroun' here.

PORTER: She used to collect 'em. She'd go out in back and fish 'em out of the incinerator.

ELEVATOR BOY: What'n hell for?

PORTER: Mr. Abrams says she used to cut out the Campbell soup kids. Them red-tomato-headed kewpie dolls that go with the soup advertisements. You seen 'em, ain'tcha?

ELEVATOR BOY: Uh-huh.

PORTER: She made a collection of 'em. Filled a big lot of scrapbooks with them paper kiddies an' took 'em down to the Children's Hospitals on Xmas Eve an' Easter Sunday, exactly twicet a year. Sounds better, don't it? [*referring to gramophone, which resumes its faint, wheedling music*] Eliminated some a that crankin' noise . . .

ELEVATOR BOY: I didn't know that she'd been nuts *that* long.

PORTER: Who's nuts an' who ain't? If you ask me the world is populated with people that's just as peculiar as she is.

ELEVATOR BOY: Hell. She don't have brain *one*.

PORTER: There's important people in Europe got less'n she's got. Tonight they're takin' her off 'n' lockin' her up. They'd do a lot better to leave 'er go an' lock up some a them maniacs over there. She's harmless; they ain't. They kill millions of people an' go scot free!

ELEVATOR BOY: An ole woman like her is disgusting, though, imaginin' somebody's raped her.

PORTER: Pitiful, not disgusting. Watch out for them cigarette ashes.

ELEVATOR BOY: What's uh diff'rence? So much dust you can't see it. All a this here goes out in the morning, don't it?

PORTER: Uh-huh.

ELEVATOR BOY: I think I'll take a couple a those ole records as curiosities for my girl friend. She's got a portable in 'er bedroom, she says it's better with music!

PORTER: Leave 'em alone. She's still got 'er property rights.

ELEVATOR BOY: Aw, she's got all she wants with them dream-lovers of hers!

PORTER: *Hush up!* [*He makes a warning gesture as Miss Collins enters from bedroom. Her appearance is that of a ravaged woman. She leans exhaustedly in the doorway, hands clasped over her flat, virginal bosom.*]

MISS COLLINS [*breathlessly*]: Oh, Richard—Richard . . .

PORTER [*coughing*]: Miss—Collins.

ELEVATOR BOY: Hello, Miss Collins.

MISS COLLINS [*just noticing the men*]: Goodness! You've arrived already! Mother didn't tell me you were here! [*Self-consciously she touches her ridiculous corkscrew curls with the faded pink ribbon tied through them. Her manner becomes that of a slightly coquettish but prim little Southern belle.*] I must ask you gentlemen to excuse the terrible disorder.

PORTER: That's all right, Miss Collins.

114

MISS COLLINS: It's the maid's day off. Your No'thern girls receive such excellent domestic training, but in the South it was never considered essential for a girl to have anything but prettiness and charm! [*She laughs girlishly.*] Please do sit down. Is it too close? Would you like a window open?

PORTER: No, Miss Collins.

MISS COLLINS [*advancing with delicate grace to the sofa*]: Mother will bring in something cool after while. . . . Oh, my! [*She touches her forehead.*]

PORTER [*kindly*]: Is anything wrong, Miss Collins?

MISS COLLINS: Oh, no, no, thank you, nothing! My head is a little bit heavy. I'm always a little bit—malarial—this time of year! [*She sways dizzily as she starts to sink down on the sofa.*]

PORTER [*helping her*]: Careful there, Miss Collins.

MISS COLLINS [*vaguely*]: Yes, it is, I hadn't noticed before. [*She peers at them nearsightedly with a hesitant smile.*] You gentlemen have come from the church?

PORTER: No, ma'am. I'm Nick, the porter, Miss Collins, and this boy here is Frank that runs the elevator.

MISS COLLINS [*stiffening a little*]: Oh? . . . I don't understand.

PORTER [*gently*]: Mr. Abrams just asked me to drop in here an' see if you was getting along all right.

MISS COLLINS: Oh! Then he must have informed you of what's been going on in here!

PORTER: He mentioned some kind of—disturbance.

115

MISS COLLINS: Yes! Isn't it outrageous? But it mustn't go any further, you understand. I mean you mustn't repeat it to other people.

PORTER: No, I wouldn't say nothing.

MISS COLLINS: Not a word of it, please!

ELEVATOR BOY: Is the man still here, Miss Collins?

MISS COLLINS: Oh, no. No, he's gone now.

ELEVATOR BOY: How did he go, out the bedroom window, Miss Collins?

MISS COLLINS [*vaguely*]: Yes. . . .

ELEVATOR BOY: I seen a guy that could do that once. He crawled straight up the side of the building. They called him The Human Fly! Gosh, that's a wonderful publicity angle, Miss Collins—"Beautiful Young Society Lady Raped by The Human Fly!"

PORTER [*nudging him sharply*]: Git back in your cracker box!

MISS COLLINS: Publicity? No! It would be so humiliating! Mr. Abrams surely hasn't reported it to the papers!

PORTER: No, ma'am. Don't listen to this smarty pants.

MISS COLLINS [*touching her curls*]: Will pictures be taken, you think? There's one of him on the mantel.

ELEVATOR BOY [*going to the mantel*]: This one here, Miss Collins?

MISS COLLINS: Yes. Of the Sunday School faculty picnic. I had the little kindergarteners that year and he had the older boys. We rode in the cab of a railroad locomotive from Webb to Crystal Springs. [*She covers her ears with a girlish grimace and toss of her curls.*] Oh, how the steamwhistle blew! Blew! [*giggling*] Blewwwww! It frightened me so, he put his arm round my shoulders! But she was there, too, though she had no business being. She grabbed his hat and stuck it on the back of her head and they—they *rassled* for it, they actually *rassled* together! Everyone said it was *shameless!* Don't you think that it was?

PORTER: Yes, Miss Collins.

MISS COLLINS: That's the picture, the one in the silver frame up there on the mantel. We cooled the watermelon in the springs and afterwards played games. She hid somewhere and he took ages to find her. It got to be dark and he hadn't found her yet and everyone whispered and giggled about it and finally they came back together—her hangin' on to his arm like a common little strumpet—and Daisy Belle Huston shrieked out, "Look, everybody, the seat of Evelyn's skirt!" It was—covered with— grass-stains! Did you ever hear of anything as outrageous? It didn't faze her, though, she laughed like it was something very, very amusing! Rather *triumphant* she was!

ELEVATOR BOY: Which one is him, Miss Collins?

MISS COLLINS: The tall one in the blue shirt holding onto one of my curls. He loved to play with them.

ELEVATOR BOY: Quite a Romeo—1910 model, huh?

MISS COLLINS [*vaguely*]: Do you? It's nothing, really, but I like the lace on the collar. I said to Mother, "Even if I don't wear it, Mother, it will be *so* nice for my hope chest!"

117

ELEVATOR BOY: How was he dressed tonight when he climbed into your balcony, Miss Collins?

MISS COLLINS: Pardon?

ELEVATOR BOY: Did he still wear that nifty little stick-candy-striped blue shirt with the celluloid collar?

MISS COLLINS: He hasn't changed.

ELEVATOR BOY: Oughta be easy to pick him up in that. What color pants did he wear?

MISS COLLINS [*vaguely*]: I don't remember.

ELEVATOR BOY: Maybe he didn't wear any. Shimmied out of 'em on the way up the wall! You could get him on grounds of indecent exposure, Miss Collins!

PORTER [*grasping his arm*]: Cut that or git back in your cage! Understand?

ELEVATOR BOY [*snickering*]: Take it easy. She don't hear a thing.

PORTER: Well, you keep a decent tongue or get to hell out. Miss Collins here is a lady. You understand that?

ELEVATOR BOY: Okay. She's Shoiley Temple.

PORTER: She's a *lady!*

ELEVATOR BOY: Yeah! [*He returns to the gramophone and looks through the records.*]

MISS COLLINS: I really shouldn't have created this disturbance. When the officers come I'll have to explain that to them. But you can understand my feelings, can't you?

118

PORTER: Sure, Miss Collins.

MISS COLLINS: When men take advantage of common white-trash women who smoke in public there is probably some excuse for it, but when it occurs to a lady who is single and always com*pletely* above reproach in her moral behavior, there's really nothing to do but call for police protection! Unless of course the girl is fortunate enough to have a father and brothers who can take care of the matter privately without any scandal.

PORTER: Sure. That's right, Miss Collins.

MISS COLLINS: Of course it's bound to cause a great deal of very disagreeable talk. Especially 'round the *church!* Are you gentlemen Episcopalian?

PORTER: No, ma'am. Catholic, Miss Collins.

MISS COLLINS: Oh. Well, I suppose you know in England we're known as the English Catholic church. We have direct Apostolic succession through St. Paul who christened the Early Angles—which is what the original English people were called—and established the English branch of the Catholic church over there. So when you hear ignorant people claim that our church was founded by—by Henry the *Eighth*—that horrible, *lech*erous old man who had so many wives—as many as *Blue*beard they say!—you can see how ridiculous it *is* and how thoroughly ob*nox*ious to anybody who really *knows* and under*stands* Church *His*tory!

PORTER [*comfortingly*]: Sure, Miss Collins. Everybody knows that.

MISS COLLINS: I wish they *did*, but they need to be in*struc*ted! Before he died, my father was Rector at the Church of St. Michael and St. George at Glorious Hill, Mississippi. . . . I've literally grown up right in the very *shadow* of the Episcopal

119

church. At Pass Christian and Natchez, Biloxi, Gulfport, Port Gibson, Columbus and Glorious Hill! (*with gentle, bewildered sadness*) But you know I sometimes suspect that there has been some kind of spiritual schism in the modern church. These northern dioceses have completely departed from the good old church traditions. For instance our Rector at the Church of the Holy Communion has never darkened my door. It's a fashionable church and he's terribly busy, but even so you'd think he might have time to make a stranger in the congregation feel at home. But he doesn't though! Nobody seems to have the time any more. . . . [*She grows more excited as her mind sinks back into illusion.*] I ought not to mention this, but do you know they actually take a malicious de*light* over there at the Holy Communion—where I've recently transferred my letter—in what's been going on here at night in this apartment? *Yes!!* [*She laughs wildly and throws up her hands.*] They take a malicious de-*LIGHT* in it!! [*She catches her breath and gropes vaguely about her wrapper.*]

PORTER: You lookin' for somethin', Miss Collins?

MISS COLLINS: My—handkerchief . . . [*She is blinking her eyes against tears.*]

PORTER [*removing a rag from his pocket*]: Here. Use this, Miss Collins. It's just a rag but it's clean, except along that edge where I wiped off the phonograph handle.

MISS COLLINS: Thanks. You gentlemen are very kind. Mother will bring in something cool after while. . . .

ELEVATOR BOY [*placing a record on machine*]: This one is got some kind of foreign title. [*The record begins to play Tschaikovsky's "None But the Lonely Heart."*]

MISS COLLINS [*stuffing the rag daintily in her bosom*]: Excuse me, please. Is the weather nice outside?

PORTER [*huskily*]: Yes, it's nice, Miss Collins.

MISS COLLINS [*dreamily*]: So wa'm for this time of year. I wore my little astrakhan cape to service but had to *carry* it *home,* as the weight of it actually seemed *oppres*sive to me. [*Her eyes fall shut.*] The sidewalks seem so dreadfully long in summer. . . .

ELEVATOR BOY: This ain't summer, Miss Collins.

MISS COLLINS [*dreamily*]: I used to think I'd never get to the end of that last block. And that's the block where all the trees went down in the big tornado. The walk is simply *glit*tering with sunlight. [*Pressing her eyelids*] Impossible to shade your face and I *do* perspire so freely! [*She touches her forehead daintily with the rag.*] Not a branch, not a leaf to give you a little protection! You simply *have* to en*dure* it. Turn your hideous red face away from all the front porches and walk as fast as you decently *can* till you get *by* them! Oh, dear, dear Savior, sometimes you're not so lucky and you *meet* people and have to *smile!* You can't *avoid* them unless you cut *across* and that's so *ob*vious, you know. . . . People would say you're pe-*cul*iar. . . . His house is right in the middle of that awful leaf-less block, *their* house, his and *hers,* and they have an auto-mobile and always get home early and sit on the porch and *watch* me walking by—Oh, Father in Heaven—with a ma*li*cious de*light!* [*She averts her face in remembered torture.*] She has such *penetrating* eyes, they look straight through me. She sees that terrible choking thing in my throat and the pain I have in here—[*touching her chest*]—and she points it out and laughs and whispers to him, "There she goes with her shiny big red nose, the poor old maid—that *loves* you!" [*She chokes and hides her face in the rag.*]

PORTER: Maybe you better forget all that, Miss Collins.

121

MISS COLLINS: Never, never forget it! Never, never! I left my parasol once—the one with long white fringe that belonged to Mother—I left it behind in the cloakroom at the church so I didn't have anything to cover my face with when I walked by, and I couldn't turn back either, with all those people behind me—giggling back of me, poking fun at my clothes! Oh, dear, dear! I had to walk straight forward—past the last elm tree and into that *merciless* sunlight. Oh! It beat down on me, *scorching* me! *Whips!* . . . Oh, Jesus! . . . Over my face and my body! . . . I tried to walk on fast but was dizzy and they kept closer behind me—! I stumbled, I nearly fell, and all of them burst out laughing! My face turned so *horribly* red, it got so red and wet, I knew how ugly it was in all that merciless glare—not a single shadow to hide in! And then—[*Her face contorts with fear.*]—their automobile drove up in front of their house, right where I had to pass by it, and *she* stepped out, in white, so fresh and easy, her stomach round with a baby, the first of the *six*. Oh, God! . . . And he stood smiling behind her, white and easy and cool, and they stood there waiting for me. *Waiting!* I had to keep on. What else could I do? I couldn't turn *back*, could I? *No!* I said dear *God*, strike me *dead!* He didn't, though. I put my head way down like I couldn't see them! You know what she did? She stretched out her hand to *stop* me! And *he*—he stepped up straight in front of me, *smiling*, blocking the walk with his terrible big white body! "*Lucretia*," he said, "Lucretia *Collins!*" I—I tried to speak but I couldn't, the breath went out of my body! I covered my face and—ran! . . . Ran! . . . *Ran!* [*beating the arm of the sofa*] Till I reached the end of the block—and the elm trees—*started* again. . . . Oh, Merciful Christ in Heaven, how *kind* they were! [*She leans back exhaustedly, her hand relaxed on sofa. She pauses and the music ends.*] I said to Mother, "Mother, we've got to leave town!" We *did* after that. And now after all these years he's finally remembered and come *back!* Moved away from that house and the woman and come *here*—I saw him in the back of the church one day. I wasn't sure—but it *was*. The night after that was the night that he first

122

broke in—and indulged his senses with me. . . . He doesn't realize that I've changed, that I can't feel again the way that I used to feel, now that he's got six children by that Cincinnati girl—three in high school already! Six! Think of that? Six children! I don't know what he'll say when he knows another one's coming! He'll probably blame *me* for it because a man always *does!* In spite of the fact that he *forced* me!

ELEVATOR BOY [*grinning*]: Did you say—a *baby*, Miss Collins?

MISS COLLINS [*lowering her eyes but speaking with tenderness and pride*]: Yes—I'm expecting a *child*.

ELEVATOR BOY: *Jeez!* [*He claps his hand over his mouth and turns away quickly.*]

MISS COLLINS: Even if it's not legitimate, I think it has a perfect right to its father's name—don't you?

PORTER: Yes. Sure, Miss Collins.

MISS COLLINS: A child is innocent and pure. No matter how it's conceived. And it must *not* be made to suffer! So I intend to dispose of the little property Cousin Ethel left me and give the child a private education where it won't come under the evil influence of the Christian church! I want to make sure that it doesn't grow up in the shadow of the cross and then have to walk along blocks that scorch you with terrible sunlight! [*The elevator buzzer sounds from the hall.*]

PORTER: Frank! Somebody wants to come up. [*The Elevator Boy goes out. The elevator door bangs shut. The Porter clears his throat.*] Yes, it'd be better—to go off some place else.

MISS COLLINS: If only I had the courage—but I don't. I've grown so used to it here, and people outside—it's always so *hard* to *face* them!

PORTER: Maybe you won't—have to face nobody, Miss Collins. [*The elevator door clangs open.*]

MISS COLLINS [*rising fearfully*]: Is someone coming—here?

PORTER: You just take it easy, Miss Collins.

MISS COLLINS: If that's the officers coming for Richard, tell them to go away. I've decided not to prosecute Mr. Martin. [*Mr. Abrams enters with the Doctor and the Nurse. The Elevator Boy gawks from the doorway. The Doctor is the weary, professional type, the Nurse hard and efficient. Mr. Abrams is a small, kindly person, sincerely troubled by the situation.*]

MISS COLLINS [*shrinking back, her voice faltering*]: I've decided not to—prosecute Mr. Martin . . .

DOCTOR: Miss Collins?

MR. ABRAMS [*with attempted heartiness*]: Yes, this is the lady you wanted to meet, Dr. White.

DOCTOR: Hmmm. [*briskly to the Nurse*] Go in her bedroom and get a few things together.

NURSE: Yes, sir. [*She goes quickly across to the bedroom.*]

MISS COLLINS [*fearfully shrinking*]: Things?

DOCTOR: Yes, Miss Tyler will help you pack up an overnight bag. [*smiling mechanically*] A strange place always seems more homelike the first few days when we have a few of our little personal articles around us.

MISS COLLINS: A strange—place?

DOCTOR [*carelessly, making a memorandum*]: Don't be disturbed, Miss Collins.

MISS COLLINS: I know! [*Excitedly*] You're come from the Holy Communion to place me under arrest! On moral charges!

MR. ABRAMS: Oh, no, Miss Collins, you got the wrong idea. This is a doctor who—

DOCTOR [*impatiently*]: Now, now, you're just going away for a while till things get straightened out. [*He glances at his watch.*] Two-twenty-five! Miss Tyler?

NURSE: Coming!

MISS COLLINS [*with slow and sad comprehension*]: Oh. . . . I'm going away. . . .

MR. ABRAMS: She was always a lady, Doctor, such a perfect lady.

DOCTOR: Yes. No doubt.

MR. ABRAMS: It seems too bad!

MISS COLLINS: Let me—write him a note. A pencil? Please?

MR. ABRAMS: Here, Miss Collins. [*She takes the pencil and crouches over the table. The Nurse comes out with a hard, forced smile, carrying a suitcase.*]

DOCTOR: Ready, Miss Tyler?

NURSE: All ready, Dr. White. [*She goes up to Miss Collins.*] Come along, dear, we can tend to that later!

125

MR. ABRAMS [*sharply*]: Let her finish the note!

MISS COLLINS [*straightening with a frightened smile*]: It's—finished.

NURSE: All right, dear, come along. [*She propels her firmly toward the door.*]

MISS COLLINS [*turning suddenly back*]: Oh, Mr. Abrams!

MR. ABRAMS: Yes, Miss Collins?

MISS COLLINS: If he should come again—and find me gone—I'd rather you didn't tell him—about the baby. . . . I think it's better for *me* to tell him *that*. [*Gently smiling*] You know how men *are*, don't you?

MR. ABRAMS: Yes, Miss Collins.

PORTER: Goodbye, Miss Collins. [*The Nurse pulls firmly at her arm. She smiles over her shoulder with a slight apologetic gesture.*]

MISS COLLINS: Mother will bring in—something cool—after while . . . [*She disappears down the hall with the Nurse. The elevator door clangs shut with the metallic sound of a locked cage. The wires hum.*]

MR. ABRAMS: She wrote him a note.

PORTER: What did she write, Mr. Abrams?

MR. ABRAMS: "Dear—Richard. I'm going away for a while. But don't worry, I'll be back. I have a secret to tell you. Love—Lucretia." [*He coughs.*] We got to clear out this stuff an' pile it down in the basement till I find out where it goes.

126

PORTER [*dully*]: Tonight, Mr. Abrams?

MR. ABRAMS [*roughly to hide his feeling*]: No, no, not tonight, you old fool. Enough has happened tonight! [*Then gently*] We can do it tomorrow. Turn out that bedroom light—and close the window. [*Music playing softly becomes audible as the men go out slowly, closing the door, and the light fades out.*]

CURTAIN

AUTO-DA-FÉ

A Tragedy in One Act

CHARACTERS

MME. DUVENET

ELOI,* her son

* Pronounced Ell-wah. The part is created for Mr. John Abbott.

The front porch of an old frame cottage in the Vieux Carré of New Orleans. There are palm or banana trees, one on either side of the porch steps: pots of geraniums and other vivid flowers along the low balustrade. There is an effect of sinister antiquity in the setting, even the flowers suggesting the richness of decay. Not far off on Bourbon Street the lurid procession of bars and hot spots throws out distance-muted strains of the jukeorgans and occasional shouts of laughter. Mme. Duvenet, a frail woman of sixty-seven, is rocking on the porch in the faint, sad glow of an August sunset. Eloi, her son, comes out the screendoor. He is a frail man in his late thirties, a gaunt, ascetic type with feverish dark eyes.

Mother and son are both fanatics and their speech has something of the quality of poetic or religious incantation.

MME. DUVENET: Why did you speak so crossly to Miss Bordelon?

ELOI [*standing against the column*]: She gets on my nerves.

MME. DUVENET: You take a dislike to every boarder we get.

ELOI: She's not to be trusted. I think she goes in my room.

MME. DUVENET: What makes you think that?

ELOI: I've found some evidence of it.

MME. DUVENET: Well, I can assure you she doesn't go in your room.

ELOI: Somebody goes in my room and roots through my things.

131

MME. DUVENET: Nobody ever touches a thing in your room.

ELOI: My room is my own. I don't want anyone in it.

MME. DUVENET: You know very well that I have to go in to clean it.

ELOI: I don't want it cleaned.

MME. DUVENET: You want the room to be filthy?

ELOI: Just don't go in it to clean it or anything else.

MME. DUVENET: How could you live in a room that was never cleaned?

ELOI: I'll clean it myself when cleaning is necessary.

MME. DUVENET: A person would think that you were concealing something.

ELOI: What would I have to conceal?

MME. DUVENET: Nothing that I can imagine. That's why it's so strange that you have such a strong objection to even your mother going into your room.

ELOI: Everyone wants a little privacy, Mother.

MME. DUVENET [*stiffly*]: Your privacy, Eloi, shall be regarded as sacred.

ELOI: Huh.

MME. DUVENET: I'll just allow the filth to accumulate there.

132

ELOI [*sharply*]: What do you mean by "the filth"?

MME. DUVENET [*sadly*]: The dust and disorder that you would rather live in than have your mother come in to clean it up.

ELOI: Your broom and your dustpan wouldn't accomplish much. Even the air in this neighborhood is unclean.

MME. DUVENET: It is not as clean as it might be. I love clean window curtains, I love white linen, I want immaculate, spotless things in a house.

ELOI: Then why don't we move to the new part of town where it's cleaner?

MME. DUVENET: The property in this block has lost all value. We couldn't sell our place for what it would cost us to put new paint on the walls.

ELOI: I don't understand you, Mother. You harp on purity, purity all the time, and yet you're willing to stay in the midst of corruption.

MME. DUVENET: I harp on nothing. I stay here because I have to. And as for corruption, I've never allowed it to touch me.

ELOI: It does, it does. We can't help breathing it here. It gets in our nostrils and even goes in our blood.

MME. DUVENET: I think you're the one that harps on things around here. You won't talk quietly. You always fly off on some tangent and raise your voice and get us all stirred up for no good reason.

ELOI: I've had about all that I can put up with, Mother.

133

MME. DUVENET: Then what do you want to do?

ELOI: Move, move. This asthma of mine, in a pure atmosphere uptown where the air is fresher, I know that I wouldn't have it nearly so often.

MME. DUVENET: I leave it entirely to you. If you can find someone to make an acceptable offer, I'm willing to move.

ELOI: You don't have the power to move or the will to break from anything that you're used to. You don't know how much we've been affected already!

MME. DUVENET: By what, Eloi?

ELOI: This fetid old swamp we live in, the Vieux Carré! Every imaginable kind of degeneracy springs up here, not at arm's length, even, but right in our presence!

MME. DUVENET: Now I think you're exaggerating a little.

ELOI: You read the papers, you hear people talk, you walk past open windows. You can't be entirely unconscious of what goes on! A woman was horribly mutilated last night. A man smashed a bottle and twisted the jagged end of it in her face.

MME. DUVENET: They bring such things on themselves by their loose behavior.

ELOI: Night after night there are crimes taking place in the parks.

MME. DUVENET: The parks aren't all in the Quarter.

ELOI: The parks aren't all in the Quarter but decadence is. This is the primary lesion, the—focal infection, the—chancre! In medical language, it spreads by—metastasis! It creeps through the capillaries and into the main blood vessels. From there it is spread all through the surrounding tissue! Finally nothing is left outside the decay!

MME. DUVENET: Eloi, you are being unnecessarily violent in your speech.

ELOI: I feel that strongly about it.

MME. DUVENET: You mustn't allow yourself to sound like a fanatic.

ELOI: You take no stand against it?

MME. DUVENET: You know the stand that I take.

ELOI: I know what ought to be done.

MME. DUVENET: There ought to be legislation to make for reforms.

ELOI: Not only reforms but action really drastic!

MME. DUVENET: I favor that, too, within all practical bounds.

ELOI: Practical, practical. You can't be practical, Mother, and wipe out evil! The town should be razed.

MME. DUVENET: You mean this old section torn down?

ELOI: Condemned and demolished!

MME. DUVENET: That's not a reasonable stand.

ELOI: It's the stand I take.

MME. DUVENET: Then I'm afraid you're not a reasonable person.

ELOI: I have good precedence for it.

MME. DUVENET: What do you mean?

ELOI: All through the Scriptures are cases of cities destroyed by the justice of fire when they got to be nests of foulness!

MME. DUVENET: Eloi, Eloi.

ELOI: Condemn it, I say, and purify it with fire!

MME. DUVENET: You're breathing hoarsely. That's what brings on asthma, over-excitement, not just breathing bad air!

ELOI [*after a thoughtful pause*]: I *am* breathing hoarsely.

MME. DUVENET: Sit down and try to relax.

ELOI: I can't any more.

MME. DUVENET: You'd better go in and take an amytal tablet.

ELOI: I don't want to get to depending too much on drugs. I'm not very well, I'm never well any more.

MME. DUVENET: You never will take the proper care of yourself.

ELOI: I can hardly remember the time when I really felt good.

MME. DUVENET: You've never been quite as strong as I'd like you to be.

ELOI: I seem to have chronic fatigue.

MME. DUVENET: The Duvenet trouble has always been mostly with nerves.

ELOI: Look! I had a sinus infection! You call that nerves?

MME. DUVENET: No, but—

ELOI: Look! This asthma, this choking, this suffocation I have, do you call that nerves?

MME. DUVENET: I never agreed with the doctor about that condition.

ELOI: You hate all doctors, you're rabid on the subject!

MME. DUVENET: I think all healing begins with faith in the spirit.

ELOI: How can I keep on going when I don't sleep?

MME. DUVENET: I think your insomnia's caused by eating at night.

ELOI: It soothes my stomach.

MME. DUVENET: Liquids would serve that purpose!

ELOI: Liquids don't satisfy me.

MME. DUVENET: Well, something digestible, then. A little hot cereal maybe with cocoa or Postum.

ELOI: All that kind of slop is nauseating to look at!

MME. DUVENET: I notice at night you won't keep the covers on you.

ELOI: I can't stand covers in summer.

MME. DUVENET: You've got to have something over your body at night.

ELOI: Oh, Lord, oh, Lord.

MME. DUVENET: Your body perspires and when it's exposed, you catch cold!

ELOI: You're rabid upon the subject of catching cold.

MME. DUVENET: Only because you're unusually prone to colds.

ELOI [*with curious intensity*]: It isn't a cold! It is a sinus infection!

MME. DUVENET: Sinus infection and all catarrhal conditions are caused by the same things as colds!

ELOI: At ten every morning, as regular as clockwork, a headache commences and doesn't let up till late in the afternoon.

MME. DUVENET: Nasal congestion is often the cause of headache.

ELOI: Nasal congestion has nothing to do with this one!

MME. DUVENET: How do you know?

ELOI: It isn't in that location!

MME. DUVENET: Where is it, then?

138

ELOI: It's here at the base of the skull. And it runs around here.

MME. DUVENET: Around where?

ELOI: Around here!

MME. DUVENET [*touching his forehead*]: Oh! There!

ELOI: No, no, are you blind? I said *here!*

MME. DUVENET: Oh, here!

ELOI: *Yes! Here!*

MME. DUVENET: Well, that could be eyestrain.

ELOI: When I've just changed my glasses?

MME. DUVENET: You read consistently in the wrong kind of light.

ELOI: You seem to think I'm a saboteur of myself.

MME. DUVENET: You actually are.

ELOI: You just don't know. [*darkly*] There's lots of things that you don't know about, Mother.

MME. DUVENET: I've never pretended nor wished to know a great deal. [*They fall into a silence, and Mme. Duvenet rocks slowly back and forth. The light is nearly gone. A distant juke-box can be heard playing "The New San Antonio Rose." She speaks, finally, in a gentle, liturgical tone.*] There are three simple rules I wish that you would observe. One: you should wear undershirts whenever there's changeable weather! Two: don't sleep without covers, don't kick them off in the night! Three:

139

chew your food, don't gulp it. Eat like a human being and not like a dog! In addition to those three very simple rules of common hygiene, all that you need is faith in spiritual healing! [*Eloi looks at her for a moment in weary desperation. Then he groans aloud and rises from the steps.*] Why that look, and the groan?

ELOI [*intensely*]: You—just—don't—*know!*

MME. DUVENET: Know what?

ELOI: Your world is so simple, you live in a fool's paradise!

MME. DUVENET: Do I indeed!

ELOI: Yes, Mother, you do indeed! I stand in your presence a stranger, a person unknown! I live in a house where nobody knows my name!

MME. DUVENET: You tire me, Eloi, when you become so excited!

ELOI: You just don't know. You rock on the porch and talk about clean white curtains! While I'm all flame, all burning, and no bell rings, nobody gives an alarm!

MME. DUVENET: What are you talking about?

ELOI: Intolerable burden! The conscience of all dirty men!

MME. DUVENET: I don't understand you.

ELOI: How can I speak any plainer?

MME. DUVENET: You go to confession!

ELOI: The priest is a cripple in skirts!

MME. DUVENET: How can you say that!

ELOI: Because I have seen his skirts and his crutches and heard his meaningless mumble through the wall!

MME. DUVENET: Don't speak like that in my presence!

ELOI: It's worn-out magic, it doesn't burn any more!

MME. DUVENET: Burn any more? Why should it!

ELOI: Because there needs to be burning!

MME. DUVENET: For what?

ELOI [*leaning against the column*]: For the sake of burning, for God, for the purification! Oh, God, oh, God. I can't go back in the house, and I can't stay out on the porch! I can't even breathe very freely, I don't know what is about to happen to me!

MME. DUVENET: You're going to bring on an attack. Sit down! Now tell me quietly and calmly what is the matter? What have you had on your mind for the last ten days?

ELOI: How do you know that I've had something on my mind?

MME. DUVENET: You've had something on your mind since a week ago Tuesday.

ELOI: Yes, that's true. I have. I didn't suppose you'd no-ticed . . .

MME. DUVENET: What happened at the post office?

ELOI: How did you guess it was there?

141

MME. DUVENET: Because there is nothing at home to explain your condition.

ELOI [*leaning back exhaustedly*]: No.

MME. DUVENET: Then obviously it was something where you work.

ELOI: Yes . . .

MME. DUVENET: What was it, Eloi? [*Far down the street a tamale vendor cries out in his curiously rich haunting voice: "Re-ed ho-ot, re-ed ho-ot, re-e-ed!" He moves in the other direction and fades from hearing.*] What *was* it, Eloi?

ELOI: A letter.

MME. DUVENET: You got a letter from someone? And that upset you?

ELOI: I didn't get any letter.

MME. DUVENET: Then what did you mean by "a letter"?

ELOI: A letter came into my hands by accident, Mother.

MME. DUVENET: While you were sorting the mail?

ELOI: Yes.

MME. DUVENET: What was there about it to prey on your mind so much?

ELOI: The letter was mailed unsealed, and something fell out.

MME. DUVENET: Something fell out of the unsealed envelope?

ELOI: Yes!

MME. DUVENET: What was it fell out?

ELOI: A picture.

MME. DUVENET: A what?

ELOI: A picture!

MME. DUVENET: What kind of a picture? [*He does not answer. The jukebox starts playing again the same tune with its idiotic gaiety in the distance.*] Eloi, what kind of a picture fell out of the envelope?

ELOI [*gently and sadly*]: Miss Bordelon is standing in the hall and overhearing every word I say.

MME. DUVENET [*turning sharply*]: She's not in the hall.

ELOI: Her ear is clapped to the door!

MME. DUVENET: She's in her bedroom reading.

ELOI: Reading what?

MME. DUVENET: How do I know what she's reading? What difference does it make what she is reading!

ELOI: She keeps a journal of everything said in the house. I feel her taking shorthand notes at the table!

MME. DUVENET: Why, for what purpose, would she take shorthand notes on our conversation?

ELOI: Haven't you heard of hired investigators?

143

MME. DUVENET: Eloi, you're talking and saying such horrible things!

ELOI [*gently*]: I may be wrong. I may be wrong.

MME. DUVENET: Eloi, of course you're mistaken! Now go on and tell me what you started to say about the picture.

ELOI: A lewd photograph fell out of the envelope.

MME. DUVENET: A what?

ELOI: An indecent picture.

MME. DUVENET: Of whom?

ELOI: Of two naked figures.

MME. DUVENET: Oh! . . . That's all it was?

ELOI: You haven't looked at the picture.

MME. DUVENET: Was it so bad?

ELOI: It passes beyond all description!

MME. DUVENET: As bad as all that?

ELOI: No. Worse. I felt as though something exploded, blew up in my hands, and scalded my face with acid!

MME. DUVENET: Who sent this horrible photograph to you, Eloi?

ELOI: It wasn't to me.

144

MME. DUVENET: Who was it addressed to?

ELOI: One of those—opulent—antique dealers on—Royal . . .

MME. DUVENET: And who was the sender?

ELOI: A university student.

MME. DUVENET: Isn't the sender liable to prosecution?

ELOI: Of course. And to years in prison.

MME. DUVENET: I see no reason for clemency in such a case.

ELOI: Neither did I.

MME. DUVENET: Then what did you do about it?

ELOI: I haven't done anything yet.

MME. DUVENET: Eloi! You haven't reported it to the authorities yet?

ELOI: I haven't reported it to the authorities yet.

MME. DUVENET: I can't imagine one reason to hesitate!

ELOI: I couldn't proceed without some investigation.

MME. DUVENET: Investigation? Of what?

ELOI: Of all the circumstances around the case.

MME. DUVENET: What circumstances are there to think of but the fact that somebody used the mails for that purpose!

145

ELOI: The youth of the sender has something to do with the case.

MME. DUVENET: The sender was young?

ELOI: The sender was only nineteen.

MME. DUVENET: And are the sender's parents still alive?

ELOI: Both of them still living and in the city. The sender happens to be an only child.

MME. DUVENET: How do you know these facts about the sender?

ELOI: Because I've conducted a private investigation.

MME. DUVENET: How did you go about that?

ELOI: I called on the sender, I went to the dormitory. We talked in private and everything was discussed. The attitude taken was that I had come for money. That I was intending to hold the letter for blackmail.

MME. DUVENET: How perfectly awful.

ELOI: Of course I had to explain that I was a federal employee who had some obligation to his employers, and that it was really excessively fair on my part to even delay the action that ought to be taken.

MME. DUVENET: The action that has to be taken!

ELOI: And then the sender began to be ugly. Abusive. I can't repeat the charges, the evil suggestions! I ran from the room. I left my hat in the room. I couldn't even go back to pick it up!

146

MME. DUVENET: Eloi, Eloi. Oh, my dear Eloi. When did this happen, the interview with the sender?

ELOI: The interview was on Friday.

MME. DUVENET: Three days ago. And you haven't done anything yet?

ELOI: I thought and I thought and I couldn't take any action!

MME. DUVENET: Now it's too late.

ELOI: Why do you say it's too late?

MME. DUVENET: You've held the letter too long to take any action.

ELOI: Oh, no, I haven't. I'm not paralyzed any longer.

MME. DUVENET: But if you report on the letter now they will ask why you haven't reported on it sooner!

ELOI: I can explain the responsibility of it!

MME. DUVENET: No, no, it's much better not to do anything now!

ELOI: I've got to do something.

MME. DUVENET: You'd better destroy the letter.

ELOI: And let the offenders go scot free?

MME. DUVENET: What else can you do since you've hesitated so long!

ELOI: There's got to be punishment for it!

MME. DUVENET: Where is the letter?

ELOI: I have it here in my pocket.

MME. DUVENET: You have that thing on your person?

ELOI: My inside pocket.

MME. DUVENET: Oh, Eloi, how stupid, how foolish! Suppose something happened and something like that was found on you while you were unconscious and couldn't explain how you got it.

ELOI: Lower your voice! That woman is listening to us!

MME. DUVENET: Miss Bordelon? No!

ELOI: She is, she is. She's hired as investigator. She claps her ear to the wall when I talk in my sleep!

MME. DUVENET: Eloi, Eloi.

ELOI: They've hired her to spy, to poke and pry in the house!

MME. DUVENET: Who do you mean?

ELOI: The sender, the antique dealer!

MME. DUVENET: You're talking so wildly you scare me. Eloi, you've got to destroy that letter at once!

ELOI: Destroy it?

MME. DUVENET: Yes!

ELOI: How?

MME. DUVENET: Burn it! [*Eloi rises unsteadily. For a third time the distant jukeorgan begins to grind out "The New San Antonio Rose," with its polka rhythm and cries of insane exultation.*]

ELOI [*faintly*]: Yes, yes—burn it!

MME. DUVENET: Burn it this very instant!

ELOI: I'll take it inside to burn it.

MME. DUVENET: No, burn it right here in my presence.

ELOI: You can't look at it.

MME. DUVENET: My God, my God, I would pluck out my eyes before they would look at that picture!

ELOI [*hoarsely*]: I think it is better to go in the kitchen or basement.

MME. DUVENET: No, no, Eloi, burn it here! On the porch!

ELOI: Somebody might see.

MME. DUVENET: What of it?

ELOI: It might be thought that it was something of mine.

MME. DUVENET: Eloi, Eloi, take it out and burn it! Do you hear me? Burn it now! This instant!

ELOI: Turn your back. I'll take it out of my pocket.

MME. DUVENET [*turning*]: Have you matches, Eloi?

ELOI [*sadly*]: Yes, I have them, Mother.

MME. DUVENET: Very well, then. Burn the letter and burn the terrible picture. [*Eloi fumblingly removes some papers from his inside pocket. His hand is shaking so that the picture falls from his grasp to the porch steps. Eloi groans as he stoops slowly to pick it up.*] Eloi! What is the matter?

ELOI: I—dropped the picture.

MME. DUVENET: Pick it up and set fire to it quickly!

ELOI: Yes . . . [*He strikes a match. His face is livid in the glow of the flame and as he stares at the slip of paper, his eyes seem to start from his head. He is breathing hoarsely. He draws the flame and the paper within one inch of each other but seems unable to move them any closer. All at once he utters a strangled cry and lets the match fall.*]

MME. DUVENET [*turning*]: Eloi, you've burned your fingers!

ELOI: Yes!

MME. DUVENET: Oh, come in the kitchen and let me put soda on it! [*Eloi turns and goes quickly into the house. She starts to follow.*] Go right in the kitchen! We'll put on baking soda! [*She reaches for the handle of the screen door. Eloi slips the latch into place. Madame Duvenet pulls the door and finds it locked.*] Eloi! [*He stares at her through the screen. A note of terror comes into her voice.*] Eloi! You've latched the door! What are you thinking of, Eloi? [*Eloi backs slowly away and out of sight.*] Eloi, Eloi! Come back here and open this door! [*A door slams inside the house, and the boarder's voice is raised in surprise and anger. Mme. Duvenet is now calling frantically.*]

150

Eloi, Eloi! Why have you locked me out? What are you doing in there? Open the screendoor, please! [*Eloi's voice is raised violently. The woman inside cries out with fear. There is a metallic clatter as though a tin object were hurled against a wall. The woman screams; then there is a muffled explosion. Mme. Duvenet claws and beats at the screen door.*] Eloi! Eloi! Oh, answer me, Eloi! [*There is a sudden burst of fiery light from the interior of the cottage. It spills through the screen door and out upon the clawing, witch-like figure of the old woman. She screams in panic and turns dizzily about. With stiff, grotesque movements and gestures, she staggers down the porch steps, and begins to shout hoarsely and despairingly.*] Fire! Fire! The house is on fire, on fire, the house is on fire!

CURTAIN

LORD BYRON'S LOVE LETTER

CHARACTERS

THE SPINSTER

THE OLD WOMAN

THE MATRON

THE HUSBAND

LORD BYRON'S LOVE LETTER

The parlor of a faded old residence in the French Quarter of New Orleans in the late nineteenth century. The shuttered doors of the room open directly upon the sidewalk and the noise of the Mardi Gras festivities can be faintly distinguished. The interior is very dusky. Beside a rose-shaded lamp, the Spinster, a woman of forty, is sewing. In the opposite corner, completely motionless, the Old Woman sits in a black silk dress. The doorbell tinkles.

SPINSTER [*rising*]: It's probably someone coming to look at the letter.

OLD WOMAN [*rising on her cane*]: Give me time to get out.

[*She withdraws gradually behind the curtains. One of her claw-like hands remains visible, holding a curtain slightly open so that she can watch the visitors. The Spinster opens the door and the Matron, a middle-aged woman, walks into the room.*]

SPINSTER: Won't you come in?

MATRON: Thank you.

SPINSTER: You're from out of town?

MATRON: Oh, yes, we're all the way from Milwaukee. We've come for Mardi Gras, my husband and I. [*She suddenly notices a stuffed canary in its tiny pink and ivory cage.*] Oh, this poor little bird in such a tiny cage! It's much too small to keep a canary in!

SPINSTER: It isn't a live canary.

OLD WOMAN [*from behind the curtains*]: No. It's stuffed.

155

MATRON: Oh. [*She self-consciously touches a stuffed bird on her hat.*] Winston is out there dillydallying on the street, afraid he'll miss the parade. The parade comes by here, don't it?

SPINSTER: Yes, unfortunately it does.

MATRON: I noticed your sign at the door. Is it true that you have one of Lord Byron's love letters?

SPINSTER: Yes.

MATRON: How very interesting! How did you get it?

SPINSTER: It was written to my grandmother, Irénée Marguerite de Poitevent.

MATRON: How very interesting! Where did she meet Lord Byron?

SPINSTER: On the steps of the Acropolis in Athens.

MATRON: How very, *very* interesting! I didn't know that Lord Byron was ever in Greece.

SPINSTER: Lord Byron spent the final years of his turbulent life in Greece.

OLD WOMAN [*still behind the curtains*]: He was exiled from England!

SPINSTER: Yes, he went into voluntary exile from England.

OLD WOMAN: Because of scandalous gossip in the Regent's court.

SPINSTER: Yes, involving his half-sister!

156

OLD WOMAN: It was false—completely.

SPINSTER: It was never confirmed.

OLD WOMAN: He was a passionate man but not an evil man.

SPINSTER: Morals are such ambiguous matters, I think.

MATRON: Won't the lady behind the curtains come in?

SPINSTER: You'll have to excuse her. She prefers to stay out.

MATRON [*stiffly*]: Oh. I see. What was Lord Byron doing in Greece, may I ask?

OLD WOMAN [*proudly*]: *Fighting for freedom!*

SPINSTER: Yes, Lord Byron went to Greece to join the forces that fought against the infidels.

OLD WOMAN: He gave his life in defense of the universal cause of freedom!

MATRON: What was that, did she say?

SPINSTER [*repeating automatically*]: He gave his life in defense of the universal cause of freedom.

MATRON: Oh, how very interesting!

OLD WOMAN: Also he swam the Hellespont.

SPINSTER: Yes.

OLD WOMAN: And burned the body of the poet Shelley who was drowned in a storm on the Mediterranean with a volume of Keats in his pocket!

157

MATRON [*incredulously*]: Pardon?

SPINSTER [*repeating*]: And burned the body of the poet Shelley who was drowned in a storm on the Mediterranean with a volume of Keats in his pocket.

MATRON: Oh. How very, very interesting! Indeed. I'd like so much to have my husband hear it. Do you mind if I just step out for a moment to call him in?

SPINSTER: Please do. [*The Matron steps out quickly, calling, "Winston! Winston!"*]

OLD WOMAN [*poking her head out for a moment*]: Watch them carefully! Keep a sharp eye on them!

SPINSTER: Yes. Be still. [*The Matron returns with her husband who has been drinking and wears a paper cap sprinkled with confetti.*]

MATRON: Winston, remove that cap. Sit down on the sofa. These ladies are going to show us Lord Byron's love letter.

SPINSTER: Shall I proceed?

MATRON: Oh, yes. This—uh—is my husband—Mr. Tutwiler.

SPINSTER [*coldly*]: How do you do.

MATRON: I am *Mrs.* Tutwiler.

SPINSTER: Of course. Please keep your seat.

MATRON [*nervously*]: He's been—celebrating a little.

OLD WOMAN [*shaking the curtain that conceals her*]: Ask him please to be careful with his cigar.

SPINSTER: Oh, that's all right, you may use this bowl for your ashes.

OLD WOMAN: Smoking is such an unnecessary habit!

HUSBAND: Uh?

MATRON: This lady was telling us how her Grandmother happened to meet Lord Byron. In Italy, wasn't it?

SPINSTER: No.

OLD WOMAN [*firmly*]: In Greece, in Athens, on the steps of the Acropolis! We've mentioned that *twice*, I believe. Ariadne, you may read them a passage from the journal first.

SPINSTER: Yes.

OLD WOMAN: But please be careful what you choose to read!

[*The Spinster has removed from the secretary a volume wrapped in tissue and tied with a ribbon.*]

SPINSTER: Like many other young American girls of that day and this, my Grandmother went to Europe.

OLD WOMAN: The year before she was going to be presented to society!

MATRON: How old was she?

OLD WOMAN: Sixteen! Barely sixteen! She was very beautiful, too! Please show her the picture, show these people the picture! It's in the front of the journal. [*The Spinster removes the picture from the book and hands it to the Matron.*]

159

MATRON [*taking a look*]: What a lovely young girl. [*passing it to the Husband*] Don't you think it resembles Agnes a little?

HUSBAND: Uh.

OLD WOMAN: Watch out! Ariadne, you'll have to *watch* that man. I believe he's been drinking. I *do* believe that he's been—

HUSBAND [*truculently*]: Yeah? What is she saying back there?

MATRON [*touching his arm warningly*]: Winston! Be *quiet*.

HUSBAND: Uh!

SPINSTER [*quickly*]: Near the end of her tour, my Grandmother and her Aunt went to Greece, to study the classic remains of the oldest civilization.

OLD WOMAN [*correcting*]: The oldest *European* civilization.

SPINSTER: It was an early morning in April of the year eighteen hundred and—

OLD WOMAN: Twenty-seven!

SPINSTER: Yes. In my Grandmother's journal she mentions—

OLD WOMAN: Read it, read it, *read* it.

MATRON: Yes, *please* read it to us.

SPINSTER: I'm trying to find the place, if you'll just be patient.

MATRON: Certainly, excuse me. [*She punches her Husband who is nodding.*] Winston!

160

SPINSTER: Ah, here it is.

OLD WOMAN: Be *careful!* Remember where to *stop* at, Ariadne!

SPINSTER: Shhh! [*She adjusts her glasses and seats herself by the lamp.*] "We set out early that morning to inspect the ruins of the Acropolis. I know I shall never forget how extraordinarily pure the atmosphere was that morning. It seemed as though the world were not very old but very, very young, almost as though the world had been newly created. There was a taste of earliness in the air, a feeling of freshness, exhilarating my senses, exalting my spirit. How shall I tell you, dear Diary, the way the sky looked? It was almost as though I had moistened the tip of my pen in a shallow bowl full of milk, so delicate was the blue in the dome of the heavens. The sun was barely up yet, a tentative breeze disturbed the ends of my scarf, the plumes of the marvelous hat which I had bought in Paris and thrilled me with pride whenever I saw them reflected! The papers that morning, we read them over our coffee before we left the hotel, had spoken of possible war, but it seemed unlikely, unreal: nothing was real, indeed, but the spell of golden antiquity and rose-colored romance that breathed from this fabulous city."

OLD WOMAN: Skip that part! Get on to where she meets him!

SPINSTER: Yes. . . . [*She turns several pages and continues.*] "Out of the tongues of ancients, the lyrical voices of many long-ago poets who dreamed of the world of ideals, who had in their hearts the pure and absolute image—"

OLD WOMAN: *Skip* that part! Slip down to where—

SPINSTER: Yes! *Here! Do* let us manage without any more *interruptions!* "The carriage came to a halt at the foot of the hill and my Aunt, not being too well—"

161

OLD WOMAN: She had a sore throat that morning.

SPINSTER: "—preferred to remain with the driver while I undertook the rather steep climb on foot. As I ascended the long and crumbling flight of old stone steps—"

OLD WOMAN: Yes, yes, that's the place! [*The Spinster looks up in annoyance. The Old Woman's cane taps impatiently behind the curtains.*] Go *on*, Ariadne!

SPINSTER: "I could not help observing continually above me a man who walked with a barely perceptible limp—"

OLD WOMAN [*in hushed wonder*]: Yes—Lord Byron!

SPINSTER: "—and as he turned now and then to observe beneath him the lovely panorama—"

OLD WOMAN: Actually he was watching the girl behind him!

SPINSTER [*sharply*]: Will you *please* let me finish? [*There is no answer from behind the curtains, and she continues to read.*] "I was irresistibly impressed by the unusual nobility and refinement of his features!" [*She turns a page.*]

OLD WOMAN: The handsomest man that ever walked the earth!

[*She emphasizes the speech with three slow but loud taps of her cane.*]

SPINSTER [*flurriedly*]: "The strength and grace of his throat, like that of a statue, the classic outlines of his profile, the sensitive lips and the slightly dilated nostrils, the dark lock of hair that fell down over his forehead in such a way that—"

OLD WOMAN [*tapping her cane rapidly*]: Skip that, it goes on for pages!

SPINSTER: ". . . When he had reached the very summit of the Acropolis he spread out his arms in a great, magnificent gesture like a young god. Now, thought I to myself, Apollo has come to earth in modern dress."

OLD WOMAN: Go on, skip that, get on to where she *meets* him!

SPINSTER: "Fearing to interrupt his poetic trance, I slackened my pace and pretended to watch the view. I kept my look thus carefully averted until the narrowness of the steps compelled me to move close by him."

OLD WOMAN: Of course he pretended not to see she was coming!

SPINSTER: "Then finally I faced him."

OLD WOMAN: Yes!

SPINSTER: "Our eyes came together!"

OLD WOMAN: Yes! Yes! That's the part!

SPINSTER: "A thing which I don't understand had occurred between us, a flush as of recognition swept through my whole being! Suffused my—"

OLD WOMAN: Yes . . . Yes, that's the part!

SPINSTER: " 'Pardon me,' he exclaimed, 'you have dropped your glove!' And indeed to my surprise I found that I had, and as he returned it to me, his fingers ever so slightly pressed the cups of my palm."

OLD WOMAN [*hoarsely*]: *Yes!* [*Her bony fingers clutch higher up on the curtain, the other hand also appears, slightly widening the aperture.*]

163

SPINSTER: "Believe me, dear Diary, I became quite faint and breathless, I almost wondered if I could continue my lonely walk through the ruins. Perhaps I stumbled, perhaps I swayed a little. I leaned for a moment against the side of a column. The sun seemed terribly brilliant, it hurt my eyes. Close behind me I heard that voice again, almost it seemed I could feel his breath on my—"

OLD WOMAN: Stop *there!* That will be quite enough! [*The Spinster closes the journal.*]

MATRON: Oh, is that all?

OLD WOMAN: There's a great deal more that's not to be read to people.

MATRON: Oh.

SPINSTER: I'm sorry. I'll show you the letter.

MATRON: How nice! I'm dying to see it! Winston? *Do* sit *up!*

[*He has nearly fallen asleep. The Spinster produces from the cabinet another small packet which she unfolds. It contains the letter. She hands it to the Matron, who starts to open it.*]

OLD WOMAN: Watch out, watch *out*, that woman can't *open* the letter!

SPINSTER: No, no, please, you mustn't. The contents of the letter are strictly private. I'll hold it over here at a little distance so you can see the writing.

OLD WOMAN: Not too close, she's holding up her glasses! [*The Matron quickly lowers her lorgnette.*]

SPINSTER: Only a short while later Byron was killed.

MATRON: How did he die?

OLD WOMAN: He was killed in action, defending the cause of freedom! [*This is uttered so strongly the husband starts.*]

SPINSTER: When my Grandmother received the news of Lord Byron's death in battle, she retired from the world and remained in complete seclusion for the rest of her life.

MATRON: Tch-tch-tch! How dreadful! I think that was foolish of her. [*The cane taps furiously behind the curtains.*]

SPINSTER: You don't understand. When a life is completed, it ought to be put away. It's like a sonnet. When you've written the final couplet, why go on any further? You only destroy the part that's already written!

OLD WOMAN: Read them the poem, the sonnet your Grandmother wrote to the memory of Lord Byron.

SPINSTER: Would you be interested?

MATRON: We'd adore it—truly!

SPINSTER: It's called *Enchantment.*

MATRON [*assuming a rapt expression*]: *Aahhh!*

SPINSTER [*reciting*]:
Un saison enchanté! I mused. Beguiled
Seemed Time herself, her erstwhile errant ways
Briefly forgotten, she stayed here and smiled,
Caught in a net of blue and golden days.

OLD WOMAN: Not blue and golden—gold and *azure* days!

SPINSTER:
Caught in a net—of gold and azure days!

165

But I lacked wit to see how lightly shoon
Were Time and you, to vagrancy so used—

[*The Old Woman begins to accompany in a hoarse undertone. Faint band music can be heard.*]

That by the touch of one October moon
From summer's tranquil spell you might be loosed!

OLD WOMAN [*rising stridently with intense feeling above the Spinster's voice*]:
Think you love is writ on my soul with chalk,
To be washed off by a few parting tears?
Then you know not with what slow step I walk
The barren way of those hibernal years—

My life a vanished interlude, a shell
Whose walls are your first kiss—and last farewell!

[*The band, leading the parade, has started down the street, growing rapidly louder. It passes by like the heedless, turbulent years. The Husband, roused from his stupor, lunges to the door.*]

MATRON: What's that, what's that? The *parade?* [*The Husband slaps the paper cap on his head and rushes for the door.*]

HUSBAND [*at the door*]: Come on, Mama, you'll miss it!

SPINSTER [*quickly*]: We usually accept—you understand?—a small sum of money, just anything that you happen to think you can spare.

OLD WOMAN: Stop him! He's gone outside! [*The Husband has escaped to the street. The band blares through the door.*]

SPINSTER [*extending her hand*]: Please—a *dollar* . . .

166

OLD WOMAN: *Fifty cents!*

SPINSTER: Or a *quarter!*

MATRON [*paying no attention to them*]: Oh, my goodness—*Winston!* He's *disappeared* in the *crowd!* Winston—*Winston! Excuse* me! [*She rushes out onto the door sill.*] *Winston!* Oh, my goodness gracious, he's off again!

SPINSTER [*quickly*]: We usually accept a little money for the display of the letter. Whatever you feel that you are able to give. As a matter of fact it's all that we have to *live* on!

OLD WOMAN [*loudly*]: One dollar!

SPINSTER: Fifty cents—or a quarter!

MATRON [*oblivious, at the door*]: Winston! *Winston!* Heavenly days. *Good-bye!* [*She rushes out on the street. The Spinster follows to the door, and shields her eyes from the light as she looks after the Matron. A stream of confetti is tossed through the doorway into her face. Trumpets blare. She slams the door shut and bolts it.*]

SPINSTER: *Canaille!* . . . *Canaille!*

OLD WOMAN: Gone? Without paying? *Cheated* us? [*She parts the curtains.*]

SPINSTER: *Yes*—the *canaille!* [*She fastidiously plucks the thread of confetti from her shoulder. The Old Woman steps from behind the curtains, rigid with anger.*]

OLD WOMAN: Ariadne, my letter! You've dropped my letter! Your Grandfather's letter is lying on the floor!

CURTAIN

THE STRANGEST KIND OF ROMANCE

A Lyric Play in Four Scenes

*The game enforces smirks; but we have seen
the moon in lonely alleys make
a grail of laughter of an empty ash can,
and through all sound of gaiety and quest
have heard a kitten in the wilderness.*
HART CRANE (*Chaplinesque*)

CHARACTERS

THE LITTLE MAN

THE LANDLADY

THE OLD MAN, her father-in-law

THE BOXER

NITCHEVO, the cat

*A furnished room in a small industrial city of the middle-western
states. It resembles any such room except that the walls are covered with inscriptions, the signatures of former occupants of it,
men who have stayed and passed along to other such places, the
itinerant, unmarried workingmen of a nation. There are two
windows. One shows the delicate branches of a tree that is sur-
rendering its leaves to late autumn. The other window admits a
view of the bristling stacks of the great manufacturing plant
which is the heart of the city.*

*The Landlady, a heavy woman of forty who moves and speaks
with a powerful sort of indolence, is showing the room to a pro-
spective roomer, the Little Man, dark and more delicate and
nervous in appearance than laborers usually are. As soon as he
enters the door behind the Landlady, his remarkably dilapidated
suitcase comes apart, spilling its contents over the floor—un-
laundered shirts, old shoes, shoe-polish, a rosary.*

LANDLADY [*laughing*]: Well! The suitcase has decided!

LITTLE MAN [*stooping to replace the scattered articles*]: It's
been working loose all day.

LANDLADY: How long have you had that suitcase?

LITTLE MAN: Since I started traveling.

LANDLADY: You must be Gulliver, then! You've stood up under
the strain a lot better than it has.

LITTLE MAN [*straightening*]: I don't know.

LANDLADY: You ain't held together by such old worn-out ropes.

171

LITTLE MAN [*smiling shyly and sadly*]: I don't know.

LANDLADY [*crossing to raise the window blind*]: About this room—I hope you ain't superstitious.

LITTLE MAN: Why?

LANDLADY: This room is one that a man lived in who had a bad run of luck.

LITTLE MAN: Oh. What happened to him? [*The Landlady suddenly observes the cat on the bed.*]

LANDLADY: Now how did that cat get in here? A little mystery, huh? She must've got up the pear tree, dropped on the roof of the porch, an' climbed in th' window. [*The Little Man sets down his valise and crosses gently smiling to the cat. He picks her up with great tenderness.*] She used to occupy this room with the Russian.

LITTLE MAN: The who?

LANDLADY: The fellow I mentioned who had the bad run of luck. I used to say I thought she brought it on him.

LITTLE MAN: They loved each other?

LANDLADY: I never seen such devotion.

LITTLE MAN: Then she couldn't have brought the bad luck on him. Nothing's unlucky that loves you. What's her name?

LANDLADY: Nitchevo.

LITTLE MAN: What?

LANDLADY: Nitchevo. That's what he called her. He told me once what it means but I've forgotten. It used to give me a pain.

LITTLE MAN: What?

LANDLADY: I'd come in here to talk. The circumstances I've got to live under are trying. I have a good deal of steam I need to blow off. He was a good listener.

LITTLE MAN: The Russian?

LANDLADY: Sympathetic, but silent. While I talked he was only watching the cat.

LITTLE MAN [*smiling a little*]: And so you don't like her?

LANDLADY: NO. [*She sits comfortably on the bed.*] I'll tell you the story. He was a Russian or something. Polacks I usually call 'em. Occupied this room before he took sick. He'd found the cat in the alley an' brought her home an' fed her an' took care of 'er an' let 'er sleep in his bed. A dirty practice, animals in the bed. Don't you think so? [*The Little Man shrugs.*] Well—the work at the plant is unhealthy for even a strong-bodied man. The Polack broke down. Tuberculosis developed. He gets an indemnity of some kind and goes West. The cat—he wanted to take her with him. I set my foot down on that. I told him she'd disappeared. He left without her. Now I can't get rid of the dirty thing.

LITTLE MAN: The cat?

LANDLADY: Twice today I thrown cold water on her when she come slinking around here looking for him. See how she stares at me? Hatred. Withering hatred. Just like one jealous woman looks at another. I guess she's waiting around for him to come home.

173

LITTLE MAN: Will he?

LANDLADY: Never in this world.

LITTLE MAN: Dead?

LANDLADY: The sixteenth of January I got the notice. Wasn't nobody else to be informed. [*The Little Man nods with a sad smile and strokes the cat.*] Some people say an animal understands. I told her this morning, He ain't coming back, he's dead. But she don't understand it.

LITTLE MAN: I think she does. She's grieving. [*holding her against his ear*] Yes, I can hear her—grieving.

LANDLADY: You're a funny one, too. How does this bedroom suit you?

LITTLE MAN: It's a beautiful room.

LANDLADY: Who're you kidding?

LITTLE MAN: You. How much?

LANDLADY: Three-fifty—in advance.

LITTLE MAN: I will take it, provided—

LANDLADY: What? Provided?

LITTLE MAN: I can do like the Russian and keep the cat here with me.

LANDLADY [*grinning*]: Oh, so you want to do like the Russian.

LITTLE MAN: Yes.

174

LANDLADY [*fixing her hair at the cracked mirror*]: My husban's a chronic invalid. An injury at the plant.

LITTLE MAN: Yeah? I'm sorry.

LANDLADY: Codeine every day. Fifty cents a pill is what it costs me. I wouldn't mind if only he wasn't such a pill sometimes himself. But who can look at suffering in a person?

LITTLE MAN: Nobody.

LANDLADY: Yes. That's how I feel. Well . . . the Russian used to help me out with man's work in the house.

LITTLE MAN: I see.

LANDLADY: How old are you? I bet I can guess! Thirty-five?

LITTLE MAN: Uh-huh. About.

LANDLADY: Eyetalian?

LITTLE MAN: Uh-huh.

LANDLADY: Wouldn't you think that I was a fortune-teller? My father was a Gypsy. He taught me a lot of the Zigeuner songs. He used to say to me, Bella, you're nine parts music—the rest is female mischief! [*She smiles at him.*] That instrument on the wall's a balalaika. Some night I'll drop in here to entertain you.

LITTLE MAN: Good. I heard you singing as I came up to the house. That's why I stopped. [*She smiles again and stands as if waiting.*]

LANDLADY: I'll call you Musso. Musso for Mussolini. You got a job?

LITTLE MAN: Not yet.

LANDLADY: Go down to the plant an' ask for Oliver Woodson.

LITTLE MAN: Oliver Woodson?

LANDLADY: Tell him Mizz Gallaway sent you. He'll put you right on the payroll.

LITTLE MAN: Good. Thanks.

LANDLADY: Linen's changed on Mondays. [*She starts to turn away.*] I got to apologize for the condition the walls are in.

LITTLE MAN: I noticed. Who did it?

LANDLADY: Every man who lived here signed his name.

LITTLE MAN: There must have been a lot.

LANDLADY: Birds of passage. You ever try to count them? Restlessness—changes.

LITTLE MAN [*smiling*]: Yeah.

LANDLADY: You'd think a man with pay-money in his pocket would have something better to do than sign his name on the walls of a rented bedroom.

LITTLE MAN: Is the Russian's name here, too?

LANDLADY: Not his name, he couldn't write—but his picture. There! [*She points to a childish cartoon of a big man.*] Right beside it, *look*—tail—whiskers—the *cat!* [*They both laugh.*] Partners in misery, huh?

176

LITTLE MAN: A large man?

LANDLADY: Tremendous! But when the disease germ struck him, it chopped him down like a piece of rotten timber . . . Statistics show that married men live longest. I'll tell you why it is. [*She straightens her blouse and adjusts the belt.*] Men that—live by themselves—get peculiar ways. All that part of their lives that was meant to be taken up with family matters is all left over—empty. You get what I mean?

LITTLE MAN: Yeah?

LANDLADY: Well . . . They fill it with makeshift things. I once had a roomer who went to the movies every night of the week. He carried a briefcase with him all of the time. Guess what he carried in it!

LITTLE MAN: What?

LANDLADY: Sanitary paper toilet seats. [*The Little Man looks away in embarrassment.*] A crank about sanitation. Another I had, had a pair of pet bedroom slippers.

LITTLE MAN: Pet—bedroom—?

LANDLADY: Slippers. Plain gray felt, nothing the least bit picturesque about them. Only one thing—the odor! Highly objectionable, after fifteen years—the length of time I reckon he must 've worn 'em! Well—the slippers disappeared—accidentally on purpose, as they say! Heavens on earth! How did I know he would die of a broken heart? He practickly did! [*She laughs.*] Life was incomplete without those bedroom slippers. [*She turns back to the walls.*] Some day I'm going to take me a wire scrubbing brush an' a bar of Fels-Naphtha an' leave them walls as clean as they was before the first roomer moved in. [*The door*

177

is pushed open. The Old Man enters. He looks like Walt Whitman.]

OLD MAN: You mustn't do that, daughter.

LANDLADY: Aw. You. Why mustn't I?

OLD MAN: These signatures are their little claims of remembrance. Their modest bids for immortality, daughter. Don't brush them away. Even a sparrow—leaves an empty nest for a souvenir. Isn't that so, young man?

LITTLE MAN: Yes.

OLD MAN: Cataracts have begun to— [*He waves his hand in front of his nearly sightless eyes.*] I'm not sure where you are.

LITTLE MAN [*stretching out his hand*]: Here.

OLD MAN: Be comforted here. For the little while you stay. And write your name on the wall! You won't be forgotten.

LANDLADY: That's enough, now, Father.

OLD MAN: I'm only looking for some empty bottles. Have you any empty bottles?

LANDLADY: How would he have empty bottles? He just moved in.

OLD MAN: I trade them in at the Bright Spot Delicatessen. I'll drop in later to finish our conversation. [*He goes out.*]

LANDLADY: My father-in-law. Don't encourage him, he'll be a nuisance to you. [*She taps her forehead.*] Alcoholic—gone!

178

LITTLE MAN [*sinking down on the bed and lifting the cat again*]: I'm—tired.

LANDLADY: I hope you'll be comfortable here. I guess that's all.

LITTLE MAN: Oliver Woodson?

LANDLADY [*at the door*]: Oh, yes—Oliver Woodson. [*She goes out. The Little Man rises and removes a stub of pencil from his pocket. Smiling a little, he goes to the wall and beneath the large and elliptical self-portrait of the Russian, he draws his own lean figure, in a few quick pencil scratches. Beneath the cat's picture, he puts an emphatic check mark. Then he smiles at the cat and stands aside to survey.*]

CURTAIN

*It is late one night that winter. The furnished room is empty
except for the cat. Through the frosted panes of the window in
the left wall a steely winter moonlight enters. The window in
the right wall admits the flickering ruddy glow of the plant and
its pulse-like throbbing is heard faintly. The Little Man enters
and switches on the suspended electric globe. He carries a small
package. He smiles at Nitchevo and unwraps the package. It is a
small bottle of cream which he brandishes before her.*

LITTLE MAN: Just a minute. [*He lowers the window shade that
faces the plant.*] Now. We forget the plant. [*He pours the
cream in a blue saucer.*] There. Supper. [*He sets it on the floor
by the bed and sits to watch her eat.*] Nitchevo, don't be nervous. There's nothing to worry about. In winter my hands get
stiff, it makes me clumsy. But I can rub them together, I can
massage the joints. And when the weather turns warmer—the
stiffness will pass away. Then I won't jam up the machine any
more. Today Mr. Woodson got mad. He bawled me out. Because my clumsy fingers jammed the machine. He stood behind
me and watched me and grunted—like this! [*He utters an ominous grunt.*] Oh, it was like a knife stuck in me, between my
ribs! Because, you see, I . . . have to *keep* this job, to provide
the supper. Well . . . I began to shake! Like this! [*He imitates
shaking.*] And he kept standing behind me, watching and grunting. My hands went faster and faster, they broke the rhythm.
All of a sudden a part was put out of place, the machine was
jammed, the belt conveyor stopped! SCR-E-E-ECH! Every man
along the line looked at me! Up and down and all along the line
they turned and stared—at *me!* Mr. Woodson grabbed me by
the shoulder! "There you go," he said, "you clumsy Dago!
Jammed up the works again, you brainless Spick!" [*He covers
his face.*] Oh, Nitchevo—I lost my dignity—I cried. . . . [*He
draws his breath in a shuddering sob.*] But now we forget about
that, that's over and done! It's night, we're alone together—the

180

room is warm—we sleep. . . . [*He strips off his shirt and lies back on the bed. There is a knock at the door and he sits up quickly. He makes a warning gesture to the cat. But the caller is not to be easily discouraged. The knock is repeated, the door is thrust open. It is the Landlady in a soiled but fancy negligee.*]

LANDLADY [*resentfully but coyly*]: Oh—you were playing possum.

LITTLE MAN: I'm—not dressed.

LANDLADY: Nobody needs to be bashful on my account. I thought you'd gone out and left on the light in your room. We got to economize on electric current.

LITTLE MAN: I always turn it off when I go out.

LANDLADY: I don't believe you ever go out, except to the plant.

LITTLE MAN: I'm on the night shift now.

LANDLADY: The graveyard shift, they call it. What is the trouble with you and Oliver Woodson?

LITTLE MAN: Trouble? Why?

LANDLADY: I met him in the Bright Spot Delicatessen. "Oh, by way," I said to him, "how's that feller I sent you getting along, that Eyetalian feller?" "Aw, him!" said Mr. Woodson. "Say, what's the matter with him? Isn't he doing okay?" "Naw, he jams things up!" "Well," I said, "give him time, I think he's nervous. Maybe he tries too hard."

LITTLE MAN: What did he say?

LANDLADY: He grunted. [*She smiles. The Little Man pours the rest of the cream in the cat's saucer. He is trembling.*] You

181

must try an' get over being so nervous. Maybe what you need is more amusement. [*She sits on the edge of the bed, with the balalaika.*] Sit back down! There's room for two on this sofa! [*She pats the space beside her. He gingerly sits back down at a considerable distance. His hands knot anxiously together. She plays a soft chord on the balalaika and hums with a sidelong glance at the nervous roomer.*] Tired?

LITTLE MAN: Yes.

LANDLADY: Some nights I hear you—talking through the door. Who is he talking to, I used to wonder. [*She chuckles.*] At first I imagined you had a woman in here. Well, I'm a tolerant woman. I know what people need is more than food and more than work at the plant. [*She plays dreamily for a moment.*] So when I heard that talking I was pleased. I said to myself—"That lonely little man has found a woman!" I only hoped it wasn't one picked up—you know—on the street. Women like that aren't likely to be very clean. Female hygiene's a lot more—complicated. Well . . . [*The Little Man looks down in an agony of embarrassment.*]

LITTLE MAN: It wasn't—a woman.

LANDLADY: I know. I found that out. Just you. Carrying on a one-sided conversation with a cat! Funny, yes—but kind of pitiful, too. You a man not even middle-aged yet—devoting all that care and time and affection—on what? A stray alleycat you inherited just by chance from the man who stayed here before you, that fool of a Russian! The strangest kind of a romance . . . a man—and a cat! What we mustn't do, is disregard nature. Nature says—"Man take woman or—man be lonesome!" [*She smiles at him coyly and moves a little closer.*] Nature has certainly never said, "Man take cat!"

LITTLE MAN [*suddenly, awkwardly rising*]: Nature has never said anything to me.

LANDLADY [*impatiently*]: Because you wouldn't listen!

LITTLE MAN: Oh, I listened. But all I ever heard was my own voice—asking me troublesome questions!

LANDLADY: You hear *me*, don't you?

LITTLE MAN: I hear you singing when I come home sometimes. That's very good, I like it.

LANDLADY: Then why don't you stop in the parlor and have a chat? Why do you act so bashful? [*She rises and stands back of him.*] We could talk—have fun! When you took this room you gave me a false impression.

LITTLE MAN: What do you mean?

LANDLADY: Have you forgotten the conversation we had?

LITTLE MAN: I don't remember any conversation.

LANDLADY: You said you wanted to do just like the Russian.

LITTLE MAN: I meant about the cat, to have her with me!

LANDLADY: I told you he also helped about the house!

LITTLE MAN: I'm on the night shift now!

LANDLADY: Quit dodging the issue! [*There is a pause and then she touches his shoulder.*] I thought I explained things to you. My husband's a chronic invalid, codeine, now, twice a day! Naturally I have—lots of steam to blow off! [*The Little Man moves nervously away. She follows ponderously, reaching above her to switch off the electric globe.*] Now—that's better, ain't it?

LITTLE MAN: I don't think I know—exactly.

LANDLADY: You ain't satisfied with the room?

LITTLE MAN: I like the room.

LANDLADY: I had the idea you wasn't satisfied with it.

LITTLE MAN: The room is home. I like it.

LANDLADY: The way you avoided having a conversation—almost ran past the front room every night. Why don't we talk together? The cat's got your tongue?

LITTLE MAN: You wouldn't be talking—to me.

LANDLADY: I'm talking to you—direckly!

LITTLE MAN: Not to *me*.

LANDLADY: You! Me! Where is any third party?

LITTLE MAN: There isn't a second party.

LANDLADY: What?

LITTLE MAN: You're only talking to something you think is me.

LANDLADY: Now we *are* getting in deep.

LITTLE MAN: You made me say it. [*turning to face her*] I'm not like you, a solid, touchable being.

LANDLADY: Words—wonderful! The cat's let go of your tongue?

LITTLE MAN: You're wrong if you think I'm—a person! I'm not—no person! At all . . .

LANDLADY: What are you, then, little man?

LITTLE MAN [*sighing and shrugging*]: A kind of a—ghost of a—man . . .

LANDLADY [*laughing*]: So you're not Napoleon, you're Napoleon's ghost!

LITTLE MAN: When a body is born in the world—it can't back out. . . .

LANDLADY: Huh?

LITTLE MAN: But sometimes—

LANDLADY: What?

LITTLE MAN [*with a bewildered gesture*]: The body is only—a shell. It may be alive—when what's inside—is too afraid to come out! It stays locked up and alone! Single! Private! That's how it is—with me. You're not talking to me—but just what you *think* is me!

LANDLADY [*laughing gently*]: Such a lot of words. You've thrown me the dictionary. All you needed to say was that you're lonesome. [*She touches his shoulder.*] Plain old lonesomeness, that's what's the matter with you! [*He turns to her and she gently touches his face.*] Nature says, "Don't be lonesome!" [*The curtain begins to fall.*] Nature says—"*Don't*—be lonesome!"

CURTAIN

It is again late at night. The Little Man enters with snow on his turned up collar and knitted black wool cap.

He carries the usual little package of cream for his friend the cat. Again he follows his nightly routine of lowering the shade on the glare of the plant, pouring the cream in the blue saucer, and the sighing relaxation on the bed.

LITTLE MAN: Nitchevo—don't worry—don't be nervous! [*A needless admonition for Nitchevo doesn't have a care in the world. The Little Man, smiling, watches her as he half-reclines on the bed.*] As long as we stick together there's nothing to fear. There's only danger when two who belong to each other get separated. We won't get separated—never! Will we? [*There is a rap at the door.*] Bella? [*The door is pushed open and the Old Man steps inside.*]

OLD MAN: May I come in? [*The Little Man nods.*] Don't mention this visit to my daughter-in-law. She doesn't approve of my having social relations with her roomers. Where is a chair?

LITTLE MAN [*shoving one toward him*]: Here.

OLD MAN: Thank you. I won't stay long.

LITTLE MAN: You may stay as long as you wish.

OLD MAN: That's very generous of you. But I won't do it. I know how tiresome I am, a tiresome old man who makes his need of companionship a nuisance. I don't suppose you—have a little tobacco?

LITTLE MAN [*producing some*]: Yes—here. Shall I roll it for you?

OLD MAN: Oh, no, no, no. I have a wonderful lightness in my fingers!

LITTLE MAN: Mine shake, they're always clumsy.

OLD MAN: Yes. I understand that. So I—dropped in. I thought we would have a talk.

LITTLE MAN [*embarrassed*]: I don't—talk much.

OLD MAN: Fools hate silence. I like it. I see you have books. From the public library?

LITTLE MAN: One or two. I own them.

OLD MAN: As I was passing outside, I heard some clinking.

LITTLE MAN: Clinking?

OLD MAN: Yes—like bottles. I collect empty bottles which I exchange at the Bright Spot Delicatessen.

LITTLE MAN: The bottle you heard was only a little cream bottle. It's under the bed.

OLD MAN: Oh. That wouldn't do any good. You drink cream?

LITTLE MAN: The cat.

OLD MAN [*nodding*]: Ohhh, so the cat is present! That's what made the air in the room so soft and full of sweetness! Nitchevo —where are you?

LITTLE MAN: She's having her supper.

OLD MAN: Well, I won't disturb her until she's finished. You are devoted to animals?

187

LITTLE MAN: To Nitchevo.

OLD MAN: Be careful.

LITTLE MAN: Of what?

OLD MAN: You may *lose* her. That's the trouble with love, the chance of loss.

LITTLE MAN: Nitchevo wouldn't leave me.

OLD MAN: Not on purpose, maybe. But life is full of accidents, chances, possibilities—not all of which are always very good ones. Do you know that?

LITTLE MAN: Yes.

OLD MAN: A truck might run her down.

LITTLE MAN: Nitchevo was brought up on the street.

OLD MAN: The luxuries of her present existence may have dulled her faculties a little.

LITTLE MAN: You don't understand Nitchevo. She hasn't forgotten how dangerous life can be for a lonely person.

OLD MAN: But she hasn't control of the universe in her hands!

LITTLE MAN: No. Why should she?

OLD MAN: Other things might happen. You work at the plant?

LITTLE MAN: Yes.

OLD MAN [*a fanatical light coming into his clouded eyes*]: Uh-huh! I know those fellows that operate the plant, I know the

188

bosses. They *know* I know them, too. They know I know their tricks. That's why they hate me. Look. Suppose the demand for what they make slacked off. There's two things they could do. They could cut down on the price and so put the product within the purchasing power of more consumers. Listen! I've read books on the subject! But, no! There's another thing they could do. They could cut down on the number of things they make—create a scarcity! See? And boost the price still higher! And so maintain the rich man's margin of profit! Which do you think they'd do? Why, God Almighty—*Nitchevo* knows the answer! They'd do what they've always done. [*He chuckles and rises and begins to sing in a hoarse cracked voice.*]

> Hold up, hold up the Profit,
> Ye Minions of the Boss!
> Lift high the Royal Profit,
> It must not suffer loss!

[*There is a pounding on the wall and vocal objection outside.*]

LITTLE MAN: Mrs. O'Fallon—disturbed.

OLD MAN: Yes, yes! What they'll cut down is production. Less and less men will be needed to run the machines. Fewer and fewer will stand at the belt conveyor. More and more workers will fall into the hands of the social agencies. Independence goes—then pride—then hope. Finally even the ability of the heart to feel shame or despair or anything at all—goes, too. What's left? A creature like me. Whose need of companionship has become a nuisance to people. Well, somewhere along the line of misadventures—is the cat!

LITTLE MAN: Nitchevo?

OLD MAN [*nodding sagaciously*]: You are not able to buy the cream any more.

189

LITTLE MAN: Well?

OLD MAN: Well, cats are *capricious!*

LITTLE MAN: She isn't a fair-weather friend.

OLD MAN: You think she'd be faithful to you? In adversity, even?

LITTLE MAN: She'd be faithful to me.

OLD MAN [*beaming slowly*]: Good! Good! [*He touches his eyelids.*]. A beautiful trust. A rare and beautiful trust. It makes me cry a little. That's all that life has to give in the way of perfection.

LITTLE MAN: What?

OLD MAN: The warm and complete understanding of two or three in a close-walled room with the windows blind to the world.

LITTLE MAN [*nodding*]: Yes.

OLD MAN [*alternatingly tender and vociferous*]: The roof is thin. Above it, the huge and glittering wheel of heaven which spells a mystery to us. Fine—invisible—cords of wonder—attach us to it. And so we are saved and purified and exalted. We three! You and me and—Nitchevo, the cat! [*He lifts her against his ear.*] Listen! She purrs! Mmm, such a soft and sweet and powerful sound it is. It's the soul of the universe—throbbing in her! [*He hands her back to the Little Man.*] Take her and hold her close! Close! Never let her be separated from you. For while you're together—none of the evil powers on earth can destroy you. Not even the imbecile child which is chance—nor the mad, insatiable wolves in the hearts of men! [*The sound of exterior protest gathers volume. A window bangs open and a*

190

woman shouts for an officer. The Old Man crosses to the window that faces the plant. He raises the blind and the flickering red glare of the pulsing forges shines on his bearded face.]
There she is!

LITTLE MAN: The plant?

OLD MAN: Uh-huh. [*in a quiet, conversational tone*] The day before yesterday I went down to the plant. I asked the Superin tendent about a job. "Oliver Woodson," I said, "this corpora· tion's too big for me to fight with. I've come with the olive branch. I want a job." "You're too old," he told me. "Never mind," I said, "take down my name!" "But, Pop," he said to me, "you're nearly blind!" "Never mind," I said, "take down my name!" "Okay, Pop," said Mr. Oliver Woodson. "What's your name?" "My name is Man," I said. "My name is Man. Man is my name," I said, "spelt M-A-N." "Okay," said Oliver Woodson. "Where do you live?" "I live on a cross," I said. "On what?" "On a cross! I live on a cross, on a cross! [*His voice rising louder and louder.*] Cupidity and Stupidity, that is the two-armed cross on which you have nailed me! Stupidity and cupidity, that is the two-armed cross on which you have nailed me!"

LITTLE MAN: What did he say, then? The Superintendent?

OLD MAN: The Superintendent? Said, "Hush up, be still! I'll send for the wagon!"

WOMAN ROOMER [*shouting in the hall outside*]: I ain't gonna live in no house with a lunatic! I called the police, he's gonna send for th' wagon!

LITTLE MAN [*sadly*]: She's going to send for the wagon.

OLD MAN: There! You see? I speak for the people. For me, they send for the wagon! Never mind. Take down my name.

191

It's Man! [*He leans out the window and shakes his fist at the plant. The forges blaze higher and their steady pulse seems to quicken with the Old Man's frenzy.*] I see you and I hear you! Boom-boom-boom! The pulse of a diseased heart!

LANDLADY [*in the hall*]: Be still, you drunken old fool, you've woke up the house!

WOMAN ROOMER [*outside*]: Terrible, terrible, terrible! Lunatics in the house!

OLD MAN: A fire-breathing monster you are! But listen to me! Because I'm going to speak The Malediction! Go on, go on, you niggardly pimps of the world! You entrepreneurs of deception, you traders of lies! We stand at bay but we are not defeated. The passion of our resistance is gathering force. We can Boom-Boom, too, we're going to Boom! It's only a little while we give you license! We say, Feed on, Feed on! You race of gluttons! Devour the flesh of thy brother, drink his blood! Glut your monstrous bellies on corruption! And when you're too fat to move—that fist will clench, which is the fist of God—to strike! Strike! *STRIKE!* [*He smashes a pane of the window. At this moment the door is burst open. Light spills in from the hall.*]

WOMAN ROOMER [*outside the doorway*]: Watch out! He'll kill somebody!

LANDLADY: Mrs. O'Fallon, be still, get out of the way! Officer, go on in! [*A police officer enters, followed by the Landlady in a wrapper. A group of frightened roomers, gray and bloodless-looking, huddle behind her in the doorway. The Little Man stands clutching the cat against his chest. The Old Man's rage is spent. He stands with head hanging in the banal glow of the electric bulb which the Landlady switches on.*]

LANDLADY [*to the Old Man*]: Ahh, you drunken old fool, my patience is gone. Officer, take him away. Lock him up till he comes to his senses. [*The officer grasps the Old Man's arm.*]

OFFICER: Come along, old man.

WOMAN ROOMER [*in the crowd at the door*]: A dangerous, criminal character!

LANDLADY [*to the group*]: Go on, go on back to your beds. The excitement is over. [*The Old Man seems barely conscious as he is pushed out the door. The others retreat behind him. The Little Man makes a dumb, protesting gesture, still clutching Nitchevo against his chest with one arm. The Landlady slams the door on the others. She turns angrily to face the Little Man.*] You! You're responsible for it! Haven't I told you not to encourage him in his drunken ravings? Well! . . . Why don't you say something? [*She jerks the window down.*] Christ. You're not a man at all, you're a poor excuse. Put down that cat! Throw that animal down! [*She snatches Nitchevo from him and casts her to the floor.*] She hates me.

LITTLE MAN: She doesn't like unkindness. [*He stares at her.*]

LANDLADY [*uneasily*]: Why that look? What's the meaning of it?

LITTLE MAN: I'm not looking at you. I'm looking at all the evil in the world. Turn out the light. I've lived too long in a room that was nothing but windows and always at noon and with no curtains to draw. Turn out the light. [*She reaches slowly above her and switches it off. He suddenly goes to her and plunges his head against her chest.*] O beautiful, cruel Zigeuner! Sing to me, sing to me! Comfort me in the dark!

[*At first she stands stiff and hostile. Then she relents and embraces his crouching body, and begins to sing, softly.*]

CURTAIN

A morning in spring. The branches outside the windows of the furnished room bear delicate new leaves which cast their trembling shadows through the panes. On the white iron bed is seated the Boxer in his undershirt paring his corns with a penknife. With a faint creaking, the door is pushed open. The Little Man comes in. His manner is dazed, he looks as though he had had a long illness.

LITTLE MAN [*faintly*]: *Ni*-tchevo?

BOXER [*grinning*]: Sorry, you've got the wrong party—my name is Bill! [*He points to a space on the wall where his signature is scrawled in great letters. A great X mark has been drawn through the portraits of the Russian, the Cat, and the Little Man.*]

LITTLE MAN: This was—my old room.

BOXER: Well, it ain't any more. Unless the landlady rooked me.

LITTLE MAN: You've—moved in here?

BOXER: Yep. I've hung my boxing gloves on the wall. And there's my silver trophies. [*He points to gloves suspended from a nail and several silver cups on the bureau.*]

LITTLE MAN: There was—a cat.

BOXER: A cat?

LITTLE MAN: Yes.

BOXER: Yours?

LITTLE MAN: Yes. She was mine—by adoption. I thought I might—hoped—find her here.

BOXER [*looking at him with humorous curiosity*]: I can't help you out.

LITTLE MAN: You haven't seen one? A gray one? [*He touches his chest.*] White-spotted?

BOXER: Why, I've seen dozens of cats of every description— [*Away in the house somewhere the Landlady commences to sing one of her haunting Zigeuner songs. As he speaks the Boxer returns to paring his corns with an amiable expression.*]—I've seen gray ones, black ones, white ones, spitted, spotted, and sputted! My relations with cats is strictly—*laissez faire!* Know what that means, buddy? Live and let live—a motto. I've never gone *out* of my way—[*looking up reflectively*]—to *injure* a cat. But when one gets *in* my way, I usually *kick* it! [*The Little Man stares at him speechlessly.*] Any more information I can give you?

LITTLE MAN: You see, I worked at the plant.

BOXER: So?

LITTLE MAN: I was fired, I—couldn't handle the work! My—fingers—froze up on me! On the way home, I—something happened. They took me to the Catholic Sisters of Mercy! [*The Boxer grunts.*] I had no idea how many weeks I was there. Observation—mental. When I got out—I wondered about my cat, and that was only this morning. I've—come to get her.

BOXER: I haven't seen her, buddy.

LITTLE MAN [*desperately*]: She hasn't—climbed in the window?

195

BOXER: No. If she did she wouldn't have got a very cordial reception.

LITTLE MAN: She hasn't—been *around*, then? [*His voice breaks, his lips tremble. The Boxer stares at him incredulously. Suddenly he begins to laugh. Helplessly the Little Man laughs with him, breathlessly and uncontrollably. For several moments they laugh together, then all at once the Little Man's face puckers up. He covers his face and sobs. The Boxer grunts with amazement. This is entirely too much. He strides to the door.*]

BOXER [*shouting*]: Bella! Bella! Hey, Bella! [*The Landlady answers. After a moment or two she appears in the door. Her large simplicity is gone. She has frizzed her hair and has on a tight-fitting dress and flashy jewelry. In her now is a sinister, gleaming richness.*]

LANDLADY: Aw. *YOU*. They tole me you got laid off at th' plant. I'm sorry. The room 'as been taken. It's now occupied by this young gentleman here. Your stuff, your few belongings, are packed in the downstairs closet. On your way out you may as well pick them up. [*The Little Man claws in his .pockets and pulls out a large dirty rag. He blows his nose on it.*] I can't afford to let my rooms stay vacant. I got to be practical, don't I? I didn't take you under false pretenses. You must remember the first conversation we had, before you even decided you'd take the room. I told you there wasn't nothing soft in my nature. That I was a character perfectly fair and decent—but not sentimental. It's luck in this world, plain luck—and you've got to buck it!

LITTLE MAN: You—came in, nights and—sang.

BOXER: Huh!

LITTLE MAN [*wonderingly*]: Sang. . . .

LANDLADY: What of it? I gave you free entertainment. But that don't mean I was sentimental about you. [*The Little Man shakes his head.*]

LITTLE MAN: Nothing?

LANDLADY: What?

LITTLE MAN: *Nothing?*

BOXER [*annoyed*]: What is this? What's this going on here? Is this my room or is it somebody else's? [*He grabs his gloves from the wall.*] Return me the fin I paid you and I'll move out!

LANDLADY: Just hold your horses a minute!

BOXER: Mine or his?

LANDLADY: Yours, horse-mouth! Take it easy!

BOXER: Naw, I won't. I don't like this kind of business! I rent a room, I want no crackpot visitors coming an' cryin' over some—cat's disappearance!

LANDLADY: Easy, for God's sake! Is this a national crisis? Mr.— Chile con carne! Whatever it is! Please go.

LITTLE MAN [*recovering his dignity*]: I'm going. I only wanted to ask you. Where is the cat?

LANDLADY [*grandly*]: That question I cannot answer. I turned her out.

LITTLE MAN: When?

LANDLADY: I don't remember. Two or three weeks ago, maybe.

LITTLE MAN [*despairingly*]: No!

BOXER: Christ.

LITTLE MAN: No, no, no!

LANDLADY [*angrily, to them both*]: Be still! What do you think I am? The nerve a some people . . . Expeck me to play nurse-maid to a sick alley cat? [*There is a pause.*]

LITTLE MAN: Sick?

LANDLADY: Yes! Whining! Terrific!

LITTLE MAN: What was—the matter with her?

LANDLADY: How should I know? Am I a—*vettinerry?* She cried all night and made an awful disturbance. Yes, like you're making now! I turned her out. And when she come slinking back here, I thrown cold water on her three or four times! Finally, finally, she took no for an answer! That is all I have to say on the subjeck.

LITTLE MAN [*staring at her*]: Mean—ugly—fat! [*He repeats it faster.*] Mean, ugly, fat, mean, ugly, fat! [*She slaps him furiously in the face. The Boxer grabs his shoulders and shoves him out the door with a kick.*]

BOXER: Now, God damn it! A *mad*house!

LANDLADY: Ahhh! Th'—

LITTLE MAN [*screaming through the door*]: *Where* is she? Nitchevo, Nitchevo! Where is she? Where did she go? Nitchevo, Nitchevo! Where!

LANDLADY [*screaming back at him*]: Holy God, what do I care where that dirty cat went! She might've gone to the devil for all I care! Get out of the house and stop screaming! I'll call the police! [*The Little Man does not answer and turns away from the door where the Boxer is blocking him.*]

BOXER: Huh! Yes—a *mad*house.

LANDLADY: Out of his mind. Completely. [*She wipes her face on her sleeve and adjusts her clothes.*] Going? Can you hear?

BOXER: Yeah. Going back downstairs.

LANDLADY: God. I hate for people to make a scene like that. Imagine! Holding me responsible for a sick cat. [*She sniffles a little.*] Mean, ugly, fat. . . . I guess I *am.* But who *isn't?*

[*She sinks exhaustedly on the bed. The Boxer stands at the window rolling a cigarette.*]

BOXER: He's gone out back of the house.

LANDLADY: What's he doing back there?

BOXER: Poking around in the alley and calling the cat. [*The Little Man calls in the distance: "Nitchevo!"*]

LANDLADY: Useless. He'll never find her. [*There is a sudden burst of joyful shouting. The Boxer leans out the window and chuckles. A softer, warmer quality appears in the slanting sunlight. There is distant music.*] Now what's going on?

BOXER: A celebration.

LANDLADY: Celebration of what?

BOXER [*lighting his cigarette and resting a foot on the sill*]: The old crackpot with the whiskers has found the cat.

LANDLADY: Found her? Who did you say?

BOXER: The old man, your father-in-law.

LANDLADY: The old man couldn't have found her! [*She gets up languidly and moves to the window.*] How could he have found her? The old man's blind.

BOXER: Anyhow, he found her. And there they go. [*The Landlady gazes wonderingly out the window. The Boxer slips his arm about her waist. The light is golden, the music is faint and tender.*]

LANDLADY: Well, well, well. And so they are leaving together. The funniest pair of lovers! The ghost of a man—and a cat named Nitchevo! I'm glad. . . . Good-bye! [*The music sounds louder and triumphant.*]

CURTAIN

THE LONG GOOD-BYE

CHARACTERS

JOE

MYRA

MOTHER

SILVA

BILL

FOUR MOVERS

THE LONG GOOD-BYE

Apartment F, third floor south, in a tenement apartment situated in the washed-out middle of a large mid-western American city. Outside the trucks rumble on dull streets and children cry out at their games in the areaways between walls of dusty-tomato-colored brick. Through the double front windows in the left wall, late afternoon sunlight streams into the shabby room. Beyond the windows is the door to the stair hall, and in the center of the back wall a large door opening on a corridor in the apartment where a telephone stand is located. A door in the right wall leads to a bedroom. The furnishings are disheveled and old as if they had witnessed the sudden withdrawal of twenty-five years of furious, desperate living among them and now awaited only the moving men to cart them away. From the apartment next door comes the sound of a radio broadcasting the baseball game from Sportsman's Park. Joe, a young man of twenty-three, is sitting at a table by the double windows, brooding over a manuscript. In front of him is a portable typewriter with a page of the manuscript in it, and on the floor beside the table is a shabby valise. Joe wears an undershirt and washpants. The noise of the broadcast game annoys him and he slams down the windows, but the sound is as loud as ever. He raises them and goes out the door on the right and slams other windows. The shouting of the radio subsides and Joe comes back in lighting a cigarette, a desperate scowl on his face. Silva, an Italian youth, small, graceful and good-natured, opens the entrance door and comes in. He is about Joe's age. By way of greeting he grins and then takes off his shirt.

JOE: Radios, baseball games! That's why I write nothing but crap!

SILVA: Still at it?

JOE: All night and all day.

SILVA: How come?

JOE: I had a wild hair. Couldn't sleep.

SILVA [*glancing at page in machine*]: You're burning the candle at both ends, Kid . . . [*He moves from the table across the room.*] And in my humble opinion the light ain't worth it. I thought cha was moving today.

JOE: I am. [*He flops in table-chair and bangs out a line. Then he removes the sheet.*] Phone the movers. They oughta been here.

SILVA: Yeh? Which one?

JOE: Langan's Storage.

SILVA: Storin' this stuff?

JOE: Yeh.

SILVA: What for? Why don't you sell it?

JOE: For six bits to the junk man?

SILVA: Store it you gotta pay storage. Sell it you got a spot a cash to start on.

JOE: Start on what?

SILVA: Whatever you're going to start on.

JOE: I got a spot a cash. Mother's insurance. I split it with Myra, we both got a hundred and fifty. Know where I'm going?

SILVA: No. Where?

JOE: Rio. Or Buenos Aires. I took Spanish in high school.

SILVA: So what?

JOE: I know the language. I oughta get on okay.

SILVA: Working for Standard Oil?

JOE: Maybe. Why not? Call the movers.

SILVA [*going to the phone*]: You better stay here. Take your money outa the bank and go on the Project.

JOE: No. I'm not gonna stay here. All of this here is dead for me. The goldfish is dead. I forgot to feed it.

SILVA [*into the phone*]: Lindell 0124. . . . Langan's Storage? This is the Bassett apartment. Why ain't the movers come yet? . . . Aw! [*He hangs up the receiver.*] The truck's on the way. June is a big moving month. I guess they're kept busy.

JOE: I shouldn't have left the bowl setting right here in the sun. It probably cooked the poor bastard.

SILVA: He stinks. [*Silva picks up the bowl.*]

JOE: What uh you do with him?

SILVA: Dump 'im into the tawlut.

JOE: The tawlut's turned off.

SILVA: Oh, well. [*He goes out the bedroom door.*]

JOE: Why is it that Jesus makes a distinction between the goldfish an' the sparrow! [*He laughs.*] There is no respect for dead bodies.

205

SILVA [*coming back in*]: You are losing your social consciousness, Joe. You should say "unless they are rich"! I read about once where a millionaire buried his dead canary in a small golden casket studded with genuine diamonds. I think it presents a beautiful picture. The saffron feathers on the white satin and the millionaire's tears falling like diamonds in sunlight—maybe a boys' choir singing! Like death in the movies. Which is always a beautiful thing. Even for an artist I'd say that your hair was too long. A little hip motion you'd pass for a female Imp. Cigarette?

JOE: Thanks. Christ!

SILVA: What's the matter?

JOE: How does this stuff smell to you? [*He gives him a page of the manuscript.*]

SILVA: Hmm. I detect a slight odor of frying bacon.

JOE: Lousy?

SILVA: Well, it's not you at your best. You'd better get on the Project. We're through with the city guide.

JOE: What are you going to write next?

SILVA: God Bless Harry L. Hopkins 999 times. Naw . . . I got a creative assignment. I'm calling it "Ghosts in the Old Courthouse." Days when the slaves were sold there! . . . This is bad. This speech of the girl's—"I want to get you inside of my body—not just for the time that it takes to make love on a bed between the rattle of ice in the last highball and the rattle the milkwagons make—"

JOE [*tearing the page from his hands*]: I must've been nuts.

206

SILVA: You must've had hot britches!

JOE: I did. Summer and celibacy aren't a very good mix. Buenos Aires. . . .

1ST MOVER [*from the hall outside*]: Langan's Storage!

JOE [*going to the door*]: Right here. [*He opens the door and the four burly Movers crowd in, sweating, shuffling, looking about with quick, casual eyes.*] Take out the back stuff first, will yuh, boys?

1ST MOVER: Sure.

SILVA: Hot work, huh?

2ND MOVER: Plenty.

3RD MOVER [*walking in hastily*]: "I got a pocketful of dreams!" What time's it, kid?

JOE: Four-thirty-five.

3RD MOVER: We oughta get time an' a ha'f w'en we finish this job. How'd the ball game come out?

JOE: Dunno. [*He watches them, troubled.*]

2ND MOVER: What's it to you, Short Horn? Get busy! [*They laugh and go out the rear corridor. Later they are heard knocking down a bed.*]

SILVA [*noting Joe's gloom*]: Let's get out of this place. It's depressing.

JOE: I got to look out for the stuff.

207

SILVA: Come on get a beer. There's a twenty-six-ounce-a-dime joint open up on Laclede.

JOE: Wait a while, Silva.

SILVA: Okay. [*The Movers come through with parts of a bed. Joe watches them, motionless, face set.*]

JOE: That is the bed I was born on.

SILVA: Jeez! And look how they handle it—just like it was an ordinary bed!

JOE: Myra was born on that bed, too. [*The Movers go out the door.*] Mother died on it.

SILVA: Yeah? She went pretty quick for cancer. Most of 'em hang on longer an' suffer a hell of a lot.

JOE: She killed herself. I found the empty bottle that morning in a wastebasket. It wasn't the pain, it was the doctor an' hospital bills that she was scared of. She wanted us to have the insurance.

SILVA: I didn't know that.

JOE: Naw. We kept it a secret—she an' me an' the doctor. Myra never found out.

SILVA: Where is Myra now?

JOE: Last I heard, in Detroit. I got a card from her. Here.

SILVA: Picture of the Yacht Club. What's she doin'—yachting?

JOE [*gruffly*]: Naw, I dunno what she's doin'. How should I know?

SILVA: She don't say? [*Joe doesn't answer.*] She was a real sweet kid—till all of a sudden she—

JOE: Yeh. Ev'rything broke up—when Mom died.

SILVA [*picking up a magazine*]: Four bit magazines! No wonder you stick up your nose at the Project. Hemingway! You know he's got a smooth style. [*Joe stands as if entranced as the Movers pass through to the rear.*] He's been with the Loyalist forces in Spain. Fighting in front-line trenches, they say. And yet some a the critics say that he wears a toupee on his chest! Reactionaries! [*Silva begins to read. Myra comes quietly into the room—young, radiant, vibrant with the glamor that memory gives.*]

JOE: You got a date tonight, Myra?

MYRA: Uh-huh.

JOE: Who with?

MYRA: Bill.

JOE: Who's Bill?

MYRA: Fellow I met at the swimming meet out at Bellerive Country Club.

JOE: I don't think a swimming pool's the best place in the world to pick up your boyfriends, Myra.

MYRA: Sure it is. If you look good in a Jantzen. [*She slips off her kimono.*] Get my white summer formal. No, I better. You got sweaty hands. [*She goes out the bedroom door.*]

JOE: What happened to Dave and Hugh White and that—that K. City boy?

MYRA [*coming back with a white evening dress on*]: Who? Them? My God, I don't know. Here. Hook this for me.

JOE: I guess what you've got in your heart's a revolving door.

MYRA: You know it. The radio's a great institution, huh, Joe? [*Rapidly brushing her hair*] I get so tired of it. Pop's got it on all the time. He gripes my soul. Just setting there, setting there, setting there! Never says nothing no more.

JOE: You oughta watch your English. It's awful.

MYRA: Hell, I'm not a bookworm. How's it look?

JOE: Smooth. Where you going?

MYRA: Chase Roof. Bill is no piker. His folks have got lotsa mazooma. They live out in Huntleigh—offa Ladue. Christ, it's— whew! Open that window! Cloudy?

JOE: No. Clear as a bell.

MYRA: That's good. Dancing under the stars! [*The doorbell rings.*] That's him. Get the door. [*Joe faces the door as Bill enters.*]

JOE: Why go to Switzerland, huh?

BILL: What? [*He laughs indifferently.*] Oh, yeah. She ready?

JOE: Sit down. She'll be right out.

BILL: Good.

JOE [*sweeping papers off the sofa*]: You see we read the papers. Keep up with events of the day. Sport sheet?

BILL: No, thanks.

JOE: The Cards won a doubleheader. Joe Medwick hit a homerun with two men on in the second. Comics?

BILL: No, thanks. I've seen the papers.

JOE: Oh. I thought you might've missed 'em because it's so early.

BILL: It's eight-forty-five.

JOE: It's funny, isn't it?

BILL: What?

JOE: The chandelier. I thought you were looking at it.

BILL: I hadn't noticed—particularly.

JOE: It always reminds me a little of mushroom soup. [*Bill regards him without amusement.*] Myra says that you live in Huntleigh Village.

BILL: Yes?

JOE: It must be very nice out there. In summer.

BILL: We like it. [*He stands up.*] Say, could you give your little sister a third-alarm—or whatever it takes?

JOE: She'll be out when she's ready.

BILL: That's what I'm afraid of.

JOE: Is this your first date, Bill?

211

BILL: How do you mean?

JOE: In my experience girls don't always pop right out of their boudoirs the minute a guy calls for 'em.

BILL: No? But you sort of expect more speed of a swimming champ. [*Calling*] Hey! Myra!

MYRA [*facing the wall as though it were a mirror*]: Yeh, Bill, I'm coming right out!

JOE: Excuse me, will you?

BILL: Oh, yes. [*He faces Myra.*]

JOE: This Bill of yours is a son-of-a-bitch. If I'd stayed in the room with him another minute I'd have busted him one.

MYRA: Then you'd better stay out. 'Cause I like him. What're you doing tonight, Joe?

JOE: Stay home and write.

MYRA: You stay home and write too much. Broke? Here's a dollar. Get you a date with that girl who writes poetry. Doris. She oughta bat out a pretty good sonnet under the proper influences. Oh, hell—I'm not gonna wear any stockings. Coming, Bill! Look! How is the back of my neck? Is it filthy? Christ! [*She sprays herself with perfume.*] You gotta bathe three times a day to keep fresh in this weather. Doris. Is that her name? I bet that she could be had without too much effort!

JOE: Myra. Don't talk that way.

MYRA: You kill me!

JOE: Naw, it doesn't sound right in a kid your age.

MYRA: I'm twice your age! G'bye, Joe!

JOE: G'bye, Myra.

MYRA [*facing Bill with a dazzling smile*]: Hello, darling!

BILL: Hi. Let's get outa this sweatbox.

MYRA: Yeah. [*They go out. The Movers come in with a dresser.*]

1ST MOVER: Easy.

2ND MOVER: Got it?

1ST MOVER: Yep. Who the fuck closed that door?

JOE: I'll get it. Careful down those stairs.

SILVA [*glancing up from the magazine*]: A broken mirror is seven years' bad luck.

JOE: Aw. Is that right? The stork must've dropped us through a whole bunch of 'em when we were born. How's the story?

SILVA: It's good strong stuff.

JOE [*glancing at the title*]: Butterfly and the Tank. I read that one.

CHILD [*from the street below*]: Fly, Sheepie, fly! Fly, Sheepie, fly!

JOE [*reflectively*]: Fly, Sheepie, fly! You ever played that game?

213

SILVA: Naw. Kids that play games are sissies in our neighborhood.

JOE: We played it. Myra an' me. Up and down fire escapes, in an' out basements. . . . Jeez! We had a swell time. What happens to kids when they grow up?

SILVA: They grow up. [*He turns a page.*]

JOE: Yeh, they grow up. [*The sound of roller skates on the sidewalk rises in the silence, as the light fades. Only the door to the bedroom on the right is clear in a spotlight.*]

MOTHER [*softly from the bedroom*]: Joe? Oh, Joe!

JOE: Yes, Mother? [*Mother appears in the door—a worn, little woman in a dingy wrapper with an expression that is personally troubled and confused.*]

MOTHER: Joe, aren't you going to bed?

JOE: Yes. In a minute.

MOTHER: I think you've written enough tonight, Joe.

JOE: I'm nearly finished. I just wanta finish this sentence.

MOTHER: Myra's still out.

JOE: She went to the Chase Roof.

MOTHER: Couldn't you go along with her sometimes? Meet the boys that she goes out with?

JOE: No, I can't horn in on her dates. Hell, if I had a job I couldn't pay tips for that crowd!

MOTHER: I'm worried about her.

JOE: What for? She says she's older than I am, Mom, an' I guess she's right.

MOTHER: No, she's only a baby. You talk to her, Joe.

JOE: Okay.

MOTHER: I regret that she took that job now, Joe. She should've stayed on at high school.

JOE: She wanted things—money, clothes—you can't blame her. 'S Dad out?

MOTHER: Yes. . . . She's given up her swimming.

JOE: She got kicked off the Lorelei team.

MOTHER: What for, Joe?

JOE: She broke training rules all the time. Hell, I can't stop her.

MOTHER: She listens to you.

JOE: Not much.

MOTHER: Joe—

JOE: Yes?

MOTHER: Joe, it's come back on me, Joe.

JOE [*facing her slowly*]: What?

MOTHER: The operation wasn't no use. And all it cost us, Joe, the bills not paid for it yet!

JOE: Mother—what makes you think so?

MOTHER: The same pain's started again.

JOE: How long?

MOTHER: Oh, some time now.

JOE: Why didn't you—?

MOTHER: Joe . . . what's the use?

JOE: Maybe it's—not what you think! You've got to go back. For examination, Mom!

MOTHER: No. This is the way I look at it, Joe. Like this. I've never liked being cramped. I've always wanted to have space around me, plenty of space, to live in the country on the top of a hill. I was born in the country, raised there, and I've hankered after it lots in the last few years.

JOE: Yes. I know. [*Now he speaks to himself.*] Those Sunday afternoon rides in the country, the late yellow sun through an orchard, the twisted shadows, the crazy old wind-beaten house, vacant, lopsided, and you pointing at it, leaning out of the car, trying to make Dad stop—

MOTHER: Look! That house, it's for sale! It oughta go cheap! Twenty acres of apple, a henhouse, and look, a nice barn! It's rundown now but it wouldn't cost much to repair! Stop, Floyd, go slow along here!

JOE: But he went by fast, wouldn't look, wouldn't listen! The snake-fence darted away from the road and a wall of stone rose and the sun disappeared for a moment. Your face was dark, your face looked desperate, Mother, as though you were starv-

216

ing for something you'd seen and almost caught in your hands—but not quite. And then the car stopped in front of a roadside stand. "We need eggs." A quarter, a dime—you borrowed a nickel from Dad. And the sun was low then, slanting across winter fields, and the air was cold. . . .

MOTHER: Some people think about death as being laid down in a box under earth. But I don't. To me it's the opposite, Joe, it's being let out of a box. And going upwards, not down. I don't take stock in heaven, I never did. But I do feel like there's lots of room out there and you don't have to pay rent on the first of each month to any old tightfisted Dutchman who kicks about how much water you're using. There's freedom, Joe, and freedom's the big thing in life. It's funny that some of us don't ever get it until we're dead. But that's how it is and so we've got to accept it. The hard thing to me is leaving things not straightened out. I'd like to have some assurance, some definite knowledge of what you were going to do, of how things'll work out for you. . . . Joe!

JOE: Yes?

MOTHER: What would you do with three hundred dollars?

JOE: I'm not going to think about that.

MOTHER: I want you to, Joe. The policy's in your name. It's in the right hand drawer of the chiffonier, folded up under the handkerchief box and it's got . . . [*Her voice fades out and two of the Movers come in carrying a floorlamp.*]

JOE [*clearing his throat*]: Where's the shade to that lamp?

[*Mother slips quietly out as the sunlight brightens.*]

1ST MOVER: It's comin'. [*He knocks the lamp slightly against the wall.*]

217

JOE: God damn you! Why don't you look what you're doing?

2ND MOVER: What's eating you?

1ST MOVER: Lissen, buddy—

JOE: You don't care about people's things! Any old way is all right!

SILVA [*looking up from the magazine*]: Joe, take it easy. They're not going to damage this stuff.

JOE: They're not going to damage it—no!

1ST MOVER: Damage it? Shit! [*The two Movers laugh as they go out.*]

SILVA: If they break a thing you collect on it.

3RD MOVER [*entering with some cardboard boxes*]: What's in these here boxes?

JOE: China. Glass things. So don't go tossing 'em around like—

SILVA: Joe, let's get outa this place. I can't concentrate on a story with all this commotion. What uh yuh stayin' here for anyhow, screwball? It's only—makin' yuh feel—depressed, ain't it?

JOE: You go on if you want. I've got to wait here.

4TH MOVER [*coming in with a handful of bottles*]: Some empty powder an' perfume bottles offa that dresser—you want 'em or not?

JOE: Leave 'em here on the floor. [*The 4th Mover takes up a chair from the room and goes out the door to the stair hall. Joe examines the articles on the floor. He removes the stopper from a perfume bottle and sniffs. The light in the room dims again and the front door is caught in a spotlight. Myra's voice can be heard in the hall outside.*]

MYRA: Bill, I had a swell time.

BILL: Zat all? . . . It's dark. They're all in bed. [*Joe rises and straightens attentively.*]

MYRA [*appearing in the doorway*]: Joe's light's still on.

BILL: I'll be quiet, honey. We don't have to make any noise. I'm a *wee* little mouthie!

MYRA [*kissing him*]: Yes, and you've got to go home.

BILL: C'mere closer. Unh!

MYRA: Bill!

BILL: Whatsamatter? Aren't you the little freestyle swimming an' fancy diving champion of St. Louis?

MYRA: What if I am?

BILL: Well, I can do a swell breaststroke, too—outa water.

MYRA: Shut up. I want to go to bed.

BILL: So do I.

MYRA: Goodnight.

BILL: Lissen!'

MYRA: What?

BILL: I go out with debutantes.

MYRA: What of it?

BILL: Nothing. Except that . . .

MYRA: How should I take that remark?

BILL: Okay, I'll tell you. I'll take "Goodnight I've had a swell time" from the V.P. Queen! But when girls like you try to sell me that stuff—

JOE [*stepping into the spotlighted area*]: Get out!

BILL: Aw. It's big brother. I thought you'd be out on the milk-route by now.

JOE: Get out, you stinking—

MYRA: Joe!

JOE: Before I hang one on you! [*Bill laughs weakly and goes out.*]

MYRA: You were right about him. He's no good. [*Joe looks at her.*] Joe, what do they mean by—'girls like me'?

JOE [*bending slowly and removing a small object from the floor*]: I guess they mean—this.

MYRA [*without looking*]: What?

JOE: Something he—dropped from his pocket.

MYRA [*dully*]: Oh. [*raising her voice*] Joe, I don't want you to think I—

JOE: Shut up. . . . Mother's sick.

MYRA [*excitedly*]: Oh, I know, I know, it's all a rotten dirty mess! The Chase Roof, dancing under the stars! . . . And then on the way home, puking over the side of the car—puking! And then he stops in the park and tries to— Oh, Christ, I want to have a good time! You don't think I have it sewing hooks an' eyes on corsets down at Werber & Jacobs? Nights I wanta get out, Joe, I wanta go places, have fun! But I don't want things like him crawling on me, worse than filthy cockroaches!

JOE: Hush up!

MOTHER [*faintly from another room*]: Joe—Myra . . . [*She moans.*]

MYRA [*frightened*]: What's that?

JOE: It's Mother, she's sick, she's—[*Myra runs out hall door and the lights come up again.*]—dead!

SILVA: What?

JOE: Nothing. You want some perfume?

SILVA: What kinda perfume?

JOE: Carnation.

SILVA: Naw. I resent the suggestion. [*The Movers crowd in again.*]

1ST MOVER [*to 3rd Mover*]: Quit horsin' around on a job. Git them rugs.

3RD MOVER: Awright, straw boss. They should've put in a pinch hitter. Meighan or Flowers.

2ND MOVER: Flowers? He couldn't hit an elephant's ass. Grab an end a the sofa. Hup!

4TH MOVER: Cabbage for supper nex' door.

WOMAN [*calling mournfully from the street*]: May-zeeee! Oh, *May*-zeeee!

3RD MOVER: In that game a' Chicago . . . [*The Movers carry the sofa and other furniture out the entrance door. Joe removes a picture from wall.*]

SILVA [*looking up from the magazine*]: Myra's, huh?

JOE: One she had in the rotogravure, time she broke a record in the Mississippi Valley relays.

SILVA [*taking the picture*]: She had a sweet shape on her, huh?

JOE: Yes.

SILVA: What makes a girl go like that.

JOE: Like what?

SILVA: You know.

JOE: No, I *don't* know! Why don't you get out of here and leave me alone?

SILVA: Because I don't want to. Because I'm reading a story. Because I think you're nuts.

JOE: Yeah? Gimme that picture. [*He bends over his suitcase to pack the photograph with his things and as he does so the lights dim a little and Myra comes in. She is appreciably cheaper and more sophisticated and wears a negligee she could not have bought with her monthly salary.*]

MYRA: I wish you'd quit having that dago around the place.

JOE [*rising*]: Silva?

MYRA: Yeah. I don't like the way he looks at me.

JOE: Looks at you?

MYRA: Yeh. I might as well be standing naked in front of him the way that he looks. [*Joe laughs harshly.*] You think it's funny—him looking at me that way?

JOE: Yes. It *is* funny.

MYRA: My sense a the comical don't quite agree with yours.

JOE [*looking at her*]: You're getting awfully skittish—objecting to guys looking at you.

MYRA: Well, that boy is repulsive.

JOE: Because he don't live somewhere offa Ladue?

MYRA: No. Because he don't take a bath.

JOE: That's not true. Silva takes a shower ev'ry morning at the party headquarters.

MYRA: Party headquarters! You better try to associate with people that will do you some good instead of—radical dagoes and niggers an'—

JOE: Shut up! My God, you're getting common. Snobbishness, that's always the first sign. I've never known a snob yet that wasn't fundamentally as common as dirt!

MYRA: Is it being a snob not to like dirty people?

JOE: Dirty people are what *you* run around with! Geezers in fifty dollar suits with running sores on the back of their necks. You better have your blood tested!

MYRA: You—you—you can't insult me like that! I'm going to—call Papa—tell him to—

JOE: I used to have hopes for you, Myra. But not any more. You're goin' down the toboggan like a greased pig. Take a look at yourself in the mirror. Why did Silva look at you that way? Why did the newsboy whistle when you walked past him last night? Why? 'Cause you looked like a whore—like a cheap one, Myra, one he could get for six! [*Myra looks at him, stunned, but does not answer for a moment.*]

MYRA [*quietly*]: You never would have said a thing to me like that—when Mother was living.

JOE: No. When Mother was living, you wouldn't have been like this. And stayed on here in the house.

MYRA: The house? This isn't a house. It's five rooms and a bath and I'm getting out as quick as I can and I mean it! I'm not going to hang around here with a bunch of long-haired lunatics with eyes that strip the clothes off you, and then be called— dirty names!

JOE: If my sister was clean . . . I'd kill any fellow that dared to look at her that way!

224

MYRA: You got a swell right—you that just loaf around all day writing crap that nobody reads. You never do nothing, nothing, you don't make a cent! If I was Papa—I'd kick you out of this place so fast it would— Ahhhhh! [*She turns away in disgust.*]

JOE: Maybe that won't be necessary.

MYRA: Oh, no? You been saying that a long time. They'll move every stick a furniture out a this place before they do you!

[*She laughs and goes out. The lights come up.*]

JOE [*to himself*]: Yeah. . . . [*The 1st and 2nd Movers come back and start rolling the carpet. Joe watches them and then speaks aloud.*] Every stick a furniture out—before me! [*He laughs.*]

SILVA: What?

JOE: I got a card from her last week.

SILVA: Who?

JOE: Myra.

SILVA: Yeah. You told me that. [*He throws the magazine aside.*] I wonder where your old man is.

JOE: Christ. I don't know.

SILVA: Funny an old bloke like him just quittin' his job and lamming out to God knows where—after fifty—or fifty-five years of livin' a regular middle-class life.

JOE: I guess he got tired of living a regular middle-class life.

SILVA: I used to wonder what he was thinking about nights—sitting in that big overstuffed chair. [*The 3rd and 4th Movers have come back and now they remove the big chair. Joe takes his shirt from the chair as they pass and slowly puts it on.*]

JOE: So did I. I'm still wondering. He never said a damn thing.

SILVA: Naw?

JOE: Just sat there, sat there, night after night after night. Well, he's gone now, they're all gone.

SILVA [*with a change of tone*]: You'd better go, too.

JOE: Why don't you go on ahead an' wait for me, Silva. I'll be along in a while.

SILVA: Because I don't like the way you're acting and for some goddam reason I feel—responsible for you. You might take a notion to do a Steve Brody out one a them windows.

JOE [*laughing shortly*]: For Chrissakes what would I do that for?

SILVA: Because your state of mind is abnormal. I've been lookin' at you. You're starin' off into space like something's come loose in your head. I know what you're doing. You're taking a morbid pleasure in watchin' this junk hauled off like some dopes get in mooning around a bone orchard after somebody's laid under. This place is done for, Joe. You can't help it. [*Far down at the end of the block an organ grinder has started winding out an old blues tune of ten or fifteen years ago. It approaches gradually with a melancholy gaiety throughout rest of play.*] Write about it some day. Call it "An Elegy for an Empty Flat." But right now my advice is to get out of here and get drunk! 'Cause the world goes on. And you've got to keep going on with it.

JOE: But not so fast that you can't even say good-bye.

SILVA: Good-bye? 'S not in my vocabulary! Hello's the word nowadays.

JOE: You're kidding yourself. You're saying good-bye all the time, every minute you live. Because that's what life is, just a long, long good-bye! [*with almost sobbing intensity*] To one thing after another! Till you get to the last one, Silva, and that's—good-bye to yourself! [*He turns sharply to the window.*] Get out of here now, get out and leave me alone!

SILVA: Okay. But I think you're weeping like Jesus and it makes me sick. [*He begins to put on his shirt.*] I'll see you over at Weston's if I can still see. [*grinning wryly*] Remember, kid, what Socrates said. "Hemlock's a damn bad substitute for a twenty-six-ounce glass a beer!" [*He laughs and puts on his hat.*] So long. [*Silva goes out the door, leaving Joe in the bare room. The yellow stains on the walls, the torn peeling paper with its monotonous design, the fantastically hideous chandelier now show up in cruel relief. The sunlight through the double windows is clear and faded as weak lemon water and a fly is heard buzzing during a pause in the organ grinder's music. The tune begins again and is drowned in the starting roar of the moving van which ebbs rapidly away. Joe walks slowly to the windows.*]

CHILD [*calling in the street*]: Olly—olly—oxen-free! Olly—olly —oxen-free! [*Joe looks slowly about him. His whole body contracts in a spasm of nostalgic pain. Then he grins wryly, picks up his suitcase and goes over to the door. He slips a hand to his forehead in a mocking salute to the empty room, then thrusts the hand in his pocket and goes slowly out.*] Olly—olly—oxen-free! [*Scattered shouting and laughter floats up to the room. The music is now fading.*]

SLOW CURTAIN

HELLO FROM BERTHA

CHARACTERS

GOLDIE

BERTHA

LENA

GIRL

HELLO FROM BERTHA

A bedroom in "the valley"—a notorious red-light section along the river-flats of East St. Louis. In the center is a massive brass bed with tumbled pillows and covers on which Bertha, a large blonde prostitute, is lying restlessly. A heavy old-fashioned dresser with gilt knobs, gaudy silk cover and two large kewpie dolls stands against the right wall. Beside the bed is a low table with empty gin bottles. An assortment of lurid magazines is scattered carelessly about the floor. The wallpaper is grotesquely brilliant—covered with vivid magnified roses—and is torn and peeling in some places. On the ceiling are large yellow stains. An old-fashioned chandelier, fringed with red glass pendants, hangs from the center. Goldie comes in at the door in the left wall. She wears a soiled double-piece dress of white and black satin, fitted closely to her almost fleshless body. She stands in the doorway, smoking a cigarette, and stares impatiently at Bertha's prostrate figure.

GOLDIE: Well, Bertha, what are you going to do? [*For a moment there is no answer.*]

BERTHA [*with faint groan*]: I dunno.

GOLDIE: You've got to decide, Bertha.

BERTHA: I can't decide nothing.

GOLDIE: Why can't you?

BERTHA: I'm too tired.

GOLDIE: That's no answer.

BERTHA [*tossing fretfully*]: Well, it's the only answer I know. I just want to lay here and think things over.

GOLDIE: You been layin' here thinkin' or somethin' for the past two weeks. [*Bertha makes an indistinguishable reply.*] You got to come to some decision. The girls need this room.

BERTHA [*with hoarse laugh*]: Let 'em have it!

GOLDIE: They can't with you layin' here.

BERTHA [*slapping her hand on bed*]: Oh, God!

GOLDIE: Pull yourself together, now, Bertha. [*Bertha tosses again and groans.*]

BERTHA: What's the matter with me?

GOLDIE: You're sick.

BERTHA: I got a sick headache. Who slipped me that Mickey Finn last night?

GOLDIE: Nobody give you no Mickey Finn. You been layin' here two solid weeks talkin' out of your head. Now, the sensible thing for you to do, Bertha, is to go back home or—

BERTHA: Go back nowhere!—I'm stayin' right here till I get on my feet. [*She stubbornly averts her face.*]

GOLDIE: The valley's no place for a girl in your condition. Besides we need this room.

BERTHA: Leave me be, Goldie. I wanta get in some rest before I start workin'.

GOLDIE: Bertha, you've got to decide! [*The command hangs heavily upon the room's florid atmosphere for several long moments. Bertha slowly turns her head to Goldie.*]

BERTHA [*faintly*]: What is it I got to decide?

GOLDIE: Where you're going from here? [*Bertha looks at her silently for a few seconds.*]

BERTHA: Nowhere. Now leave me be, Goldie. I've got to get in my rest.

GOLDIE: If I let you be, you'd just lay here doin' nothin' from now till the crack of doom! [*Bertha's reply is indistinguishable.*] Liseen here! If you don't make up your mind right away, I'm gonna call the ambulance squad to come get you! So you better decide right this minute.

BERTHA [*her body stiffening slightly at this threat*]: I can't decide nothing. I'm too tired—worn out.

GOLDIE: All right! [*She snaps her purse open.*] I'll take this nickel and I'll make the call right now. I'll tell 'em we got a sick girl over here who can't talk sense.

BERTHA [*thickly*]: Go ahead. I don't care what happens to me now.

GOLDIE [*changing her tactics*]: Why don't you write another letter, Bertha, to that man who sells . . . hardware or something in Memphis?

BERTHA [*with sudden alertness*]: Charlie? You leave his name off your dirty tongue!

GOLDIE: That's a fine way for you to be talking, me keeping you here just out of kindness and you not bringing in a red, white or blue cent for the last two weeks! Where do you—

BERTHA: Charlie's a real . . . sweet. Charlie's a . . . [*Her voice trails into a sobbing mumble.*]

GOLDIE: What if he is? All the better reason for you to write him to get you out of this here tight spot you're in, Bertha.

BERTHA [*aroused*]: I'll never ask him for another dime! Get that? He's forgotten all about me, my name and everything else. [*She runs her hand slowly down her body.*] Somebody's cut me up with a knife while I been sleeping.

GOLDIE: Pull yourself together, Bertha. If this man's got money, maybe he'll send you some to help you git back on your feet.

BERTHA: Sure he's got money. He owns a hardware store. I reckon I ought to know, I used to work there! He used to say to me, Girlie, any time you need something just let Charlie know. . . . We had good times together in that back room!

GOLDIE: I bet he ain't forgotten it neither.

BERTHA: He's found out about all the bad things I done since I quit him and . . . come to St. Louie. [*She slaps the bed twice with her palm.*]

GOLDIE: Naw, he ain't, Bertha. I bet he don't know a thing. [*Bertha laughs weakly.*]

BERTHA: It's you that's been writing him things. All the dirt you could think of about me! Your filthy tongue's been clacking so fast that—

GOLDIE: Bertha! [*Bertha mutters an indistinguishable vulgarity.*] I been a good friend to you, Bertha.

BERTHA: Anyhow he's married now.

GOLDIE: Just write him a little note on a postcard and tell him you've had some tough breaks. Remind him of how he said he would help you if ever you needed it, huh?

BERTHA: Leave me alone a while, Goldie. I got an awful feeling inside of me now.

GOLDIE [*advancing a few steps and regarding Bertha more critically*]: You want to see a doctor?

BERTHA: No. [*There is a pause.*]

GOLDIE: A priest? [*Bertha's fingers claw the sheet forward.*]

BERTHA: No!

GOLDIE: What religion are you, Bertha?

BERTHA: None.

GOLDIE: I thought you said you was Catholic once.

BERTHA: Maybe I did. What of it?

GOLDIE: If you could remember, maybe we could get some sisters or something to give you a room like they did for Rose Kramer for you to rest in, and get your strength back—huh, Bertha?

BERTHA: I don't want no sisters to give me nothing! Just leave me be in here till I get through resting.

GOLDIE: Bertha, you're . . . bad sick, Bertha!

BERTHA [*after a slight pause*]: Bad?

GOLDIE: Yes, Bertha. I don't want to scare you but . . .

BERTHA [*hoarsely*]: You mean I'm dying?

235

GOLDIE [*after a moment's consideration*]: I didn't say that.

[*There is another pause.*]

BERTHA: No, but you meant it.

GOLDIE: We got to provide for the future, Bertha. We can't just let things slide.

BERTHA [*attempting to sit up*]: If I'm dying I want to write Charlie. I want to—tell him some things.

GOLDIE: If you mean a confession, honey, I think a priest would be—

BERTHA: No, no priest! I want Charlie!

GOLDIE: Father Callahan would—

BERTHA: No! No! I want Charlie!

GOLDIE: Charlie's in Memphis. He's running his hardware business.

BERTHA: Yeah. On Central Avenue. The address is 563.

GOLDIE: I'll write him and tell what condition you're in, huh, Bertha?

BERTHA [*after a reflective pause*]: No. . . . Just tell him I said hello. [*She turns her face to the wall.*]

GOLDIE: I gotta say more than that, Bertha.

BERTHA: That's all I want you to say. Hello from—Bertha.

GOLDIE: That wouldn't make sense, you know that.

BERTHA: Sure it would. Hello from Bertha to Charlie with all her love. Don't that make sense?

GOLDIE: No!

BERTHA: Sure it does.

GOLDIE [*turning to the door*]: I better call up the hospital and get them to send out the ambulance squad.

BERTHA: No, you don't! I'd rather just die than that.

GOLDIE: You're in no condition to stay in the valley, Bertha. A girl in your shape's got to be looked out for proper or anything's likely to happen. [*Outside, in the reception room, someone has started the nickel phonograph. It is playing "The St. Louis Blues." A hoarse male voice joins in the refrain and there is a burst of laughter and the slamming of a door.*]

BERTHA [*after a slight pause*]: You're telling me, sister. [*She elevates her shoulders.*] I know the rules of this game! [*She stares at Goldie with brilliant, faraway eyes.*] When you're out you're out and there's no comeback for you neither! [*She shakes her head and then slowly reclines again. She knots her fingers and pounds the bed several times; then her hand relaxes and slips over the side of the bed.*]

GOLDIE: Now, pull yourself together, Bertha, and I'll have you moved to a nice, clean ward where you'll get good meals and a comfortable bed to sleep in.

BERTHA: Die in, you mean! Help me outa this bed! [*She struggles to rise.*]

237

GOLDIE [*going to her*]: Don't get excited, now, Bertha.

BERTHA: Help me up. Yes! Where's my kimono?

GOLDIE: Bertha, you're not in any shape to go crawling around out of bed!

BERTHA: Shut up, you damned crepe-hanger! Get Lena in here. She'll help me out with my things.

GOLDIE: What've you decided on, Bertha?

BERTHA: To go.

GOLDIE: Where?

BERTHA: That's my business.

GOLDIE [*after a pause*]: Well, I'll call Lena. [*Bertha has risen painfully and now she totters toward the dresser.*]

BERTHA: Wait a minute, you! Look under that tray. The comb and brush tray. [*She sinks, panting, into a rocker.*] You'll find five bucks stuck under there.

GOLDIE: Bertha, you ain't got no money under that tray.

BERTHA: You trying to tell me I'm broke?

GOLDIE: You been broke for ten days, Bertha. Ever since you took sick you been out of money.

BERTHA: You're a liar!

GOLDIE [*angrily*]: Don't call me names, Bertha! [*They glare at each other. A Girl, in what looks like a satin gymnasium out-*

fit, appears in doorway and glances in curiously. She grins and disappears.]

BERTHA [*finally*]: Get Lena in here. She won't cheat me.

GOLDIE [*going to the dresser*]: Look, Bertha. Just to satisfy you. See under the tray? Nothing there but an old postcard you once got from Charlie.

BERTHA [*slowly*]: I been robbed. Yes, I been robbed. [*with increasing velocity*] Just because I'm too sick an' tired an' done in to look out for myself, I get robbed! If I was in my strength, you know what I'd do? I'd bust this place wide open! I'd get back my money you stole or take it out of your hide, you old—

GOLDIE: Bertha, you spent your last dime. You bought gin with it.

BERTHA: No!

GOLDIE: It was Tuesday night, the night you got sick, you bought yourself a quart of dry gin that night. I swear you did, Bertha!

BERTHA: I wouldn't believe your dying word on a Bible! Get Lena in here! It's a frame-up! [*She rises and staggers toward the door.*] Lena! Lena! *Get me police headquarters!*

GOLDIE [*alarmed*]: No, Bertha!

BERTHA [*still louder*]: GET ME POLICE HEADQUAR-TERS! [*Collapsing with weakness against the side of the door, she sobs bitterly and covers her eyes with one hand. The electric phonograph starts again. There is the shuffling of dancers outside.*]

GOLDIE: Bertha, be calm. Settle down here now.

239

BERTHA [*turning on her*]: Don't tell me to be calm, you old slut. Get me police headquarters quick or I'll—! [*Goldie catches her arm and they struggle but Bertha wrenches free.*] I'll report this robbery to the police if it's the last thing I do! You'd steal the pennies off a dead nigger's eyes, that's how bighearted you are! You come in here and try to soft-soap me about priests and confessions and—GET ME POLICE HEADQUARTERS! [*She pounds the wall, and sobs.*]

GOLDIE [*helplessly*]: Bertha, you need a good bromide. Get back in bed, honey, and I'll bring you a double bromide and a box of aspirin.

BERTHA [*rapidly, with eyes shut, head thrown back and hands clenched*]: You'll bring me back my twenty-five dollars you stole from under that comb and brush tray!

GOLDIE: Now, Bertha—

BERTHA [*without changing her position*]: You'll bring it back or I'll have you prosecuted! [*Her tense lips quiver; a shining thread of saliva dribbles down her chin. She stands like a person in a catatonic trance.*] I've got friends in this town. Big shots! [*exultantly*] Lawyers, politicians! *I can beat any God damn rap you try to hang on me!* [*Her eyes flare open.*] *Va-grancy, huh?* [*She laughs wildly.*] That's a laugh, ain't it! I got my constitutional rights!

[*Her laughter dies out and she staggers to the rocker and sinks into it. Goldie watches her with extreme awe. Then she edges cautiously past Bertha and out the door with a frightened gasp.*]

BERTHA: Oh, Charlie, Charlie, you were such a sweet, sweet! [*Her head rocks and she smiles in agony.*] You done me dirt more times than I could count, Charlie—stood me up, married a little choirsinger— Oh, God! I love you so much it makes my guts ache to look at your blessed face in the picture! [*Her ecstasy fades and the look of schizophrenic suspicion returns.*] Where's that hellcat gone to? Where's my ten dollars? Hey, *YOU!!* Come back in here with that money! I'll brain you if ever I catch you monkeying around with any money belonging to me! . . . Oh, Charlie . . . I got a sick headache, Charlie. No, honey. Don't go out tonight. [*She gets up from the rocker.*] Hey, you! Bring me a cold ice pack—my head's aching. I got one hell of a hangover, baby! [*She laughs.*] Vagrancy, huh? Vagrancy your Aunt Fanny! Get me my lawyer. I got influence in this town. Yeah. My folks own half the oil wells in the state of—of—Nevada. [*She laughs.*] Yeah, that's a laugh, ain't it? [*Lena, a dark Jewish girl in pink satin trunks and blouse, comes in the door. Bertha looks at her with half-opened eyes.*] Who're you?

LENA: It's me, Lena.

BERTHA: Oh. Lena, huh? Set down an' take a load off yer feet. Have a cigarette, honey. I ain't feeling good. There ain't any cigarettes here. Goldie took 'em. She takes everything I got. Set down an'—take a—

LENA [*in doorway*]: Goldie told me you weren't feelin' so good this evening so I thought I'd just look in on you, honey.

BERTHA: Yeah, that's a laugh, ain't it? I'm all right. I'll be on the job again tonight. You bet. I always come through, don't I, kid? Ever known me to quit? I may be a little down on my luck right now but—that's all! [*She pauses, as if for agreement.*] That's all, ain't it, Lena? I ain't old. I still got my looks. Ain't I?

LENA: Sure you have, Bertha. [*There is a pause.*]

BERTHA: Well, what're you grinning about?

LENA: I ain't grinning, Bertha.

BERTHA [*herself slightly smiling*]: I thought maybe you thought there was something funny about me saying I still had my looks.

LENA [*after a pause*]: No, Bertha, you got me wrong.

BERTHA [*hoarsely*]: Listen, sweetheart, I know the Mayor of this God damn little burg. Him and me are like that. See? I can beat any rap you try to hang on me and I don't give a damn what. Vagrancy, huh? That's a sweet laugh to me! Get me my traveling bag, will you, Lena? Where is it? I been thrown out of better places than this. [*She rises and drags herself vaguely about the room and then collapses on bed. Lena moves toward the bed.*] God, I'm too tired. I'll just lay down till my head stops swimming. . . . [*Goldie appears in the doorway. She and Lena exchange significant glances.*]

GOLDIE: Well, Bertha, have you decided yet?

BERTHA: Decided what?

GOLDIE: What you're gonna do?

BERTHA: Leave me be. I'm too tired.

GOLDIE [*casually*]: Well, I've called up the hospital, Bertha. They're sending an ambulance around to get you. They're going to put you up in a nice clean ward.

BERTHA: Tell 'em to throw me in the river and save the state some money. Or maybe they're scared I'd pollute the water. I guess they'll have to cremate me to keep from spreadin' infection. Only safe way of disposin' of Bertha's remains. That's a sweet laugh, ain't it? Look at her, Lena, that slut that calls herself Goldie. She thinks she's bighearted. Ain't that a laugh? The only thing big about her is the thing that she sits on. Yeah, the old horse! She comes in here talking soft about callin' a priest an' havin' me stuck in the charity ward. Not me. None a that stuff for me, I'll tell you!

GOLDIE [*with controlled fury*]: You better watch how you talk. They'll have you in the straitjacket, that's what!

BERTHA [*suddenly rising*]: Get the hell out! [*She throws a glass at Goldie, who screams and runs out. Bertha then turns to Lena.*] Set down and take a letter for me. There's paper under that kewpie.

LENA [*looking on the dresser*]: No, there ain't, Bertha.

BERTHA: Ain't? I been robbed a that, too! [*Lena walks to the table by the bed and picks up a tablet.*]

LENA: Here's a piece, Bertha.

BERTHA: All right. Take a letter. To Mr. Charlie Aldrich, owner of the biggest hardware store in the City of Memphis. Got that?

LENA: What's the address, Bertha?

BERTHA: It's 563 Central Avenue. Got it? Yeah, that's right. Mr. Charlie Aldrich. Dear Charlie. They're fixing to lock me up in the city bughouse. On a charge of criminal responsibility without due process of law. Got that? [*Lena stops writing.*] And I'm as sane as you are right this minute, Charlie. There's nothing wrong with my upper story and there never will be. Got that? [*Lena looks down and pretends to write.*] So come on down here, Charlie, and bail me out of here, honey, for old times' sake. Love and kisses, your old sweetheart, Bertha.

. . . Wait a minute. Put a P.S. and say how's the wife and your— No! Scratch it out! That don't belong in there. Scratch it all out, the whole damn thing! [*There is a painful silence. Bertha sighs and turns slowly on the bed, pushing her damp hair back.*] Get you a clean sheet of paper. [*Lena rises and tears another sheet from the tablet. A young Girl sticks her head in the door.*]

GIRL: Lena!

LENA: Coming.

BERTHA: Got it?

LENA: Yes.

BERTHA: That's right. Now just say this. Hello from Bertha—to Charlie—with all her love. Got that? Hello from Bertha—to Charlie . . .

LENA [*rising and straightening her blouse*]: Yes.

BERTHA: With all . . . her love . . . [*The music in the outer room recommences.*]

CURTAIN

THIS PROPERTY IS CONDEMNED

CHARACTERS

WILLIE, a young girl

TOM, a boy

THIS PROPERTY IS CONDEMNED

A railroad embankment on the outskirts of a small Mississippi town on one of those milky white winter mornings peculiar to that part of the country. The air is moist and chill. Behind the low embankment of the tracks is a large yellow frame house which has a look of tragic vacancy. Some of the upper windows are boarded, a portion of the roof has fallen away. The land is utterly flat. In the left background is a billboard that says "GIN WITH JAKE" and there are some telephone poles and a few bare winter trees. The sky is a great milky whiteness: crows occasionally make a sound of roughly torn cloth.

The girl Willie is advancing precariously along the railroad track, balancing herself with both arms outstretched, one clutching a banana, the other an extraordinarily dilapidated doll with a frowsy blond wig.

She is a remarkable apparition—thin as a beanpole and dressed in outrageous cast-off finery. She wears a long blue velvet party dress with a filthy cream lace collar and sparkling rhinestone beads. On her feet are battered silver kid slippers with large ornamental buckles. Her wrists and her fingers are resplendent with dimestore jewelry. She has applied rouge to her childish face in artless crimson daubs and her lips are made up in a preposterous Cupid's bow. She is about thirteen and there is something ineluctably childlike and innocent in her appearance despite the makeup. She laughs frequently and wildly and with a sort of precocious, tragic abandon.

The boy Tom, slightly older, watches her from below the embankment. He wears corduroy pants, blue shirt and a sweater and carries a kite of red tissue paper with a gaudily ribboned tail.

TOM: Hello. Who are you?

WILLIE: Don't talk to me till I fall off. [*She proceeds dizzily. Tom watches with mute fascination. Her gyrations grow wider and wider. She speaks breathlessly.*] Take my—crazy doll—will you?

TOM [*scrambling up the bank*]: Yeh.

WILLIE: I don't wanta—break her when—I fall! I don't think I can—stay on much—longer—do you?

TOM: Naw.

WILLIE: I'm practically—off—right now! [*Tom offers to assist her.*] No, don't touch me. It's no fair helping. You've got to do it—all—by yourself! God, I'm wobbling! I don't know what's made me so nervous! You see that watertank way back yonder?

TOM: Yeah?

WILLIE: That's where I—started—from! This is the furthest—I ever gone—without once—falling off. I mean it will be—if I can manage to stick on—to the next—telephone—pole! Oh! Here I go! [*She becomes completely unbalanced and rolls down the bank.*]

TOM [*standing above her now*]: Hurtcha self?

WILLIE: Skinned my knee a little. Glad I didn't put my silk stockings on.

TOM [*coming down the bank*]: Spit on it. That takes the sting away.

WILLIE: Okay.

TOM: That's animal's medicine, you know. They always lick their wounds.

WILLIE: I know. The principal damage was done to my bracelet, I guess. I knocked out one of the diamonds. Where did it go?

TOM: You never could find it in all them cinders.

WILLIE: I don't know. It had a lot of shine.

TOM: It wasn't a genuine diamond.

WILLIE: How do you know?

TOM: I just imagine it wasn't. Because if it was you wouldn't be walking along a railroad track with a banged-up doll and a piece of a rotten banana.

WILLIE: Oh, I wouldn't be so sure. I might be peculiar or something. You never can tell. What's your name?

TOM: Tom.

WILLIE: Mine's Willie. We've both got boy's names.

TOM: How did that happen?

WILLIE: I was expected to be a boy but I wasn't. They had one girl already. Alva. She was my sister. Why ain't you at school?

TOM: I thought it was going to be windy so I could fly my kite.

WILLIE: What made you think that?

TOM: Because the sky was so white.

WILLIE: Is that a sign?

TOM: Yeah.

WILLIE: I know. It looks like everything had been swept off with a broom. Don't it?

TOM: Yeah.

WILLIE: It's perfectly white. It's white as a clean piece of paper.

TOM: Uh-huh.

WILLIE: But there isn't a wind.

TOM: Naw.

WILLIE: It's up too high for us to feel it. It's way, way up in the attic sweeping the dust off the furniture up there!

TOM: Uh-huh. Why ain't you at school?

WILLIE: I quituated. Two years ago this winter.

TOM: What grade was you in?

WILLIE: Five A.

TOM: Miss Preston.

WILLIE: Yep. She used to think my hands was dirty until I explained that it was cinders from falling off the railroad tracks so much.

TOM: She's pretty strict.

WILLIE: Oh, no, she's just disappointed because she didn't get married. Probably never had an opportunity, poor thing. So she has to teach Five A for the rest of her natural life. They started teaching algebra an' I didn't give a goddam what X stood for so I quit.

TOM: You'll never get an education walking the railroad tracks.

WILLIE: You won't get one flying a red kite neither. Besides . . .

TOM: What?

WILLIE: What a girl needs to get along is social training. I learned all of that from my sister Alva. She had a wonderful popularity with the railroad men.

TOM: Train engineers?

WILLIE: Engineers, firemen, conductors. Even the freight sup'rintendent. We run a boardinghouse for railroad men. She was I guess you might say The Main Attraction. Beautiful? Jesus, she looked like a movie star!

TOM: Your sister?

WILLIE: Yeah. One of 'em used to bring her regular after each run a great big heart-shaped red silk box of assorted chocolates and nuts and hard candies. Marvelous?

TOM: Yeah. [*The cawing of crows sounds through the chilly air.*]

WILLIE: You know where Alva is now?

TOM: Memphis?

WILLIE: Naw.

TOM: New Awleuns?

WILLIE: Naw.

TOM: St. Louis?

WILLIE: You'll never guess.

TOM: Where is she then? [*Willie does not answer at once.*]

WILLIE [*very solemnly*]: She's in the bone orchard.

TOM: What?

WILLIE [*violently*]: Bone orchard, cemetery, graveyard! Don't you understand English?

TOM: Sure. That's pretty tough.

WILLIE: You don't know the half of it, buddy. We used to have some high old times in that big yellow house.

TOM: I bet you did.

WILLIE: Musical instruments going all of the time.

TOM: Instruments? What kind?

WILLIE: Piano, victrola, Hawaiian steel guitar. Everyone played on something. But now it's—awful quiet. You don't hear a sound from there, do you?

TOM: Naw. Is it empty?

WILLIE: Except for me. They got a big sign stuck up.

TOM: What does it say?

WILLIE [*loudly but with a slight catch*]: "THIS PROPERTY IS CONDEMNED!"

TOM: You ain't still living there?

WILLIE: Uh-huh.

TOM: What happened? Where did everyone go?

WILLIE: Mama run off with a brakeman on the C. & E. I. After that everything went to pieces. [*A train whistles far off.*] You hear that whistle? That's the Cannonball Express. The fastest thing on wheels between St. Louis, New Awleuns an' Memphis. My old man got to drinking.

TOM: Where is he now?

WILLIE: Disappeared. I guess I ought to refer his case to the Bureau of Missing Persons. The same as he done with Mama when she disappeared. Then there was me and Alva. Till Alva's lungs got affected. Did you see Greta Garbo in *Camille?* It played at the Delta Brilliant one time las' spring. She had the same what Alva died of. Lung affection.

TOM: Yeah?

WILLIE: Only it was—very beautiful the way she had it. You know. Violins playing. And loads and loads of white flowers. All of her lovers come back in a beautiful scene!

TOM: Yeah?

WILLIE: But Alva's all disappeared.

TOM: Yeah?

WILLIE: Like rats from a sinking ship! That's how she used to describe it. Oh, it—wasn't like death in the movies.

TOM: Naw?

253

WILLIE: She says, "Where is Albert? Where's Clemence?" None of them was around. I used to lie to her, I says, "They send their regards. They're coming to see you tomorrow." "Where's Mr. Johnson?" she asked me. He was the freight sup'rintendent, the most important character we ever had in our rooming house. "He's been transferred to Grenada," I told her. "But wishes to be remembered." She known I was lying.

TOM: Yeah?

WILLIE: "This here is the payoff!" she says. "They all run out on me like rats from a sinking ship!" Except Sidney.

TOM: Who was Sidney?

WILLIE: The one that used to give her the great big enormous red silk box of American Beauty choc'lates.

TOM: Oh.

WILLIE: He remained faithful to her.

TOM: That's good.

WILLIE: But she never did care for Sidney. She said his teeth was decayed so he didn't smell good.

TOM: Aw!

WILLIE: It wasn't like death in the movies. When somebody dies in the movies they play violins.

TOM: But they didn't for Alva.

WILLIE: Naw. Not even a goddam victrola. They said it didn't agree with the hospital regulations. Always singing around the house.

TOM: Who? Alva?

WILLIE: Throwing enormous parties. This was her favorite number. [*She closes her eyes and stretches out her arms in the simulated rapture of the professional blues singer. Her voice is extraordinarily high and pure with a precocious emotional timbre.*]

> You're the only star
> In my blue hea-ven
> And you're shining just
> For me!

This is her clothes I got on. Inherited from her. Everything Alva's is mine. Except her solid gold beads.

TOM: What happened to them?

WILLIE: Them? She never took 'em off.

TOM: Oh!

WILLIE: I've also inherited all of my sister's beaux. Albert and Clemence and even the freight sup'rintendent.

TOM: Yeah?

WILLIE: They all disappeared. Afraid that they might get stuck for expenses I guess. But now they turn up again, all of 'em, like a bunch of bad pennies. They take me out places at night. I've got to be popular now. To parties an' dances an' all of the railroad affairs. Lookit here!

TOM: What?

WILLIE: I can do bumps! [*She stands in front of him and shoves her stomach toward him in a series of spasmodic jerks.*]

TOM: Frank Waters said that . . .

WILLIE: What?

TOM: You know.

WILLIE: Know what?

TOM: You took him inside and danced for him with your clothes off.

WILLIE: Oh. Crazy Doll's hair needs washing. I'm scared to wash it though 'cause her head might come unglued where she had that compound fracture of the skull. I think that most of her brains spilled out. She's been acting silly ever since. Saying an' doing the most outrageous things.

TOM: Why don't you do that for me?

WILLIE: What? Put glue on your compound fracture?

TOM: Naw. What you did for Frank Waters.

WILLIE: Because I was lonesome then an' I'm not lonesome now. You can tell Frank Waters that. Tell him that I've inherited all of my sister's beaux. I go out steady with men in responsible jobs. The sky sure is white. Ain't it? White as a clean piece of paper. In Five A we used to draw pictures. Miss Preston would give us a piece of white foolscap an' tell us to draw what we pleased.

TOM: What did you draw?

WILLIE: I remember I drawn her a picture one time of my old man getting conked with a bottle. She thought it was good, Miss Preston, she said, "Look here. Here's a picture of Charlie Chaplin with his hat on the side of his head!" I said, "Aw, naw, that's not Charlie Chaplin, that's my father, an' that's not his hat, it's a bottle!"

TOM: What did she say?

WILLIE: Oh, well. You can't make a school-teacher laugh.

> You're the only star
> In my blue hea-VEN . . .

The principal used to say there must've been something wrong with my home atmosphere because of the fact that we took in railroad men an' some of 'em slept with my sister.

TOM: Did they?

WILLIE: She was The Main Attraction. The house is sure empty now.

TOM: You ain't still living there, are you?

WILLIE: Sure.

TOM: By yourself?

WILLIE: Uh-huh. I'm not supposed to be but I am. The property is condemned but there's nothing wrong with it. Some county investigator come snooping around yesterday. I recognized her by the shape of her hat. It wasn't exactly what I would call stylish-looking.

TOM: Naw?

WILLIE: It looked like something she took off the lid of the stove. Alva knew lots about style. She had ambitions to be a de-

257

signer for big wholesale firms in Chicago. She used to submit her pictures. It never worked out.

You're the only star
In my blue hea-ven . . .

TOM: What did you do? About the investigators?

WILLIE: Laid low upstairs. Pretended like no one was home.

TOM: Well, how do you manage to keep on eating?

WILLIE: Oh, I don't know. You keep a sharp lookout you see things lying around. This banana, perfectly good, for instance. Thrown in a garbage pail in back of the Blue Bird Café. [*She finishes the banana and tosses away the peel.*]

TOM [*grinning*]: Yeh. Miss Preston for instance.

WILLIE: Naw, not her. She gives you a white piece of paper, says "Draw what you please!" One time I drawn her a picture of— Oh, but I told you that, huh? Will you give Frank Waters a message?

TOM: What?

WILLIE: Tell him the freight sup'rintendent has bought me a pair of kid slippers. Patent. The same as the old ones of Alva's. I'm going to dances with them at Moon Lake Casino. All night I'll be dancing an' come home drunk in the morning! We'll have serenades with all kinds of musical instruments. Trumpets an' trombones. An' Hawaiian steel guitars. Yeh! Yeh! [*She rises excitedly.*] The sky will be white like this.

TOM [*impressed*]: Will it?

WILLIE: Uh-huh. [*She smiles vaguely and turns slowly toward him.*] White—as a clean—piece of paper . . . [*then excitedly*] I'll draw—pictures on it!

TOM: Will you?

WILLIE: Sure!

TOM: Pictures of what?

WILLIE: Me dancing! With the freight sup'rintendent! In a pair of patent kid shoes! Yeh! Yeh! With French heels on them as high as telegraph poles! An' they'll play my favorite music!

TOM: Your favorite?

WILLIE: Yeh. The same as Alva's. [*breathlessly, passionately*]

> You're the only STAR—
> In my blue HEA-VEN . . .

I'll—

TOM: What?

WILLIE: I'll—wear a corsage!

TOM: What's that?

WILLIE: Flowers to pin on your dress at a formal affair! Rose-buds! Violets! And lilies-of-the-valley! When you come home it's withered but you stick 'em in a bowl of water to freshen 'em up.

TOM: Uh-huh.

WILLIE: That's what Alva done. [*She pauses, and in the silence the train whistles.*] The Cannonball Express . . .

TOM: You think a lot about Alva. Don't you?

WILLIE: Oh, not so much. Now an' then. It wasn't like death in the movies. Her beaux disappeared. An' they didn't have violins playing. I'm going back now.

TOM: Where to, Willie?

WILLIE: The watertank.

TOM: Yeah?

WILLIE: An' start all over again. Maybe I'll break some kind of continuous record. Alva did once. At a dance marathon in Mobile. Across the state line. Alabama. You can tell Frank Waters everything that I told you. I don't have time for inexperienced people. I'm going out now with popular railroad men, men with good salaries, too. Don't you believe me?

TOM: No. I think you're drawing an awful lot on your imagination.

WILLIE: Well, if I wanted to I could prove it. But you wouldn't be worth convincing. [*She smooths out Crazy Doll's hair.*] I'm going to live for a long, long time like my sister. An' when my lungs get affected I'm going to die like she did—maybe not like in the movies, with violins playing—but with my pearl earrings on an' my solid gold beads from Memphis. . . .

TOM: Yes?

WILLIE [*examining Crazy Doll very critically*]: An' then I guess—

TOM: What?

WILLIE [*gaily but with a slight catch*]: Somebody else will inherit all of my beaux! The sky sure is white.

TOM: It sure is.

WILLIE: White as a clean piece of paper. I'm going back now.

TOM: So long.

WILLIE: Yeh. So long. [*She starts back along the railroad track, weaving grotesquely to keep her balance. She disappears. Tom wets his finger and holds it up to test the wind. Willie is heard singing from a distance.*]

> You're the only star
> In my blue heaven—

[*There is a brief pause. The stage begins to darken.*]

> An' you're shining just—
> For me!

CURTAIN

TALK TO ME LIKE THE RAIN
AND LET ME LISTEN . . .

CHARACTERS

MAN

WOMAN

CHILD'S VOICE (offstage)

TALK TO ME LIKE THE RAIN
AND LET ME LISTEN . . .

A furnished room west of Eighth Avenue in midtown Manhattan. On a folding bed lies a Man in crumpled underwear, struggling out of sleep with the sighs of a man who went to bed very drunk. A Woman sits in a straight chair at the room's single window, outlined dimly against a sky heavy with a rain that has not yet begun to fall. The Woman is holding a tumbler of water from which she takes small, jerky sips like a bird drinking. Both of them have ravaged young faces like the faces of children in a famished country. In their speech there is a sort of politeness, a sort of tender formality like that of two lonely children who want to be friends, and yet there is an impression that they have lived in this intimate situation for a long time and that the present scene between them is the repetition of one that has been repeated so often that its plausible emotional contents, such as reproach and contrition, have been completely worn out and there is nothing left but acceptance of something hopelessly inalterable between them.

MAN [*hoarsely*]: What time is it? [*The Woman murmurs something inaudible.*] What, honey?

WOMAN: Sunday.

MAN: I know it's Sunday. You never wind the clock.

[*The Woman stretches a thin bare arm out of the ravelled pink rayon sleeve of her kimono and picks up the tumbler of water and the weight of it seems to pull her forward a little. The Man watches solemnly, tenderly from the bed as she sips the water. A thin music begins, hesitantly, repeating a phrase several times as if someone in a next room were trying to remember a song on a mandolin. Sometimes a phrase is sung in Spanish. The song could be* Estrellita.

[*Rain begins; it comes and goes during the play; there is a drumming flight of pigeons past the window and a child's voice chants outside—*]

CHILD'S VOICE: Rain, rain, go away!
Come again some other day!

[*The chant is echoed mockingly by another child farther away.*]

MAN [*finally*]: I wonder if I cashed my unemployment. [*The Woman leans forward with the weight of the glass seeming to pull her; sets it down on the windowsill with a small crash that seems to startle her. She laughs breathlessly for a moment. The Man continues, without much hope.*] I hope I didn't cash my unemployment. Where's my clothes? Look in my pockets and see if I got the cheque on me.

WOMAN: You came back while I was out looking for you and picked the cheque up and left a note on the bed that I couldn't make out.

MAN: You couldn't make out the note?

WOMAN: Only a telephone number. I called the number but there was so much noise I couldn't hear.

MAN: Noise? Here?

WOMAN: No, noise there.

MAN: Where was "there"?

WOMAN: I don't know. Somebody said come over and hung up and all I got afterwards was a busy signal . . .

266

MAN: When I woke up I was in a bathtub full of melting ice cubes and Miller's High Life beer. My skin was blue. I was gasping for breath in a bathtub full of ice cubes. It was near a river but I don't know if it was the East or the Hudson. People do terrible things to a person when he's unconscious in this city. I'm sore all over like I'd been kicked downstairs, not like I fell but was kicked. One time I remember all my hair was shaved off. Another time they stuffed me into a trashcan in the alley and I've come to with cuts and burns on my body. Vicious people abuse you when you're unconscious. When I woke up I was naked in a bathtub full of melting ice cubes. I crawled out and went into the parlor and someone was going out of the other door as I came in and I opened the door and heard the door of an elevator shut and saw the doors of a corridor in a hotel. The TV was on and there was a record playing at the same time; the parlor was full of rolling tables loaded with stuff from Room Service, and whole hams, whole turkeys, three-decker sandwiches cold and turning stiff, and bottles and bottles and bottles of all kinds of liquors that hadn't even been opened and buckets of ice cubes melting . . . Somebody closed a door as I came in . . . [*The Woman sips water.*] As I came in someone was going out. I heard a door shut and I went to the door and heard the door of an elevator shut . . . [*The Woman sets her glass down.*]—All over the floor of this pad near the river—articles— clothing—scattered . . . [*The Woman gasps as a flight of pigeons sweeps past the open window.*]—Bras!—Panties!—Shirts, ties, socks—and so forth . . .

WOMAN [*faintly*]: Clothes?

MAN: Yes, all kinds of personal belongings and broken glass and furniture turned over as if there'd been a free-for-all fight going on and the pad was—raided . . .

WOMAN: Oh.

MAN: Violence must have—broken out in the—place . . .

WOMAN: You were—?

MAN: —in the bathtub on—ice . . .

WOMAN: Oh . . .

MAN: And I remember picking up the phone to ask what hotel it was but I don't remember if they told me or not . . . Give me a drink of that water. [*Both of them rise and meet in the center of the room. The glass is passed gravely between them. He rinses his mouth, staring at her gravely, and crosses to spit out the window. Then he returns to the center of the room and hands the glass back to her. She takes a sip of the water. He places his fingers tenderly on her long throat.*] Now I've recited the litany of my sorrows! [*Pause: the mandolin is heard.*] And what have you got to tell me? Tell me a little something of what's going on behind your—[*His fingers trail across her forehead and eyes. She closes her eyes and lifts a hand in the air as if about to touch him. He takes the hand and examines it upside down and then he presses its fingers to his lips. When he releases her fingers she touches him with them. She touches his thin smooth chest which is smooth as a child's and then she touches his lips. He raises his hand and lets his fingers slide along her throat and into the opening of the kimono as the mandolin gathers assurance. She turns and leans against him, her throat curving over his shoulder, and he runs his fingers along the curve of her throat and says—*] It's been so long since we have been together except like a couple of strangers living together. Let's find each other and maybe we won't be lost. Talk to me! I've been lost!—I thought of you often but couldn't call you, honey. Thought of you all the time but couldn't call. What could I say if I called? Could I say, I'm lost? Lost in the city? Passed around like a dirty *post*card among people?—And then hang up . . . I am lost in this—city . . .

WOMAN: I've had nothing but water since you left! [*She says this almost gaily, laughing at the statement. The Man holds her tight to him with a soft, shocked cry.*]—Not a thing but instant coffee until it was used up, and water! [*She laughs convulsively.*]

MAN: Can you talk to me, honey? Can you talk to me, now?

WOMAN: Yes!

MAN: Well, talk to me like the rain and—let me listen, let me lie here and—listen . . . [*He falls back across the bed, rolls on his belly, one arm hanging over the side of the bed and occasionally drumming the floor with his knuckles. The mandolin continues.*] It's been too long a time since—we levelled with each other. Now tell me things. What have you been thinking in the silence?—While I've been passed around like a dirty postcard in this city . . . Tell me, talk to me! Talk to me like the rain and I will lie here and listen.

WOMAN: I—

MAN: You've got to, it's necessary! I've got to know, so talk to me like the rain and I will lie here and listen, I will lie here and—

WOMAN: I want to go away.

MAN: You do?

WOMAN: *I want to go away!*

MAN: How?

WOMAN: *Alone!* [*She returns to window.*]—I'll register under a made-up name at a little hotel on the coast . . .

MAN: What name?

WOMAN: Anna—Jones . . . The chambermaid will be a little old lady who has a grandson that she talks about . . . I'll sit in the chair while the old lady makes the bed, my arms will hang over the—sides, and—her voice will be—peaceful . . . She'll tell me what her grandson had for supper!—tapioca and—cream . . . [*The Woman sits by the window and sips the water.*]—The room will be shadowy, cool, and filled with the murmur of—

MAN: Rain?

WOMAN: Yes. Rain.

MAN: And—?

WOMAN: Anxiety will—pass—over!

MAN: Yes . . .

WOMAN: After a while the little old woman will say, Your bed is made up, Miss, and I'll say—Thank you . . . Take a dollar out of my pocketbook. The door will close. And I'll be alone again. The windows will be tall with long blue shutters and it will be a season of rain—rain—rain . . . My life will be like the room, cool—shadowy cool and—filled with the murmur of—

MAN: Rain . . .

WOMAN: I will receive a check in the mail every week that I can count on. The little old lady will cash the checks for me and get me books from a library and pick up—laundry . . . I'll always have clean things!—I'll dress in white. I'll never be very strong or have much energy left, but have enough after a while to walk on the—esplanade—to walk on the beach without ef-fort . . . In the evening I'll walk on the esplanade along the beach. I'll have a certain beach where I go to sit, a little way from the pavillion where the band plays Victor Herbert selec-

270

tions while it gets dark . . . I'll have a big room with shutters on the windows. There will be a season of rain, rain, rain. And I will be so exhausted after my life in the city that I won't mind just listening to the rain. I'll be so quiet. The lines will disappear from my face. My eyes won't be inflamed at all any more. I'll have no friends. I'll have no acquaintances even. When I get sleepy, I'll walk slowly back to the little hotel. The clerk will say, Good evening, Miss Jones, and I'll just barely smile and take my key. I won't ever look at a newspaper or hear a radio; I won't have any idea of what's going on in the world. I will not be conscious of time passing at all . . . One day I will look in the mirror and I will see that my hair is beginning to turn grey and for the first time I will realize that I have been living in this little hotel under a made-up name without any friends or acquaintances or any kind of connections for twenty-five years. It will surprise me a little but it won't bother me any. I will be glad that time has passed as easily as that. Once in a while I may go out to the movies. I will sit in the back row with all that darkness around me and figures sitting motionless on each side not conscious of me. Watching the screen. Imaginary people. People in stories. I will read long books and the journals of dead writers. I will feel closer to them than I ever felt to people I used to know before I withdrew from the world. It will be sweet and cool this friendship of mine with dead poets, for I won't have to touch them or answer their questions. They will talk to me and not expect me to answer. And I'll get sleepy listening to their voices explaining the mysteries to me. I'll fall asleep with the book still in my fingers, and it will rain. I'll wake up and hear the rain and go back to sleep. A season of rain, rain, rain . . . Then one day, when I have closed a book or come home alone from the movies at eleven o'clock at night—I will look in the mirror and see that my hair has turned white. White, absolutely white. As white as the foam on the waves. [*She gets up and moves about the room as she continues—*] I'll run my hands down my body and feel how amazingly light and thin I have grown. Oh, my, how thin I will be. Almost transparent. Not hardly real any more. Then I will realize, I will know, sort of dimly, that I have been staying on here in this little hotel, without any—social connections, responsibilities, anxieties or disturbances of any kind—for just about fifty years. Half a century. Practically a lifetime. I won't even remember the names of the people I knew before I came here nor how it feels to be someone waiting for someone that—may not come . . . Then I will know—looking in the mirror—the first time has come for me to walk out alone once more on the esplanade with the strong wind beating on me, the white clean wind that blows from the edge of the world, from even further than that, from the cool outer edges of space, from even beyond whatever there is beyond the edges of space . . . [*She sits down again unsteadily by the window.*]—Then I'll go out and walk on the esplanade. I'll walk alone and be blown thinner and thinner.

MAN: Baby. Come back to bed.

WOMAN: And thinner and thinner and thinner and thinner and thinner! [*He crosses to her and raises her forcibly from the chair.*]—Till finally I won't have any body at all, and the wind picks me up in its cool white arms forever, and takes me away!

MAN [*pressing his mouth to her throat*]: Come on back to bed with me!

WOMAN: *I want to go away, I want to go away!* [*He releases her and she crosses to center of room sobbing uncontrollably. She sits down on the bed. He sighs and leans out the window, the light flickering beyond him, the rain coming down harder. The Woman shivers and crosses her arms against her breasts. Her sobbing dies out but she breathes with effort. Light flickers and wind whines coldly. The Man remains leaning out. At last she says to him softly—*] Come back to bed. Come on back to bed, baby . . . [*He turns his lost face to her as—*]

THE CURTAIN FALLS

SOMETHING UNSPOKEN

CHARACTERS

MISS CORNELIA SCOTT

MISS GRACE LANCASTER

SOMETHING UNSPOKEN

Miss Cornelia Scott, 60, a wealthy southern spinster, is seated at a small mahogany table which is set for two. The other place, not yet occupied, has a single rose in a crystal vase before it. Miss Scott's position at the table is flanked by a cradle phone, a silver tray of mail, and an ornate silver coffee urn. An imperial touch is given by purple velvet drapes directly behind her figure at the table. A console phonograph is at the edge of lighted area.

At rise of the curtain she is dialing a number on the phone.

CORNELIA: Is this Mrs. Horton Reid's residence? I am calling for Miss Cornelia Scott. Miss Scott is sorry that she will not be able to attend the meeting of the Confederate Daughters this afternoon as she woke up this morning with a sore throat and has to remain in bed, and will you kindly give her apologies to Mrs. Reid for not letting her know sooner. Thank you. Oh, wait a moment! I think Miss Scott has another message.

[*Grace Lancaster enters the lighted area. Cornelia raises her hand in a warning gesture.*]

—What is it, Miss Scott? [*There is a brief pause.*] Oh. Miss Scott would like to leave word for Miss Esmeralda Hawkins to call her as soon as she arrives. Thank you. Good-bye. [*She hangs up.*] You see I am having to impersonate my secretary this morning!

GRACE: The light was so dim it didn't wake me up.

[*Grace Lancaster is 40 or 45, faded but still pretty. Her blonde hair, graying slightly, her pale eyes, her thin figure, in a pink silk dressing gown, give her an insubstantial quality in sharp contrast to Miss Scott's Roman grandeur. There is between the two women a mysterious tension, an atmosphere of something unspoken.*]

CORNELIA: I've already opened the mail.

GRACE: Anything of interest?

CORNELIA: A card from Thelma Peterson at Mayo's.

GRACE: Oh, how is Thelma?

CORNELIA: She says she's "progressing nicely," whatever that indicates.

GRACE: Didn't she have something removed?

CORNELIA: Several things, I believe.

GRACE: *Oh, here's the "Fortnightly Review of Current Letters!"*

CORNELIA: Much to my astonishment. I thought I had cancelled my subscription to that publication.

GRACE: Really, Cornelia?

CORNELIA: Surely you remember. I cancelled my subscription immediately after the issue came out with that scurrilous attack on my cousin Cecil Tutwiler Bates, the only dignified novelist the South has produced since Thomas Nelson Page.

GRACE: Oh, yes, I do remember. You wrote a furious letter of protest to the editor of the magazine and you received such a conciliatory reply from an associate editor named Caroline Something or Other that you were completely mollified and cancelled the cancellation!

CORNELIA: I have never been mollified by conciliatory replies, never completely and never even partially, and if I wrote to the editor-in-chief and was answered by an associate editor, my reaction to that piece of impertinence would hardly be what you call "mollified."

GRACE [*changing the subject*]: Oh, here's the new catalogue from the Gramophone Shoppe in Atlanta!

CORNELIA [*conceding a point*]: Yes, there it is.

GRACE: I see you've checked several items.

CORNELIA: I think we ought to build up our collection of Lieder.

GRACE: You've checked a Sibelius that we already have.

CORNELIA: It's getting a little bit scratchy. [*She inhales deeply and sighs, her look fastened upon the silent phone.*] You'll also notice that I've checked a few operatic selections.

GRACE [*excitedly*]: Where, which ones, I don't see them!

CORNELIA: Why are you so excited over the catalogue, dear?

GRACE: I adore phonograph records!

CORNELIA: I wish you adored them enough to put them back in their proper places in albums.

GRACE: Oh, here's the Vivaldi we wanted!

CORNELIA: Not "we" dear. Just you.

GRACE: Not *you*, Cornelia?

CORNELIA: I think Vivaldi's a very thin shadow of Bach.

GRACE: How strange that I should have the impression you— [*The phone rings.*]—Shall I answer?

CORNELIA: If you will be so kind.

GRACE [*lifting receiver*]: *Miss Scott's* residence! [*This announcement is made in a tone of reverence, as though mentioning a seat of holiness.*] Oh, no, no, this is Grace, but Cornelia is right by my side. [*She passes the phone.*] Esmeralda Hawkins.

CORNELIA [*grimly*]: I've been expecting her call. [*into phone*] Hello, Esmeralda, my dear. I've been expecting your call. Now where are you calling me from? Of course I know that you're calling me from the meeting, *ça va sans dire, ma petite!* Ha ha! But from which phone in the house, there's two, you know, the one in the downstairs hall and the one in the chatelaine's boudoir where the ladies will probably be removing their wraps. Oh. You're on the downstairs', are you? Well, by this time I presume that practically all the daughters have assembled. Now go upstairs and call me back from there so we can talk with a little more privacy, dear, as I want to make my position very clear before the meeting commences. Thank you, dear.

[*She hangs up and looks grimly into space.*]

GRACE: The—Confederate Daughters?

CORNELIA: Yes! They're holding the Annual Election today.

GRACE: Oh, how exciting! Why aren't you at the meeting?

CORNELIA: I preferred not to go.

GRACE: You preferred *not* to go?

278

CORNELIA: Yes, I preferred not to *go* . . . [*She touches her chest breathing heavily as if she had run upstairs.*]

GRACE: But it's the annual election of officers!

CORNELIA: Yes! I told you it was! [*Grace drops the spoon. Cornelia cries out and jumps a little.*]

GRACE: I'm so sorry! [*She rings the bell for a servant.*]

CORNELIA: Intrigue, intrigue and duplicity, revolt me so that I wouldn't be able to breathe in the same atmosphere! [*Grace rings the bell louder.*] Why are you ringing that bell? You know Lucinda's not here!

GRACE: I'm so sorry. Where has Lucinda gone?

CORNELIA [*in a hoarse whisper, barely audible*]: There's a big colored funeral in town. [*She clears her throat violently and repeats the statement.*]

GRACE: Oh, dear. You have that nervous laryngitis.

CORNELIA: No sleep, no sleep last night.

[*The phone screams at her elbow. She cries out and thrusts it from her as if it were on fire.*]

GRACE [*picking up the phone*]: Miss Scott's residence. Oh. Just a moment, please.

CORNELIA [*snatching phone*]: Esmeralda, are you upstairs now?

GRACE [*in a loud whisper*]: It isn't Esmeralda, it's Mrs. C. C. Bright!

279

CORNELIA: One moment, one moment, one moment! [*She thrusts phone back at Grace with a glare of fury.*] How dare you put me on the line with that woman!

GRACE: Cornelia, I didn't, I was just going to ask you if you—

CORNELIA: *Hush!* [*She springs back from the table, glaring across it.*]—Now give me that phone. [*She takes it, and says coldly:*] What can I do for you, please? No. I'm afraid that my garden will not be open to the Pilgrims this spring. I think the cultivation of gardens is an esthetic hobby and not a competitive sport. Individual visitors will be welcome if they call in advance so that I can arrange for my gardener to show them around, but no bands of Pilgrims, not after the devastation my garden suffered last spring—Pilgrims coming with dogs—picking flowers and— You're entirely welcome, yes, good-bye! [*She returns the phone to Grace.*]

GRACE: I think the election would have been less of a strain if you'd gone to it, Cornelia.

CORNELIA: I don't know what you are talking about.

GRACE: Aren't you up for office?

CORNELIA: "Up for office"? What is "up for office"?

GRACE: Why, ha ha!—*running* for—something?

CORNELIA: Have you ever known me to "*run*" for anything, Grace? Whenever I've held an office in a society or club it's been at the *insistence* of the members because I really have an *aversion* to holding office. But this is a different thing, a different thing altogether. It's a test of something. You see I have known for some time, now, that there is a little group, a *clique*, in the Daughters, which is hostile to me!

GRACE: Oh, Cornelia, I'm sure you must be mistaken.

CORNELIA: No. There is a movement against me.

GRACE: A movement? A movement against you?

CORNELIA: An organized movement to keep me out of any important office.

GRACE: But haven't you always held some important office in the Chapter?

CORNELIA: I have never been *Regent* of it!

GRACE: Oh, you want to be *Regent?*

CORNELIA: No. You misunderstand me. I don't "*want*" to be Regent.

GRACE: Oh?

CORNELIA: I don't "want" to be anything whatsoever. I simply want to break up this movement against me and for that purpose I have rallied my forces.

GRACE: Your—*forces?* [*Her lips twitch slightly as if she had an hysterical impulse to smile.*]

CORNELIA: Yes. I still have some friends in the chapter who have resisted the movement.

GRACE: Oh?

CORNELIA: I have the solid support of all the older Board members.

GRACE: Why, then, I should think you'd have nothing to worry about!

CORNELIA: The Chapter has expanded too rapidly lately. Women have been admitted that couldn't get into a front pew at the Second Baptist Church! And that's the disgraceful truth . . .

GRACE: But since it's really a patriotic society . . .

CORNELIA: My dear Grace, there are two chapters of the Confederate Daughters in the city of Meridian. There is the Forrest chapter, which is for social riffraff, and there is *this* chapter which was *supposed* to have a *little* bit of *distinction!* I'm not a snob. I'm nothing if not democratic. You know *that!* But—[*The phone rings. Cornelia reaches for it, then pushes it to Grace.*]

GRACE: Miss Scott's residence! Oh, yes, yes, just a moment! [*She passes phone to Cornelia.*] It's Esmeralda Hawkins.

CORNELIA [*into phone*]: Are you upstairs now, dear? Well, I wondered, it took you so long to call back. Oh, but I thought you said the luncheon was over. Well, I'm glad that you fortified yourself with a bite to eat. What did the buffet consist of? Chicken à la king! Wouldn't you know it! That is so characteristic of poor Amelia! With bits of pimiento and tiny mushrooms in it? What did the ladies counting their calories do! Nibbled around the edges? Oh, poor dears!—and afterwards I suppose there was lemon sherbet with ladyfingers? What, lime sherbet! And *no* ladyfingers? *What a departure!* What a *shocking* apostasy! I'm quite stunned! Ho ho ho . . . [*She reaches shakily for her cup.*] Now what's going on? Discussing the Civil Rights Program? Then they won't take the vote for at least half an hour!—Now Esmeralda, I *do* hope that you understand my position clearly. I don't wish to hold any office in the chapter unless it's by acclamation. You know what that means, don't you? It's a parliamentary term. It means when someone is desired for an office so unanimously that no vote has to be taken. In other words, elected automatically, simply by nomination, unopposed. Yes, my dear, it's just as simple as that. I have served as Treasurer for three terms, twice as Secretary, once as Chaplain—and what a dreary office that was with those long-drawn prayers for the Confederate dead!—Altogether I've served on the Board for, let's see, fourteen years!—Well, now, my dear, the point is simply this. If Daughters feel that I have demonstrated my capabilities and loyalty strongly enough that I should simply be named as Regent without a vote being taken—by unanimous acclamation!—why, then, of course I would feel obliged to accept . . . [*Her voice trembles with emotion.*]—But if, on the other hand, the—uh—*clique!*—and you know the ones I mean!—is bold enough to propose someone else for the office—Do you understand my position? In that eventuality, hard as it is to imagine,—I prefer to bow out of the picture entirely!—The moment another nomination is made and seconded, my own must be withdrawn, at once, unconditionally! Is that quite understood, Esmeralda? Then good! Go back downstairs to the meeting. Digest your chicken à la king, my dear, and call me again on the upstairs phone as soon as there's something to tell me. [*She hangs up and stares grimly into space. Grace lifts a section of grapefruit on a tiny silver fork.*]

GRACE: They haven't had it yet?

CORNELIA: Had what, dear?

GRACE: The election!

CORNELIA: No, not yet. It seems to be—imminent, though . . .

GRACE: Cornelia, why don't you think about something else until it's over!

CORNELIA: What makes you think that I am nervous about it?

GRACE: You're—you're *breathing* so fast!

CORNELIA: I didn't sleep well last night. You were prowling about the house with that stitch in your side.

GRACE: I *am* so sorry. You know it's nothing. A muscular contraction that comes from strain.

CORNELIA: What strain does it come from, Grace?

GRACE: What strain? [*She utters a faint, perplexed laugh.*] Why!—I don't know . . .

CORNELIA: The strain of *what?* Would you like *me* to tell you?

GRACE: —Excuse me, I—[*rising*]

CORNELIA [*sharply*]: Where are you going?

GRACE: Upstairs for a moment! I just remembered I should have taken my drops of belladonna!

CORNELIA: It does no good *after* eating.

GRACE: I suppose that's right. It doesn't.

CORNELIA: But you want to escape?

GRACE: Of course not . . .

CORNELIA: Several times lately you've rushed away from me as if I'd suddenly threatened you with a knife.

GRACE: Cornelia!—I've been—jumpy!

284

CORNELIA: It's always when something is almost—*spoken*—
between us!

GRACE: I hate to see you so agitated over the outcome of a
silly club-woman's election!

CORNELIA: I'm not talking about the Daughters. I'm not even
thinking about them, I'm—

GRACE: I wish you'd dismiss it completely from your mind.
Now would be a good time to play some records. Let me put a
symphony on the machine!

CORNELIA: No.

GRACE: How about the Bach For Piano and Strings! The one
we received for Christmas from Jessie and Gay?

CORNELIA: No, I said, No, I said, No!

GRACE: Something very light and quiet, then, the old French
madrigals, maybe?

CORNELIA: Anything to avoid a talk between us? Anything to
evade a conversation, especially when the servant is not in the
house?

GRACE: Oh, here it is! This is just the thing! [*She has started
the phonograph. Landowska is playing a harpsichord selection.
The phonograph is at the edge of the lighted area or just outside it.*]

[*Cornelia stares grimly as Grace resumes her seat with an af-
fectation of enchantment, clasping her hands and closing her
eyes.*]

[*In an enchanted voice:*] Oh, how it smooths things over, how sweet, and gentle, and—pure . . .

CORNELIA: Yes! And completely dishonest!

GRACE: Music? Dishonest?

CORNELIA: Completely! It "smooths things over" instead of—speaking them out . . .

GRACE: "Music hath charms to soothe the savage breast."

CORNELIA: Yes, oh, yes, if the savage breast permits it.

GRACE: Oh, sublime—sublime . . .

CORNELIA [*grudgingly*]: Landowska is an artist of rare precision.

GRACE [*ecstatically*]: And such a noble face, a profile as fine and strong as Edith Sitwell's. After this we'll play Edith Sitwell's Façade. "Jane, Jane, tall as a crane, the morning light creaks down again . . ."

CORNELIA: Dearest, isn't there something you've failed to notice?

GRACE: Where?

CORNELIA: Right under your nose.

GRACE: Oh! You mean my flower?

CORNELIA: Yes! I mean your rose!

GRACE: Of course I noticed my rose, the moment I came in the room I saw it here!

CORNELIA: You made no allusion to it.

GRACE: I would have, but you were so concerned over the meeting.

CORNELIA: I'm not concerned over the meeting.

GRACE: Whom do I have to thank for this lovely rose? My gracious employer?

CORNELIA: You will find fourteen others on your desk in the library when you go in to take care of the correspondence.

GRACE: Fourteen other roses?

CORNELIA: A total of fifteen!

GRACE: How wonderful!—Why fifteen?

CORNELIA: How long have you been here, dearest? How long have you made this house a house of roses?

GRACE: What a nice way to put it! Why, of course! I've been your secretary for fifteen years!

CORNELIA: Fifteen years my companion! A rose for every year, a year for every rose!

GRACE: What a charming sort of a way to—observe the—occasion . . .

CORNELIA: First I thought "pearls" and then I thought, No, roses, but perhaps I should have given you something golden, ha ha!—Silence is golden they say!

GRACE: Oh, dear, that stupid machine is playing the same record over!

CORNELIA: Let it, let it, I like it!

GRACE: Just let me—

CORNELIA: Sit down!!—It was fifteen years ago this very morning, on the sixth day of November, that someone very sweet and gentle and silent!—a shy, little, quiet little widow!—arrived for the first time at Seven Edgewater Drive. The season was Autumn. I had been raking dead leaves over the rose-bushes to protect them from frost when I heard footsteps on the gravel, light, quick, delicate footsteps like Spring coming in the middle of Autumn, and looked up, and sure enough, there Spring was! A little person so thin that light shone through her as if she were made of the silk of a white parasol! [*Grace utters a short, startled laugh. Wounded, Cornelia says harshly:*] Why did you laugh? Why did you laugh like that?

GRACE: It sounded—ha ha!—it sounded like the first paragraph of a woman's magazine story.

CORNELIA: What a cutting remark!

GRACE: I didn't mean it that way, I—

CORNELIA: What other way could you mean it!'

GRACE: Cornelia, you know how I am! I'm always a little embarrassed by sentiment, aren't I?

CORNELIA: Yes, frightened of anything that betrays some feeling!

GRACE: People who don't know you well, nearly all people we know, would be astounded to hear you, Cornelia Scott, that grave and dignified lady, expressing herself in such a lyrical manner!

CORNELIA: People who don't know me well are everybody! Yes, I think even *you!*

GRACE: Cornelia, you must admit that sentiment isn't like you!

CORNELIA: *Is nothing like me but silence?* [*The clock ticks loudly.*] *Am I sentenced to silence for a lifetime?*

GRACE: It's just not like you to—

CORNELIA: Not like me, not like me, what do you know what's like me or not like me!

GRACE: You may deny it, Cornelia, as much as you please, but it's evident to me that you are completely unstrung by your anxieties over the Confederate Daughters' election!

CORNELIA: Another thinly veiled insult?

GRACE: Oh, Cornelia, please!

CORNELIA [*imitating her gesture*]: "Oh, Cornelia, please!!"

GRACE: If I've said anything wrong, I beg your pardon, I offer my very humble apologies for it.

CORNELIA: I don't want apologies from you. [*There is a strained silence. The clock ticks. Suddenly Grace reaches across to touch the veined jewelled hand of Miss Scott. Cornelia snatches her own hand away as though the touch had burned her.*]

GRACE: Thank you for the roses.

CORNELIA: I don't want thanks from you either. All that I want is a little return of affection, not much, but sometimes a little!

GRACE: You have that always, Cornelia.

CORNELIA: And one thing more: a little outspokenness, too.

GRACE: Outspokenness?

CORNELIA: Yes, outspokenness, if that's not too much to ask from such a proud young lady!

GRACE [*rising from table*]: I am not proud and I am not young, Cornelia.

CORNELIA: Sit down. Don't leave the table.

GRACE: Is that an order?

CORNELIA: I don't give orders to you, I make requests!

GRACE: Sometimes the requests of an employer are hard to distinguish from orders. [*She sits down.*]

CORNELIA: Please turn off the victrola. [*Grace rises and stops the machine.*] Grace!—Don't you feel there's—*something unspoken* between us?

GRACE: No. No, I don't.

CORNELIA: I do. I've felt for a long time something unspoken between us.

GRACE: Don't you think there is always something unspoken between two people?

CORNELIA: I see no reason for it.

GRACE: But don't a great many things exist without reason?

CORNELIA: Let's not turn this into a metaphysical discussion.

GRACE: All right. But you mystify me.

CORNELIA: It's very simple. It's just that I feel that there's something unspoken between us that ought to be spoken. . . . Why are you looking at me like that?

GRACE: How am I looking at you?

CORNELIA: With positive terror!

GRACE: Cornelia!

CORNELIA: You are, you are, but I'm not going to be shut up!

GRACE: Go on, continue, please, do!

CORNELIA: I'm going to, I will, I will, I–[*The phone rings and Grace reaches for it.*] No, no, no, let it ring! [*It goes on ringing.*] Take it off the hook!

GRACE: Do just let me–

CORNELIA: Off the hook, I told you! [*Grace takes the phone off the hook. A voice says: "Hello? Hello? Hello? Hello?"*]

GRACE [*suddenly sobbing*]: I can't stand it!

CORNELIA: *BE STILL! Someone can hear you!*

VOICE: Hello? Hello? Cornelia? Cornelia Scott? [*Cornelia seizes phone and slams it back into its cradle.*]

CORNELIA: Now stop that! Stop that silly little female trick!

291

GRACE: You say there's something unspoken. Maybe there is. I don't know. But I do know some things are better left unspoken. Also I know that when a silence between two people has gone on for a long time it's like a wall that's impenetrable between them! Maybe between us there is such a wall. One that's impenetrable. Or maybe *you* can break it. I know I can't. I can't even attempt to. You're the strong one of us two and surely you know it.—Both of us have turned gray!—But not the same kind of gray. In that velvet dressing gown you look like the Emperor Tiberius!—In his imperial toga!—Your hair and your eyes are both the color of iron! Iron gray. Invincible looking! People nearby are all somewhat—frightened of you. They feel your force and they admire you for it. They come to you here for opinions on this or that. What plays are good on Broadway this season, what books are worth reading and what books are trash and what—what records are valuable and—what is the proper attitude toward—bills in Congress!—Oh, you're a fountain of wisdom!—And in addition to that, you have your—*wealth!* Yes, you have your—*fortune!*—All of your real estate holdings, your blue chip stocks, your—bonds, your—mansion on Edgewater Drive, your—shy little—secretary, your—fabulous gardens that Pilgrims cannot go into . . .

CORNELIA: Oh, yes, now you are speaking, now you are speaking at last! Go on, please go on speaking.

GRACE: I am—very—different!—Also turning gray but my gray is different. Not iron, like yours, not imperial, Cornelia, but gray, yes, gray, the—color of a . . . *cobweb* . . . [*She starts the record again, very softly.*]—Something white getting soiled, the gray of something forgotten. [*The phone rings again. Neither of them seems to notice it.*]—And that being the case, that being the difference between our two kinds of gray, yours and mine— You mustn't expect me to give bold answers to questions that make the house shake with silence! To speak out things that are fifteen years unspoken!—That long a time can make a silence a

292

wall that nothing less than dynamite could break through and—
[*She picks up the phone.*] I'm not strong enough, bold enough,
I'm not—

CORNELIA [*fiercely*]: You're speaking into the phone!

GRACE [*into phone*]: Hello? Oh, yes, she's here. It's Esmeralda
Hawkins. [*Cornelia snatches the phone.*]

CORNELIA: What is it, Esmeralda? What are you saying, is the
room full of women? Such a babble of voices! What are you
trying to tell me? Have they held the election already? What,
what, what? Oh, this is maddening! I can't hear a word that
you're saying, it sounds like the Fourth of July, a great celebration! Ha, ha, now try once more with your mouth closer to the
phone! What, what? Would I be willing to what? You can't be
serious! Are you out of your mind? [*She speaks to Grace in a
panicky voice.*] She wants to know if I would be willing to serve
as *vice*-Regent! [*into phone*] Esmeralda! Will you listen to me?
What's going on? Are there some fresh defections? How does it
look? Why did you call me again before the vote? Louder,
please speak louder, and cup your mouth to the phone in case
they're eavesdropping! Who asked if I would accept the vice-
regency, dear? Oh, Mrs. Colby, of course!—that treacherous
witch!—*Esmeralda!!* Listen! I—WILL ACCEPT—NO OFFICE—
EXCEPT—THE HIGHEST! Did you understand that? I—
WILL ACCEPT NO OFFICE EXCEPT—*ESMERALDA!* [*She
drops phone into its cradle.*]

GRACE: Have they held the election?

CORNELIA [*dazed*]: What?—No, there's a five-minute recess
before the election begins . . .

GRACE: Things are not going well?

CORNELIA: "Would you accept the vice-Regency," she asked me, "if for some reason they don't elect you Regent?"—Then she hung up as if somebody had snatched the phone away from her, or the house had—caught fire!

GRACE: You shouted so I think she must have been frightened.

CORNELIA: Whom can you trust in this world, whom can you ever rely on?

GRACE: I think perhaps you should have gone to the meeting.

CORNELIA: I think my not being there is much more pointed.

GRACE [*rising again*]: May I be excused, now?

CORNELIA: No! Stay here!

GRACE: If that is just a request, I—

CORNELIA: That's an order! [*Grace sits down and closes her eyes.*] When you first came to this house—do you know I didn't expect you?

GRACE: Oh, but, Cornelia, you'd invited me here.

CORNELIA: We hardly knew each other.

GRACE: We'd met the summer before when Ralph was—

CORNELIA: Living! Yes, we met at Sewanee where he was a summer instructor.

GRACE: He was already ill.

CORNELIA: I thought what a pity that lovely, delicate girl hasn't found someone she could lean on, who could protect her!

294

And two months later I heard through Clarabelle Drake that he was dead . . .

GRACE: You wrote me such a sweet letter, saying how lonely you were since the loss of your mother and urging me to rest here till the shock was over. You seemed to understand how badly I needed to withdraw for a while from—old associations. I hesitated to come. I didn't until you wrote me a second letter . . .

CORNELIA: After I received yours. You wanted urging.

GRACE: I wanted to be quite sure I was really wanted! I only came intending to stay a few weeks. I was so afraid that I would outstay my welcome!

CORNELIA: How blind of you not to see how desperately I wanted to keep you here forever!

GRACE: Oh, I did see that you—[*The phone rings.*] Miss Scott's residence!—Yes, she's here.

CORNELIA [*snatching it up finally*]: Cornelia Scott speaking! Oh. It's you, Esmeralda! Well, how did it come out?—*I don't believe you! I simply don't believe you* . . . [*Grace sits down quietly at the table.*]—MRS. HORNSBY ELECTED? Well, there's a dark horse for you! Less than a year in the chapter . . . Did you—nominate—*me?*—Oh—I see! But I told you to withdraw my name if—No, no, no, don't explain, it doesn't matter, I have too much already. You know I am going into the Daughters of the Barons of Runymede! Yes, it's been established, I have a direct line to the Earl of—No, it's been straightened out, a clear line is established, and then of course I am also eligible for the Colonial Dames and for the Huguenot Society, and what with all my other activities and so forth, why, I couldn't *possibly* have taken it on if they'd—*wanted.* . . . Of course I'm going to resign from the local chapter! Oh, yes, I am! My secretary is sitting right here by me. She has her pencil, her notebook! I'm going to dictate my letter of resignation from the local chapter the moment that I hang up on this conversation. Oh, no, no, no, I'm not mad, not outraged, at all. I'm just a little—ha ha!—a little—amused . . . *MRS. HORNSBY?* Nothing succeeds like mediocrity, does it? Thanks and good-bye, Esmeralda. [*She hangs up, stunned. Grace rises.*]

GRACE: Notebook and pencil?

CORNELIA: Yes. Notebook and pencil . . . I have to—dictate a letter . . . [*Grace leaves the table. Just at the edge of the lighted area, she turns to glance at Cornelia's rigid shoulders and a slight, equivocal smile appears momentarily on her face; not quite malicious but not really sympathetic. Then she crosses out of the light. A moment later her voice comes from the outer dark.*]

GRACE: *What lovely roses! One for every year!*

CURTAIN

THE UNSATISFACTORY SUPPER

or

THE LONG STAY CUT SHORT

CHARACTERS

BABY DOLL

ARCHIE LEE

AUNT ROSE

THE UNSATISFACTORY SUPPER

The curtain rises on the porch and side yard of a shotgun cottage in Blue Mountain, Mississippi. The frame house is faded and has a greenish-gray cast with dark streaks from the roof, and there are irregularities in the lines of the building. Behind it the dusky cyclorama is stained with the rose of sunset, which is stormy looking, and the wind has a catlike whine.

Upstage from the porch, in the center of the side yard, is a very large rose bush, the beauty of which is somehow sinister looking.

A Prokofiev sort of music introduces the scene and sets a mood of grotesque lyricism.

The screen door opens with a snarl of rusty springs and latches: this stops the music.

Mrs. "Baby Doll" Bowman appears. She is a large and indolent woman, but her amplitude is not benign, her stupidity is not comfortable. There is a suggestion of Egypt in the arrangement of her glossy black hair and the purple linen dress and heavy brass jewelry that she is wearing.

Archie Lee Bowman comes out and sucks at his teeth. He is a large man with an unhealthy, chalk-white face and slack figure.

The evenly cadenced lines of the dialogue between Baby Doll and Archie Lee may be given a singsong reading, somewhat like a grotesque choral incantation, and passages may be divided as strophe and antistrophe by Baby Doll's movements back and forth on the porch.

ARCHIE LEE: The old lady used to could set a right fair table, but not any more. The food has fallen off bad around here lately.

BABY DOLL: You're right about that, Archie Lee. I can't argue with you.

ARCHIE LEE: A good mess of greens is a satisfactory meal if it's

299

cooked with salt pork an' left on th' stove till it's tender, but thrown in a platter ha'f cooked an' unflavored, it ain't even fit for hog slops.

BABY DOLL: It's hard t' spoil greens but the old lady sure did spoil 'em.

ARCHIE LEE: How did she manage t' do it?

BABY DOLL [*slowly and contemptuously*]: Well, she had 'em on th' stove for about an hour. Said she thought they wuh boilin'. I went in the kitchen. The stove was stone cold. The silly old thing had forgotten to build a fire in it. So I called her back. I said, "Aunt Rose, I think I understand why the greens aren't boilin'." "Why aren't they boilin'?" she says. "Well," I told her, "it might have something to do with the fack that the stove issen lighted!"

ARCHIE LEE: What did she say about that?

BABY DOLL: Juss threw back her head an' cackled. "Why, I thought my stove was lighted," she said. "I thought my greens wuh boilin'." Everything is *my*. My stove, my greens, my kitchen. She has taken possession of everything on the place.

ARCHIE LEE: She's getting delusions of grandeur.

[*A high, thin laugh is heard inside.*]

Why does she cackle that way?

BABY DOLL: How should I know why she cackles! I guess it's supposed to show that she's in a good humor.

ARCHIE LEE: A thing like that can become awf'ly aggravating.

BABY DOLL: It gets on my nerves so bad I could haul off and scream. And obstinate! She's just as obstinate as a mule.

ARCHIE LEE: A person can be obstinate and still cook greens.

BABY DOLL: Not if they're so obstinate they won't even look in a stove t' see if it's lighted.

ARCHIE LEE: Why don't you keep the old lady out of the kitchen?

BABY DOLL: You get me a nigger and I'll keep her out of the kitchen.

[*The screen door creaks open and Aunt Rose comes out on the porch. She is breathless with the exertion of moving from the kitchen, and clings to a porch column while she is catching her breath. She is the type of old lady, about eighty-five years old, that resembles a delicate white-headed monkey. She has on a dress of gray calico which has become too large for her shrunken figure. She has a continual fluttering in her chest which makes her laugh in a witless manner. Neither of the pair on the porch pays any apparent attention to her, though she nods and smiles brightly at each.*]

AUNT ROSE: I brought out m' scissors. Tomorrow is Sunday an' I can't stand for my house to be without flowers on Sunday. Besides, if we don't cut the roses the wind'll just blow them away.

[*Baby Doll yawns ostentatiously. Archie Lee sucks loudly at his teeth.*]

BABY DOLL [*venting her irritation*]: Will you quit suckin' your teeth?

301

ARCHIE LEE: I got something stuck in my teeth an' I can't remove it.

BABY DOLL: There's such a thing as a toothpick made for that purpose.

ARCHIE LEE: I told you at breakfast we didn't have any toothpicks. I told you the same thing at lunch and the same thing at supper. Does it have to appear in the paper for you to believe it?

BABY DOLL: There's other things with a point besides a toothpick.

AUNT ROSE [*excitedly*]: Archie Lee, son! [*She produces a spool of thread from her bulging skirt pocket.*] You bite off a piece of this thread and run it between your teeth and if that don't dislodge a morsel nothing else will!

ARCHIE LEE [*slamming his feet from porch rail to floor*]: Now listen, you all, I want you both to get this. If I want to suck at my teeth, I'm going to suck at my teeth!

AUNT ROSE: That's right, Archie Lee, you go on and suck at your teeth as much as you want to.

[*Baby Doll grunts disgustedly. Archie Lee throws his feet back on the rail and goes on sucking his teeth loudly.*]

AUNT ROSE [*hesitantly*]: Archie Lee, son, you weren't satisfied with your supper. I noticed you left a lot of greens on your plate.

ARCHIE LEE: I'm not strong on greens.

AUNT ROSE: I'm surprised to hear you say that.

302

ARCHIE LEE: I don't see why you should be. As far as I know I never declared any terrible fondness for greens in your presence, Aunt Rose.

AUNT ROSE: Well, somebody did.

ARCHIE LEE: Somebody probably did sometime and somewhere but that don't mean it was me.

AUNT ROSE: [*with a nervous laugh*]: Baby Doll, who is it dotes on greens so much?

BABY DOLL [*wearily*]: I don't know who dotes on greens, Aunt Rose.

AUNT ROSE: All these likes and dislikes, it's hard to keep straight in your head. But Archie Lee's easy t' cook for, yes, he is, easy t' cook for! Jim's a complainer, oh, my what a complainer. And Susie's household! What complainers! Every living one of them's a complainer! They're such complainers I die of nervous prostration when I'm cooking for them. But Archie Lee, here, he takes whatever you give him an' seems to love ev'ry bite of it! [*She touches his head.*] Bless you, honey, for being so easy t' cook for!

[*Archie Lee picks up his chair and moves it roughly away.*]

AUNT ROSE [*laughing nervously and digging in her capacious pocket for the scissors*]: Now I'm goin' down there an' clip a few roses befo' th' wind blows 'em away 'cause I can't stand my house to be without flowers on Sunday. An' soon as I've finished with that, I'm goin' back in my kitchen an' light up my stove an' cook you some eggs Birmingham. I won't have my menfolks unsatisfied with their supper. Won't have it, I won't stand for it! [*She gets to the bottom of the steps and pauses for breath.*]

ARCHIE LEE: What is eggs Birmingham?

AUNT ROSE: Why, eggs Birmingham was Baby Doll's daddy's pet dish.

ARCHIE LEE: That don't answer my question.

AUNT ROSE [*as though confiding a secret*]: I'll tell you how to prepare them.

ARCHIE LEE: I don't care how you prepare them, I just want to know what they are.

AUNT ROSE [*reasonably*]: Well, son, I can't say what they are without telling how to prepare them. You cut some bread slices and take the centers out of them. You put the bread slices in a skillet with butter. Then into each cut-out center you drop one egg and on top of the eggs you put the cut-out centers.

ARCHIE LEE [*sarcastically*]: Do you build a fire in th' stove?

BABY DOLL: No, you forget to do that. That's why they call them eggs Birmingham, I suppose. [*She laughs at her wit.*]

AUNT ROSE [*vivaciously*]: That's what they call them, they call them eggs Birmingham and Baby Doll's daddy was just insane about them. When Baby Doll's daddy was not satisfied with his supper, he'd call for eggs Birmingham and would stomp his feet on the floor until I'd fixed 'em! [*This recollection seems to amuse her so that she nearly falls over.*] He'd stomp his feet on th' floor!—until I'd fixed 'em. . . . [*Her laughter dies out and she wanders away from the porch, examining the scissors.*]

BABY DOLL: That old woman is going out of her mind.

ARCHIE LEE: How long is she been with us?

BABY DOLL: She come in October.

ARCHIE LEE: No, it was August. She pulled in here last August.

BABY DOLL: Was it in August? Yes, it was, it was August.

ARCHIE LEE: Why don't she go an' cackle at Susie's awhile?

BABY DOLL: Susie don't have a bed for her.

ARCHIE LEE: Then how about Jim?

BABY DOLL: She was at Jim's direckly before she came here and Jim's wife said she stole from her and that's why she left.

ARCHIE LEE: I don't believe she stole from her. Do you believe she stole from her?

BABY DOLL: I don't believe she stole from her. I think it was just an excuse to get rid of her.

[*Aunt Rose has arrived at the rose bush. The wind comes up and nearly blows her off her feet. She staggers around and laughs at her precarious balance.*]

AUNT ROSE: Oh, my gracious! Ha-ha! Oh! Ha-ha-ha!

BABY DOLL: Why, every time I lay my pocketbook down, the silly old thing picks it up and comes creeping in to me with it, and says, "Count the change."

ARCHIE LEE: What does she do that for?

BABY DOLL: She's afraid I'll accuse her of stealing like Jim's wife did.

305

AUNT ROSE [*singing to herself as she creeps around the rose bush*]:

> Rock of Ages, cleft for me,
> Let me hide myself in thee!

ARCHIE LEE: Your buck-toothed cousin named Bunny, didn't he hit on a new way of using oil waste?

BABY DOLL: He did an' he didn't.

ARCHIE LEE: That statement don't make sense.

BABY DOLL: Well, you know Bunny. He hits on something and ropes in a few stockholders and then it blows up and the stockholders all go to court. And also he says that his wife's got female trouble.

ARCHIE LEE: They've all got something because they're not mental giants but they've got enough sense to know the old lady is going to break down pretty soon and none of 'em wants it to be while she's on their hands.

BABY DOLL: That is about the size of it.

ARCHIE LEE: And I'm stuck with her?

BABY DOLL: Don't holler.

ARCHIE LEE: I'm nominated the goat!

BABY DOLL: Don't holler, don't holler!

[*Aunt Rose sings faintly by rose bush.*]

ARCHIE LEE: Then pass the old lady on to one of them others.

BABY DOLL: Which one, Archie Lee?

ARCHIE LEE: Eeeny-meeny-miney-mo. —Mo gets her.

BABY DOLL: Which is "Mo"?

ARCHIE LEE: Not me!

[*Moving slowly and cautiously around the rose bush with her scissors, Aunt Rose sings to herself. She intersperses lines of the hymn with the dialogue on the porch. A blue dusk is gathering in the yard but a pool of clear light remains upon the rose bush.*]

ARCHIE LEE [*with religious awe*]: Some of them get these lingering types of diseases and have to be given morphine, and they tell me that morphine is just as high as a cat's back.

BABY DOLL: Some of them hang on forever, taking morphine.

ARCHIE LEE: And quantities of it!

BABY DOLL: Yes, they take quantities of it!

ARCHIE LEE: Suppose the old lady broke a hipbone or something, something that called for morphine!

BABY DOLL: The rest of the folks would have to pitch in and help us.

ARCHIE LEE: Try and extract a dime from your brother Jim! Or Susie or Tom or Bunny! They're all tight as drums, they squeeze ev'ry nickel until th' buffalo bleeds!

BABY DOLL: They don't have much and what they have they hold onto.

307

ARCHIE LEE: Well, if she does, if she breaks down an' dies on us here, I'm giving you fair warning— [*He lurches heavily to his feet and spits over edge of porch.*] I'll have her burned up and her ashes put in an old Coca-Cola bottle— [*He flops down again.*] Unless your folks kick in with the price of a coffin!

[*Aunt Rose has clipped a few roses. Now she wanders toward the front of the cottage with them.*]

Here she comes back. Now tell her.

BABY DOLL: Tell her what?

ARCHIE LEE: That she's outstayed her welcome.

AUNT ROSE [*still at some distance*]: I want you children to look.

ARCHIE LEE: You going to tell her?

AUNT ROSE: I want you children to look at these poems of nature!

ARCHIE LEE: Or do I have to tell her?

BABY DOLL: You hush up and I'll tell her.

ARCHIE LEE: Then tell her right now, and no more pussy-footing.

AUNT ROSE [*now close to the porch*]: Look at them, look at them, children, they're poems of nature!

[*But the "children" stare unresponsively, not at the flowers but at Aunt Rose's face with its extravagant brightness. She laughs uncertainly and turns to Archie Lee for a more direct appeal.*]

308

Archie Lee, aren't they, aren't they just poems of nature?

[*He grunts and gets up, and as he passes Baby Doll's chair he gives it a kick to remind her. Baby Doll clears her throat.*]

BABY DOLL [*uneasily*]: Yes, they are poems of nature, Aunt Rose, there is no doubt about it, they are. And, Aunt Rose— while we are talking—step over here for a minute so I can speak to you.

[*Aunt Rose had started away from the porch, as if with a premonition of danger. She stops, her back to the porch, and the fear is visible in her face. It is a familiar fear, one that is graven into her very bones, but which she has never become inured to.*]

AUNT ROSE: What is it, honey? [*She turns around slowly.*] I know you children are feeling upset about something. It don't take a gypsy with cards to figure that out. You an' Archie Lee both are upset about something. I think you were both unsatisfied with your supper. Isn't that it, Baby Doll? The greens didn't boil long enough. Don't you think I know that? [*She looks from Baby Doll's face to Archie Lee's back with a hesitant laugh.*] I played a fool trick with my stove, I thought it was lighted and all that time it was . . .

BABY DOLL: Aunt Rose, won't you set down so we can talk comfortably?

AUNT ROSE [*with a note of hysteria*]: I don't want to set down, I don't want to set down, I can talk on my feet! I tell you, getting up an' down is more trouble than it's worth! Now what is it, honey? As soon as I've put these in water, I'm going to light up my stove an' cook you two children some eggs Birmingham. Archie Lee, son, you hear that?

ARCHIE LEE [*roughly, his back still turned*]: I don't want eggs Birmingham.

BABY DOLL: He don't want eggs Birmingham and neither do I. But while we are talking, Aunt Rose—well—Archie Lee's wondered and I've been wondering, too . . .

AUNT ROSE: About what, Baby Doll?

BABY DOLL: Well, as to whether or not you've—made any plans.

AUNT ROSE: Plans?

BABY DOLL: Yes, plans.

AUNT ROSE: What kind of plans, Baby Doll?

BABY DOLL: Why, plans for the future, Aunt Rose.

AUNT ROSE: Oh! Future! No—no, when an old maid gets to be nearly a hundred years old, the future don't seem to require much planning for, honey. Many's a time I've wondered but I've never doubted. . . .

[*Her voice dies out and there is a strain of music as she faces away from the porch.*]

I'm not forgotten by Jesus! No, my Sweet Saviour has not forgotten about me! The time isn't known to me or to you, Baby Doll, but it's known by Him and when it comes He will call me. A wind'll come down and lift me an' take me away! The way that it will the roses when they're like I am. . . .

[*The music dies out and she turns back to the tribunal on the front porch.*]

BABY DOLL [*clearing her throat again*]: That's all very well, Aunt Rose, to trust in Jesus, but we've got to remember that Jesus only helps those that—well—help themselves!

AUNT ROSE: Oh, I know that, Baby Doll! [*She laughs.*] Why, I learned that in my cradle, I reckon I must have learned that before I was born. Now when have I ever been helpless? I could count my sick days, the days that I haven't been up and around, on my fingers! My Sweet Saviour has kept me healthy an' active, active an' healthy, yes, I do pride myself on it, my age hasn't made me a burden! And when the time comes that I have to lean on His shoulder, I—

[*Archie Lee turns about roughly*]

ARCHIE LEE: All this talk about Jesus an' greens didn't boil an' so forth has got nothing at all to do with the situation! Now look here, Aunt Rose—

BABY DOLL [*getting up*]: Archie Lee, will you hold your tongue for a minute?

ARCHIE LEE: Then you talk up! And plain! What's there to be so pussyfooting about?

BABY DOLL: There's ways and there's ways of talking anything over!

ARCHIE LEE: Well, talk it over and get off the subject of Jesus! There's Susie, there's Jim, there's Tom and Jane and there's Bunny! And if none of them suits her, there's homes in the county will take her! Just let her decide on which one she is ready to visit. First thing in the morning I'll pile her things in the car and drive her out to whichever one's she's decided! Now ain't that a simple procedure compared to all of this pussyfooting around? Aunt Rose has got sense. She's counted the rooms

311

in this house! She knows that I'm nervous, she knows that I've got work to do and a workingman's got to be fed! And his house is his house and he wants it the way that he wants it! Well, Jesus Almighty, if that's not a plain, fair and square way of settling the matter, I'll wash my hands clean and leave you two women to talk it over yourselves! Yes, I'll—be God damned if—!

[*He rushes in and slams the screen door. There is a long pause in which Baby Doll looks uncomfortably at nothing, and Aunt Rose stares at the screen door.*]

AUNT ROSE [*finally*]: I thought you children were satisfied with my cooking.

[*A blue dusk has gathered in the yard. Aunt Rose moves away from the porch and there is a strain of music. The music is drowned out by the catlike whine of the wind turning suddenly angry. Baby Doll gets up from her wicker chair.*]

BABY DOLL: Archie Lee, Archie Lee, you help me in with these chairs before they blow over! [*She drags her chair to the screen door.*] It looks and sounds like a twister! Hold that screen open for me! Pull in that chair! Now this one! We better get down in the cellar! [*As an afterthought.*] Aunt Rose, come in here so we can shut this door!

[*Aunt Rose shakes her head slightly. Then she looks toward the sky, above and beyond the proscenium, where something portentous is forming. Baby Doll goes back in the house.*]

Call Aunt Rose in!

ARCHIE LEE: The stubborn old thing won't budge.

[*The door slams shut. The whine of the angry cat turns into a distant roar and the roar approaches. But Aunt Rose remains in the yard, her face still somberly but quietly thoughtful. The loose gray calico of her dress begins to whip and tug at the skeleton lines of her figure. She looks wonderingly at the sky, then back at the house beginning to shrink into darkness, then back at the sky from which the darkness is coming, at each with the same unflinching but troubled expression. Nieces and nephews and cousins, like pages of an album, are rapidly turned through her mind, some of them loved as children but none of them really her children and all of them curiously unneedful of the devotion that she had offered so freely, as if she had always carried an armful of roses that no one had ever offered a vase to receive. The flimsy gray scarf is whipped away from her shoulders. She makes an awkward gesture and sinks to her knees. Her arms let go of the roses. She reaches vaguely after them. One or two she catches. The rest blow away. She struggles back to her feet. The blue dusk deepens to purple and the purple to black and the roar comes on with the force of a locomotive as Aunt Rose's figure is still pushed toward the rose bush.]*

DIM OUT

STEPS MUST BE GENTLE

CHARACTERS

HART CRANE

GRACE, his mother

The performers, representing Hart Crane and his mother Grace, should not be too distinctly lighted unless makeup and costume provide them with a fairly close physical resemblance to the characters they play. The lighting should be cool with projection of shadows moving across them and the lecterns at which they speak at opposite sides of the stage. If the production allows the use of a "cyc," on it should be projected an abstract design which is evocative of sea, sky, and the emotional content of the duologue.

Sea sounds, with delicate mood music as the performers are lighted slowly.

GRACE: Hart?—Hart?—Son?

[*This call may be repeated a number of times in various tones, from tenderly beseeching to desperately demanding.*]

HART [*finally*]: Grace.

GRACE: At last a response to my cries. Does it take you so long, now, to recognize my voice?

HART: It's been a long while since your voice, or any voice, has interrupted my rest.

GRACE: I wake up calling incessantly in the night. How kind of you to finally respond.

HART: How was it possible to make a connection over such immense—

[*Sound*]

—distance? Of course it isn't, it's only a—hypothetical, not a possible—

[*Sound*]

—communication between us. Why have you called me, Grace?

GRACE: I want you to tell me yourself, I want no more speculations from others: WHY, WHY DID YOU DO IT?

HART: You're indulging in your usual emotionalism, Grace, breaking my rest at the floor of the sea with these outcries too strong at last not to hear.

GRACE: Ours was not a relationship, was it, that could ever permit quiet voices?

HART: Between us? No.—No . . .

GRACE: There's been such a length of time between the year nineteen thirty-two, and the year nineteen forty-seven, years devoted by me to a constant effort to sort out and try to put together the many, many bits of mystery and conflicting reports of your life between the time I last saw you in California and when I finally knew I never could again, and after—after—

[*Sea sounds: evanescent music*]

HART: —A number of us who rest here on the great bed of the sea, those of us who *chose* to rest here, paid dearly for their rest and deserve not to have it broken.

GRACE: You make it sound like a bed you've rented with your last dollar, my son, but it's not quite as you think. The name that you must have signed on the register of this place of rest has not been washed away by all the coming and going of the

318

tides. I've had my part in that: in fact, it's been my vocation, my only decent employment, from spring, 1932 till mid-summer of 1947. Have you any conception of these years between, the slightest idea, or have they no concern for you? Did you even know that my mother—*our* mother—died lingeringly in anguish, she who loved you as dearly as I did, who gave you long stays in her place on the Isle of Pines, time and again, where you worked so well, where I think you worked best, having the most peace there? Well, if you were aware that we had lost her, not a word of it reached me. Of course, of course—this is hardly a time for exchange of—recriminations . . .

HART: No, Grace.

GRACE: No, no, this is no time to speak of our—misunder-standings . . .

HART: Perhaps you mean our finally coming to understand each other too well.

GRACE: Please no more of that icy language between us!

HART: A dead man speaks this way: no other way is conceiv-able. If it is not totally inconceivable to begin with that he could speak at all except through words remembered by the living. And so to repeat: among the existing circumstances the one to be least disregarded is surely the one that I no longer exist.

GRACE: My son Hart! That may be the one circumstance among many that makes a true communication between us finally possible.

HART: All right, forget possibilities and have it your way and tell me: you are speaking to me at what point in time?

GRACE: Fifteen years after you—

319

HART: Came out on the deck of the steamship *Orizaba* at high noon, a night and half a day north of Havana, my face disfigured by a night of drunken riot in the crew's quarters. Came out on the deck in pyjamas and a coat and walked directly to the stern of the ship, folded the coat neatly over the rail, and then, and then—leapt over. —Now I've told you what, for reasons unknown, I have to pretend to know. Now you. Do you pretend not to know?

GRACE: —I know what witnesses reported.

HART: But you still say that there is a circumstance that—

GRACE: Finally makes it possible for us—

HART: To talk? —Grace, you've often talked to me in an illogical, sometimes an hysterical way, but never to this extent under—natural conditions, if such conditions ever existed between us. You don't sound well to me, Grace. You sound as if you had a fever, Grace. Aren't you coughing, Grace?

GRACE: Night employment in winter in buildings where the heat is turned off after the regular working hours was not conducive to health, but that's of no consequence now. You must suspect by now that our circumstances have become the same.

HART: I didn't quite hear that.

GRACE: Perhaps you didn't wish to.

HART: The distance, the—connection.

GRACE: All right, dismiss it as that.

HART: It's been a long while since we have existed for each other.

320

GRACE: Stop that, stop it! I exist in your blood as you exist in mine—

HART: There is no blood in bones that were cast and scattered as gambler's dice on the sea's floor and you know it.

GRACE: I speak of what did exist, and having existed once, remains—to claim what can't be denied, which must be admitted unless you regard yourself, Hart, as being completely and exclusively a product of the Crane chocolate-maker of Cleveland, Ohio. A box of his chocolates, now, is that what you claim to be only?

HART: "Sundered parentage," Grace, is that from which I chose to descend to the sea's floor—half a night and half a day north of Havana . . .

[*Sea sound and ringing of bells*]

Listen, listen! I hear them. Don't you hear them? The bells of the cathedral ringing at daybreak?—"And so it was I entered the broken world / to trace the visionary company of love / its voice an instant in the wind, I know not whither hurled / but not for long to hold each desperate choice . . ."

[*Sounds under again*]

GRACE: Hart, if only you could know how desperately I have defended your poetry with my life, because—

HART: Because?

GRACE: It was mine, too.

HART: Will you please allow me, at least, an exclusive copyright over my poetry, Grace? It was my life, not yours: allow me that.

321

GRACE: What in the name of Christ haven't I always allowed you? Over-indulgence was my one fault as your mother.

HART: Yes, of your emotions, of your self.

GRACE: Of you, you know it! Name me something which I didn't allow you, the tower room of the house, phonograph playing all night as your fists pounded out the cadences of your verse, and finally, in my heart, no matter what you shocked me into saying in California, your perversion, confessed, that ugliness spat in my face!

HART: So many allowances, God! How often I've had to beg! And I had pride—but I begged! Fell to my knees to beg! Of you? Recognition of a way of life imposed on me like a prison sentence. I had to give you the truth and you abhorred it, loathed it, that confession! From the candymaker of Cleveland? Little remittances, pittances, tight-fisted little dribbling of doles on which I had to somehow subsist in order to continue my work which I had to continue. Do you understand, Grace? I always had to beg for what I received to *feed* me!

GRACE: Feed you with *what*, Hart?

HART: With *what*, did you ask me?

GRACE: Yes, knowing the answer: the, the—sex of sailors picked up in Brooklyn, dockside bars, as if they were the thin bits of bread that symbolized Christ's flesh at Holy Communion, and their seed as if it were—His blood! Oh, but all that—

HART: Means nothing, now.

GRACE: Did it ever mean *some*thing?

HART: No, not really, Grace, but did you and the chocolate-maker predispose me toward anything but wayward kinds of love-seeking?

GRACE: —I thought we agreed that all of that is of no consequence now.

HART: While I existed, yes, it did mean much, if not everything.

GRACE: —Granted, it's all absolved and forgotten nearly but—

HART: Then can we continue this obvious impossibility, a talk between us, on a quiet level? I paid very dearly, Grace, to rest upon a quiet level. Will you please not take it from me, will you—

GRACE: Hart, please, that frigid attitude, now, at my—

[*Wind and sea sound, vast and heavy, subside before words resume.*]

HART: At your what, Grace?

GRACE: My—distance. Away.

HART: The question isn't affected at all by distance and can't be fairly called frigid since my concern for you, Grace, was—

[*Sound*]

GRACE [*overlapping*]: *Your concern for?*

HART: *My concern for you, Grace.*

GRACE: Your *concern* for me, Hart?

323

[*She laughs desperately, bitterly.*]

HART: There again—

GRACE: Again?

HART: You prefer to dismiss it and to mock it although I'm sure you still know—

GRACE: Sure that I still know what?

HART: That my concern for you, Grace, was central to my being as the heart of my body.

GRACE: If those bones thrown and scattered on the ocean's floor, like a gambler's dice, as you said, have in them no blood of mine, then how could they have a heart in them whose central concern is with me?

HART: You can't seem to believe that now I can only speak of what was, not of what is.

GRACE: What was—no matter what the distance and depth of the sea dividing us now—is still what it was, preserved—

[*Sea sound*]

—imperishably.

HART: You and dear grandmother, Grace, not only sold the house on Euclid in Cleveland but the place on the Isle of Pines.

GRACE: The place on the Isle of Pines would have been lost to Cuba, and as for the Cleveland place on Euclid, Mother Elizabeth and I were forced to sell it to go to Florida, Hart.

324

HART: I was left no place. A poet must have a place. When I begged the candyman in Cleveland to give me a loan to buy a small house, he wrote me back that his chocolate business had steadily declined since 1922 and that his new enterprise, that Cozy Country Inn, Canary Cottage in Chagrin Falls, had only possible profits in a dubious future. Still—his stinginess with me, like so much else that mattered when I existed, is irrelevant to me now—is dismissed by the judge in the big, the immense empty courtrooms of such a long time away.

GRACE: Chocolate business in Cleveland and Cozy Country Inn, Chagrin Falls: suitable monuments to a man who wrote such cheerfully vacuous letters, refusing appeals from his son, who was constructing a myth of America, far beyond the reach of the chocolate stained fingers of his—complacent small mind.

[*Sea sounds: her voice comes out of them, crying out.*]

I sold my beautiful diamonds for a song! Do you know what I was finally employed at?

HART: And the house in Cleveland and the place on the Isle of Pines. But are these the things we have to say to each other across the depth and distance, an impossible distance. —Didn't you start to tell me what you're now employed at, what you're working at now?

GRACE: Till recently: not now. Now what I'm employed at—

HART: What?

GRACE: That which you must have suspected since first you heard my voice over this tenuous connection that must break off in a moment and never be restored. I have made it my dedication, my vocation, to protect your name, your legend, against the filthy scandals that you'd seemed determined to demolish

325

them with. Despite my age, my illness, I have carried the stones to build your tower again. And it did hurt me, Hart, that you wrote of the lovely little things such as the flowers of Mexico, carried in woven straw baskets on Indian women's heads under your windows in Pueblo, the bravely common bright flowers of which you wrote in a letter *not to me*—the violets, cornflowers, white and red carnations, the carmine poppies—[*Then savagely*] A wire to you, I quote: COME AT ONCE DESPERATELY ILL AT HOME ALONE YOU CAN HELP. Close quote. Did you? Did you come to me, *did* you help?

[*Rise of sea sound*]

HART: —I—enquired of—friends in Cleveland—if the appeal was—if the circumstances were—authentic—

GRACE: Before that I wired you from California, Quote: MOTHER PASSED AWAY TONIGHT FUNERAL HERE ADVISE. Close quote. If you replied, the letter does not survive!

HART: I appealed to father to give you assistance, to make some provision for your—welfare, Grace.

GRACE: —I wonder if what you confessed in California, that obscene confession of your sexual nature hasn't a little to do with so much of such well-demonstrated grace of the heart in you, Hart.

[*Sea sound*]

HART: What have you been employed at? This time, please, no evasion!

[*Pause: sea sound and music*]

GRACE: I've been employed at nights as a scrubwoman, Hart.

326

HART: —As a—?

GRACE: *Night! Scrub! Woman!*

HART: *Oh—Grace! No!*

GRACE: It's of no consequence, now, but that was my last employment. —Traveller, stranger, son—my friend . . .

[*She closes her eyes and steps back from the lectern.*]

HART [*more and more faintly but with anguish*]: Grace—Grace—Grace—

[*His repeated calls are lost in sea sounds and music: he closes his eyes, which the Mexican painter Sequiras could only paint closed, as they contained such torment, and steps back from the lectern.*]

THE END

THE DEMOLITION DOWNTOWN

Count ten in Arabic—and try to run

CHARACTERS

MR. LANE

MRS. LANE

MR. KANE

MRS. KANE

ROSEMARY (a child)

GLADYS (a child)

THE DEMOLITION DOWNTOWN

The play is set in an upper-middle-class living room on the out-skirts of a capital city.

At the curtain's rise an attractive, youngish man is staring tensely downstage. After some moments his wife lets herself in the front door of the house, stage right or left. She is also youngish and attractive. They are Mr. and Mrs. Lane. Scattered throughout the play are the sounds of dynamite blasts and falling walls of buildings, sometimes alarmingly near.

MRS. L.: No luck.

MR. L.: Why didn't you let me know you were going out?

MRS. L.: You were upstairs. I thought you might be taking nap.

MR. L.: How could you imagine I'd be taking a nap?

MRS. L.: I suppose I'm not used to your being home before six.

MR. L.: When you came in you said, "No luck." What did you mean by no luck?

MRS. L.: I went to see if the supermarket or Kwik-chek might be open again.

MR. L.: Still closed?

MRS. L.: No sign of life on the premises of either.

MR. L.: I don't want you to go out of the house without letting me know.

MRS. L.: Has the house turned into a jail and are you the warden of it?

MR. L.: Each of us has to know where the other one is at all times.

MRS. L.: Jeff, I think it's best to act as if nothing has happened.

MR. L.: We mustn't pretend to each other.

MRS. L.: All right, we're anxious, but we don't have to act like criminals, caught and convicted, waiting for execution.

MR. L.: Neither of us leaves the house without.

MRS. L.: I told you why I went out.

MR. L.: I told you we've got to know at all times where.

MRS. L.: Didn't I just tell you why I went out?

MR. L.: When I found you'd.

MRS. L.: Gone about ten minutes to see if.

MR. L.: You'd disappeared from the house and I didn't know where you'd, and anyway we mustn't use the cars. The filling stations are shut down. Did you hear what I said? The filling stations are shut down, so we've got to reserve the gas and oil in the cars for a possible trip somewhere.

MRS. L.: We don't understand what each other.

MR. L.: We might want to go on a, we might decide to. We might want to take a little trip some place while I'm free to do it.

MRS. L.: You mean running away, and where's to run to? Don't you imagine that?

MR. L.: We don't *listen* to each other!

MRS. L.: Don't you imagine that, wouldn't you guess that the highways out of the city are barricaded?

MR. L.: There are roads not traveled on much.

MRS. L.: Do you want to know why I really went out? I really went out because I like, I need the sight of familiar places and, and. Familiar places and things, that's why I went out for ten minutes. It was good for my nerves to go out, and so was driving my car.

MR. L.: Driving a Jaguar sports car when.

MRS. L.: Oh, for the love of!

MR. L.: Hunting trips have taught me where these roads are. Roads unknown to, roads only known to, to a few people only.

MRS. L.: Jeff, for the love of, don't, don't suddenly show me a.

MR. L.: I suppose you.

MRS. L.: A yellow streak in you, Jeff. This isn't the time to.

MR. L.: To use a little precaution is.

MRS. L.: Yes, well just to see them, even shut down, it made me.

MR. L.: See what?

MRS. L.: The supermarket and Kwik-chek. I felt like someone still living a usual, normal sort of.

MR. L.: Fine, but you understand that.

MRS. L.: Oh, God, Jeff, I.

MR. L.: Not reserving the gas and oil in the cars is.

MRS. L.: Okay, okay, Mr. Lane! Get me a donkey! An old one, a mangy old donkey! For transportation! But I will *not* stay in *always!*

[*She snatches a gin bottle from the bar.*]

MR. L.: —How much is left in?

MRS. L.: About a couple of fingers. Do we have to reserve it or can we dissipate now?

MR. L.: Let's have it now. I didn't mean to shout at you.

MRS. L. [*as she shakily pours the gin in two glasses*]: No dry vermouth left, baby.

MR. L.: Baby, take off your hat. [*The request is ignored. In hat, coat, handbag in her lap she sits beside him on a sofa. The drink calms them down a little.*] Baby, will you at least take off your gloves?

MRS. L.: Gee. Drinking with my gloves on. [*She removes one of the gloves. He removes the other.*]

MR. L.: Where did you leave the Jaguar, in the garage or?

MRS. L.: I left it in front of the house.

MR. L.: Give me the key and I'll put it in the garage.

MRS. L.: There's nothing top secret about it.

MR. L.: I said please give me the key to the Jaguar, baby.

MRS. L.: I don't have the key; I don't know what I did with it.

MR. L.: I think you probably left it in the.

MRS. L.: Yes, probably, yes.

MR. L.: It's all right, baby, I'll.

[*He goes out. She finishes her drink and takes a sip of his. There is a particularly loud dynamite blast. It changes the angles of the pictures.*]

MRS. L.: Lord God in the—*Highest!* [*As Mr. L. comes back in:*] Didn't it feel good to go out for a minute?

MR. L.: What?

MRS. L.: I didn't say anything. There ought to be a reassuring statement to the people anytime now.

MR. L.: Barbarians don't, won't, can't reassure.

MRS. L.: I've heard that he comes from the intellectual class, and has a degree in—

MR. L.: Yes, in a pig's—

MRS. L.: . . . in law.

MR. L.: In violation of law and in destruction of order and disruption of—. TV dead. Radio dead. Newspapers not delivered since he seized the—

MRS. L.: Don't say "seized." Say "took over."

MR. L.: Take off your hat and coat, and put your handbag down; you're in the house.

MRS. L.: There'll be something, there has to be just something, or.

MR. L.: It's a week and a half and there's been nothing but—nothing.

MRS. L.: Any day there'll be a—

MR. L.: There'll be what? I don't expect anything.

MRS. L. [*taking off her coat*]: Isn't it lucky we have so much in the deep-freeze, Jeff?

MR. L.: Yes, since otherwise we'd. —Honey, do you know that you're still holding your handbag?

MRS. L.: —Of course I don't mind, Jeff, but the fly of your pants isn't zipped.

MR. L.: —Oh. Sorry. [*He zips the fly.*] I suppose that.

MRS. L.: Under the circumstances.

MR. L.: We have to make allowances for.

MRS. L.: I think we ought to make love, right now, on the sofa.

MR. L.: Thank you, honey, but anxiety and lovemaking? You'd find me disappointing.

MRS. L.: That's something I've never found you anytime, Jeff.

336

MR. L.: A man has a nervous system that has to be prepared for lovemaking, in the right gear for it, and.

MRS. L.: I was thinking of what might be a pleasant distraction for us.

MR. L.: Let's think of it after the blasting quits for the day.

MRS. L.: All right. I'll remind you later.

MR. L.: Yes. Later. Upstairs.

MRS. L. [*suddenly calling out*]: Sally!

MR. L.: Honey, the maid hasn't been here since the blasting began.

MRS. L.: Gee. Yes. Didn't show up for her payday. Well— [*Sound of more blasting.*] I'm glad that Rosemary and Gladys are at Sacré Coeur.

MR. L.: All schools, and Sacré Coeur is a school, have been—

MRS. L.: —What?

MR. L.: Converted to—

MRS. L.: What?

MR. L.: Barracks. I heard that from—

MRS. L.: Too many people have been guessing too wildly about too many things, and Sacré Coeur is a convent school, and.

MR. L.: The church and the new government aren't on what I'd call the friendliest terms. Would you say that they were?

MRS. L.: Oh, you seem determined to demoralize us completely when we're already demoralized, Jeff.

MR. L.: I'm not demoralized.

MRS. L.: Then why can't you sit still? Sit on the sofa and let me rub your forehead.

MR. L. [*following the suggestion*]: Not to be slightly disturbed would be— [*Sound of blasting.*] That didn't sound much further than ten or twelve blocks away.

MRS. L.: At first the blasting was only in the morning.

MR. L.: I've found out one thing. Anxiety is the most useless feeling a person can feel.

MRS. L.: I'd say it's a useful feeling, since it makes you aware of circumstances that could be, that might be not quite favorable to you.

MR. L.: Don't leave the house again without letting me know.

MRS. L.: —Jeff, in a marriage that's been as good, remarkably good, as ours has always been till just now, there shouldn't be orders. Should there?

MR. L.: Honey, don't you think it's wise to reserve the.

MRS. L.: Gas and oil in the cars. Okay. —Are we just going to rattle around here picking on each other till we forget that we love each other?

MR. L.: Oh, for.

MRS. L.: Whose sake?

338

MR. L.: The sake of consideration of.

[*Blasting.*]

MRS. L.: That rattled the windows and shook the Vertes off the wall.

MR. L.: Yes, I noticed it did.

MRS. L.: Wouldn't you think if there's all this.

MR. L.: —Demolition—downtown. [*He hangs the picture up. Immediately there's another blast and the picture is shaken down again.*]

MRS. L. [*tossing the Vertes on the sofa*]: That put the Dufy at a forty-five-degree angle. [*Mr. L. sits down and immediately springs up.*] You couldn't sit still?

MR. L.: I guess not. —You have a little twitch at the side of your mouth today.

MRS. L.: If we didn't show some symptoms of nervous uncertainty we'd be unnatural creatures.

MR. L.: Stop picking up things for no reason, looking at them with a blind look, and setting them back down. It's.

MRS. L.: It's natural for us to—

MR. L.: Not know what we're doing? —House confinement. No activity.

MRS. L.: I make up the beds and I prepare meals and I even dust the furniture and run the vacuum cleaner over the—

MR. L.: Why bother?

MRS. L.: I think we have to keep up some semblance of usual activity or we'll find ourselves climbing the walls. I didn't realize that Sally was such a poor servant till I started doing the housework myself.

MR. L.: Take your hat off, will you?

MRS. L.: I always do that in the bedroom.

MR. L.: Oh. Do you?

MRS. L.: Love, you're shaking, you're.

MR. L.: How could I feel well? Are *you* feeling well? Well, *are* you?

MRS. L.: I feel—

MR. L.: What?

MRS. L.: I always feel energetic and a little high-strung in the fall. Do you know what I think I'm going to do? I think I'm going out in the yard and rake up the dead leaves.

MR. L.: You're not going out in the yard.

MRS. L.: It would be a normal activity.

MR. L.: I think we ought to make the house look unoccupied until the—

MRS. L.: That's what I'm going to do, to work off my nervous energy. [*She goes through an upstage door. He lights a cigarette*

and burns his fingers with the match. She reenters with a rake.]
The front lawn first.

MR. L. [*seizing the rake and throwing through the dark up-stage door*]: The house is not occupied. Get it?

MRS. L.: Not a bit of it. Two lunatics live in it.

MR. L.: That's the goddamn truth. Come here.

MRS. L.: What for?

MR. L.: This. [*He pulls up her skirt and runs his hands over her buttocks.*]

MRS. L.: That's what I suggested. You said you were too nervous.

MR. L. [*feeling the front of his pants*]: Well, I guess I was right.

MRS. L.: I paid you the compliment of taking off my hat and coat in the living room.

MR. L.: Thank you. I'm sorry. The tension won't last much longer.

[*There is a pounding at the door. After some hesitation Mr. Lane unbolts it, opens it a few inches. Two little girls, Rosemary and Gladys, burst into the room. Mr. and Mrs. Lane are curiously indifferent to their homecoming.*]

ROSEMARY: Daddy! Mummy!

GLADYS: Mummy! Daddy!

MRS. L.: Why have you girls left Sacré Coeur?

ROSEMARY: It was captivated.

MR. L.: Do you mean captured?

ROSEMARY: Yes.

GLADYS: Captured.

ROSEMARY: The Sisters and the Mother Superior.

GLADYS: They were hauled away in a truck.

ROSEMARY: We ran and ran.

MRS. L.: You look like you'd been playing in a pile of cinders. Go right upstairs and bathe and go to bed.

GLADYS: Is everything all right here?

MR. L.: Perfectly, perfectly.

MRS. L.: Upstairs. Bathe. Get in bed.

ROSEMARY: A man with a black beard did a nasty thing to us.

MR. L.: What did he—?

MRS. L.: Didn't you hear me? Upstairs, I said, and bathe and get in your beds.

[*The little girls run up a flight of steps to a landing where the steps turn out of sight.*]

MR. L. [*with no real interest*]: They said that they were molested.

MRS. L.: They seemed like—

MR. L.: What?

MRS. L.: Strangers, complete strangers, to me.

MR. L.: Sacré Coeur's shut down.

MRS. L.: The nuns and that horsefaced Mother Superior hauled away in a truck. Oh. —I took a steak out of the deep-freeze this morning.

MR. L.: Oh.

MRS. L.: Yes. And some lima beans.

MR. L.: Until there's some explanation, I think we should eat in the kitchen by candlelight.

MRS. L.: Eat anywhere you want to, but I'm not going to live in a dark house, Jeff.

MR. L.: It's time for the news report.

[*He switches on the TV. Its face is blank. It gives off a crackling sound.*]

MRS. L.: An interesting news report.

MR. L.: We have to get out of here. Thank God for my hunting trips. We could—no, I guess we couldn't.

MRS. L.: What did you start to suggest?

MR. L.: Spending a week or two at Blue Lake.

MRS. L.: No, we couldn't do that. The hotels at Blue Lake had so much employment trouble that they shut down the first of September.

MR. L.: You know, I think it's possible that the new party in power, after a little preliminary shakedown, may turn out to be a rigid party but not a, not a—party that lacks human feelings.

MRS. L.: Jeff, I see your point, but the confiscation of your office building wasn't the most reassuring thing in the world. —Would you say that it was?

MR. L.: That could be more temporary than final, baby. [*The sound of a loud blast.*] The blasting sounds closer today.

MRS. L.: Maybe, baby, that's just because you're more disturbed by it today.

MR. L.: I'm naturally somewhat concerned by it but I'm not what you'd call—what did you say? Disturbed? I'm not disturbed, just waiting with concern.

MRS. L.: Is there a difference between being concerned and disturbed?

MR. L.: Disturbed is when you're sweating.

MRS. L.: You're sweating, baby. A little. Like after a hard game of tennis with a hot sun on you.

MR. L.: Do the present conditions of things make you feel nice and cool, baby?

MRS. L.: Me? I'm not thinking of me. [*She sticks her hand in his pocket.*] I'm a pickaninny. Have you got a nickel in your pocket for me to buy a licorice stick or a little bag of gumdrops?

344

MR. L.: Upstairs. Later, baby.

[*The doorbell rings.*]

MRS. L.: —Should we?

MR. L.: Yes, of course, why not.

MRS. L.: I can think of several reasons but not good ones.

MR. L.: See who's at the door, baby. Ask before you open.

MRS. L. [*approaching the door and calling out*]: Who's there?

FEMALE VOICE: Us.

MALE VOICE: Just us.

MRS. L.: Who's us?

MR. L.: Yes, I'd like to know that.

MALE VOICE: The *Kanes.*

MR. L.: The *Kanes.*

FEMALE VOICE: Don't keep us freezing out here.

MR. L.: Baby, let the Kanes in.

MRS. L.: Just a moment. I'm having a little trouble with the new bolt. Ah, there now, come in, come in, how wonderful to see you.

[*Mrs. Lane admits a pair of neighbors, Mr. and Mrs. Kane. They are the same age as the Lanes and similar to them in appearance.*]

MRS. KANE: We haven't seen you since.

MR. L.: Well, hello there, Henry.

MR. KANE: How are you doing, Jeff?

MRS. L.: Sit down, sit down.

[*The Kanes sit down: their nervousness is apparent.*]

MR. KANE: We should have phoned, but Elaine says the phone isn't working.

MRS. L.: Neither is ours.

MR. L.: Henry, how are things at the Bolster Trust?

MR. KANE: Oh, fine, I guess fine, but I, uh, haven't been down there lately.

MR. L.: Any particular reason?

MR. KANE: I thought I'd stay away till things settle down.

MRS. L.: I'm looking to see if there's any liquor and there isn't any except a bottle of sweet vermouth.

MR. KANE: We would have brought some over but we've drunk our little bar dry.

MRS. L.: We've been drinking more than usual since—

MR. L.: Since President Stane surrendered to the, uh.

MR. KANE: New regime.

MR. L.: Yes. Treasonous.

MRS. L.: We might as well drink the vermouth.

MRS. KANE: Yes. Wonderful.

MR. KANE: —Yes. [*To his wife:*] Take your coat off, honey.

MRS. KANE: It's too chilly. I'll leave it on.

MR. KANE: It's not chilly in here.

MRS. KANE: It was so chilly outside. I'll leave my coat on for a while.

MR. KANE: I'm not going to argue with you.

MR. L.: How's your kids?

MR. KANE: Snug as bugs in their beds.

[*Mr. Kane coughs.*]

MR. L.: That's a bad cough you've got there.

MRS. L.: I hope you haven't caught the new virus thing that's been going around.

MR. KANE: It's a bronchial thing, not serious but stubborn, and Dr. Brad's office is closed.

MRS. KANE: We called on the Paynes.

MR. L.: On who?

MR. KANE: *You* know the Paynes.

MR. L.: Oh, yes, sure, the Paynes. How are the Paynes doing?

MRS. KANE: Nobody answered the door.

MR. L.: They were probably out.

MRS. KANE: I don't think they were in.

MRS. L.: People stay in too much, now.

MR. L.: Hmm.

MR. KANE: Elaine here thinks we ought to drive out to Blue Lake.

MR. L.: I was thinking about that, too, and I know an unpaved road that goes to it.

MRS. KANE: It was you that brought up that subject and the hotels on Blue Lake are all shut down till the middle of May.

MR. KANE: We have a wonderful set of camping equipment that I've put in order.

MRS. KANE: Yes, just in case.

MR. L.: We've got a set, too, and I've got it ready, in case.

MRS. L.: We have a lot of tinned goods. You know, sardines and anchovies and.

MR. L.: Salmon and tuna fish and pate and.

MR. KANE: We've got a stock of that, too.

MRS. KANE [*wryly*]: Yes, a big sack of it, in case of sudden hunger on some excursion or other.

348

MR. L.: I know what you mean. Essentials.

MRS. L.: It's hard to know what essentials are, exactly.

MR. L.: Essentials are what you discover unexpected need of.

MR. KANE: Such as tinned goods and vacation clothes.

MRS. KANE: Fleece-lined coats and jackets.

MR. KANE: And spare tires in good condition.

MRS. KANE: That's right. In perfect condition.

MR. KANE: There's a cold snap tonight.

MRS. KANE: With the harvest moon shining.

MR. KANE: This is the most unpredictable time of the year.

MR. L.: Unpredictable. Yes.

MR. KANE: Completely. I know what you mean.

MRS. KANE [*winking at Mrs. L.*]: So did I. If I got this hand at bridge, I'd indicate once to my partner and let him take it from there. [*Mr. Kane laughs nervously.*] Of course I'm no good at bridge.

MR. KANE: You're pretty damn good at poker.

MR. L.: It's been too long since we've had a good game of poker.

MRS. KANE: That's right. It seems ages.

MR. L.: Yes, it seems ages and ages, but we've all been a little distracted.

MRS. KANE: A little at least.

[*There is a pause.*]

MR. KANE: What is an abattoir, Jeff?

MR. L.: An abattoir? An abattoir is a sort of a slaughter pen.

MRS. L.: Only for animals?

MR. KANE: Yes, of course, but old Hugh Wayne received a notice that said, "Kindly present yourself tomorrow, before five p.m. to the Municipal Abattoir. If you disregard this summons, a squad car will pick you up." He showed me this card, this summons, the day he got it, and he's—

MR. L.: —Not?

MR. KANE: Been seen around since.

MR. L.: We only had the barest speaking acquaintance with old Hugh Wayne. [*A dynamite blast rattles the windows.*] Hmm.

MR. KANE: Hmm.

MRS. L.: Hmm.

MRS. KANE: The closest one yet.

MRS. L.: It was the *strongest* one yet.

MR. KANE [*abruptly*]: The mountains!

MR. L.: What about the mountains?

MR. KANE: We could go to the mountains! Why don't we go to the mountains?

MR. L.: I hadn't thought of the mountains but there's the mountains to go to. And there's the Sunny Peak Road that almost nobody knows of. Two cars?

MR. KANE: One car!

MR. L.: Yes, we could all fit in one car, not too comfortably, but.

MRS. L.: Let's think about it, first.

MRS. KANE: It should be regarded as an idea before it's accepted as a decision.

MR. KANE: You girls are too nervous.

MRS. KANE: You boys are nervous, too.

MR. KANE: We've got the responsibility of decisions.

MRS. KANE: Your wives don't have that responsibility, too?

MR. KANE: Men make decisions.

MRS. KANE: Excuse me for interrupting that male prerogative for a.

MR. KANE: Mountains!

MR. L.: Mountains!

MR. KANE: Let's decide it right now.

MR. L.: Going to the mountains by the Sunny Peak Road. Hard on the rubber, but.

MR. KANE: Siphon the oil and gas in your Mercedes or our Caddy.

MR. L.: When?

MR. KANE: Now, what's wrong with right now?

MR. L.: Nothing that I can think of is wrong with an immediate little.

MR. KANE: What do you girls think?

MR. L.: Yes, how do you girls feel about it?

MRS. KANE: I think it's an inspiration.

MRS. L.: So do I.

MR. KANE: Well, let's get the siphoning going. Now, right now. [*To his wife:*] Turn off the lights while we go out the door.

[*Mrs. Kane extinguishes the living room lights. The door is heard opening and shutting.*]

MRS. KANE: They're out, now. We can turn the lights back on.

MRS. L.: Oh. Yes. Of course. [*The stage is fully lighted again.*] —To get to the Sunny Peak Road, wouldn't we have to go out some fairly well-known highway?

MRS. KANE: I think it might be reasonable to suspect so.

MRS. L.: Wouldn't there, mightn't there be some obstruction, some?

MRS. KANE: If that possibility occurred to our masterminds, it didn't seem to disturb them.

MRS. L.: —No, it didn't, did it?

MRS. KANE: No, it didn't.

MRS. L.: Perhaps they thought about it but—

MRS. KANE: What?

MRS. L.: Knew how to get around it.

MRS. KANE: Yes, that could be the reason they didn't care to discuss it in our presence.

MRS. L.: They don't want us to be nervous. [*A dynamite blast shakes all of the pictures off the walls.*] I'm not going to hang those pictures up again.

MRS. KANE: No, I wouldn't bother. [*Slight pause.*] What do you really think about this excursion to the mountains?

MRS. L.: It's a wild idea, but none of us thought of anything else.

MRS. KANE: The plan is to drive to the foot of the mountains, then get out of the car.

MRS. L.: And go on from there on foot.

353

MRS. KANE: How good are you at mountain climbing, through several feet of snow?

MRS. L.: —I've had no experience at it.

MRS. KANE: Neither have I, none at all, whatsoever.

MRS. L.: It's a desperate thing to consider, but.

MRS. KANE: The children would be better at it than we'd be.

MRS. L.: Hmm?

MRS. KANE: Hmm . . .

[*Her eyes narrow: she puts on a pair of heavy shell-rimmed glasses which give her a look of cold sagacity: she peers through them at Mrs. L.'s face which is slowly accumulating an expression of shock.*]

MRS. L.: —Hmm!

MRS. KANE: Yes.

MRS. L.: Oh, but, uh—

MRS. KANE: What "uh"?

[*Mrs. L. utters a startled, single-note laugh of incomplete disbelief. On this cue, the little girls are heard singing upstairs the marching song of the guerrilla forces which have seized the capital. Tune:* The Battle Hymn of the Republic.]

GIRLS [*singing*]: "We are crouching in the mountains where the mighty eagles fly, we are waiting in the caverns that are close up to the sky—"

MRS. KANE: The marching song of the guerrillas. Our girls know it, too, and I've learned it from them.

MRS. L. [*rushing to staircase*]: GIRLS! STOP THAT!

MRS. KANE [*slowly, fiercely*]: We can't stop them, you know. Children are creatures that know without knowing, they instinctively know without thinking or knowing, and I think that they know, well, I *know* that they know that siphoning gas out of one car into another is not a true solution and salvation. And, oh, they know we're not old, we're just a lot older than they are, and a generation gap is now a—wide—perpendicular—chasm!

MRS. L.: But they're dependent on—

MRS. KANE: Not us, now. ˙

MRS. L.: Oh, but they—

MRS. KANE [*rising*]: The agile, light-footed creatures would glance back once at their clumsy, stumbling parents, maybe call back twice, but soon they'd disappear.

MRS. L.: If we lagged behind?

MRS. KANE: The innocence of savages gives them unlimited visas, expiration date open, valid at any frontier, coming or going. . . . [*She removes her heavy-rimmed glasses, brushes fallen plaster off her coat.*] I think they know without knowing that we are just an encumbrance.

MRS. L.: Oh, Elaine!

MRS. KANE: Hmm?

MRS. L.: We mustn't think, we mustn't—talk like this!

MRS. KANE: Get with it, Jane.

MRS. L.: Oh, but—what?

MRS. KANE: About?

MRS. L.: Us!

MRS. KANE: For myself, I have a different plan, I have something else in mind.

MRS. L.: Another idea than?

MRS. KANE: Yes. Totally. In fact, I'd already made a decision before we came here. That's why I've kept on my coat, this plain gray coat. I have nothing on underneath it. Henry said, "Honey, take off your coat, why don't you?" And I said, "I feel cold, dear." Do you want to know my plan?

MRS. L.: Yes, I—

MRS. KANE: You might be interested in it. My plan is to go downtown.

MRS. L.: Are you—?

MRS. KANE: Serious? Completely. My plan is to go downtown in this plain gray coat and find the headquarters of the general and somehow get to see him.

MRS. L.: What would you—?

MRS. KANE: Get to see him, I said. Open my coat and say, "Take me." I'm counting on his being ravenous for a woman, which I think is likely. Before they took the city, they lived in mountain caves, and the general's still a young man. That's my plan. How does it impress you?

MRS L.: —Any plan, now, is a—wild thing to consider.

MRS. KANE: Does this plan of mine seem wilder than Henry's and Jeff's?

MRS. L.: —No, I—

MRS. KANE: The general has a brother. Handsome. Called "The Panther."

MRS. L.: —I have a plain—*what am I saying?*

MRS. KANE: You have a plain coat?

MRS. L.: Yes, I do. It's right here.

MRS. KANE: Strip off quick. Get into your plain coat. [*After a moment's hesitation, Mrs. L. tears off her clothes and gets into her plain coat.*] I know the marching song. Bolt the front door, the siphoning may be finished. We'll sing the marching song as loud as we can on our way downtown. And look ecstatic over the demolition.

MRS. L. [*breathlessly*]: All right! I'm ready! I'm with you!

MRS. KANE: We'll go out the back door and cut across to the boulevard and—

[*Mrs. L. pauses a moment to look about the room she won't see again. She draws a deep breath: then strides purposefully, determinedly, to the dark upstage door, followed by the "cool" Mrs. Kane. They are no sooner offstage than the biggest blast yet precipitates an avalanche of powdery plaster*

357

from the ceiling of the room. Dead on this cue, Mr. L. and Mr. Kane charge in the front door, panting like foxhounds in hot pursuit. And dead on that cue, we hear the voices of Mrs. L. and Mrs. Kane singing loudly into the diminuendo of quick distance.

MARCHING SONG:
We are crouching in the mountains where the mighty eagles fly,
We are waiting in the caverns that are close up to the sky,
But without a note of warning, with no trumpet and no drum,
From the peaks of the mountains, will our hungry legions come,
AND OUR TRUTH WILL MAKE US STRONG!

Recognizing the voices of their wives, Mr. L. and Mr. Kane turn to face each other with terrible surmise: as the voices fade in distance, Mr. L. brushes some plaster dust off Mr. Kane's jacket: a courtesy which Mr. Kane returns as—]

THE CURTAIN FALLS